One Buck
at a Time

One Buck
at a Time

*An Insider's Account of
How Dollar Tree Remade
American Retail*

Macon Brock

with Earl Swift

Beachnut Publishing
Virginia Beach, Virginia

Copyright © 2017 by Macon Brock

Distributed by John F. Blair, Publisher
1406 Plaza Drive
Winston-Salem, North Carolina 27103
blairpub.com

Dollar bill on front cover: ©*aodaodaodaod/Shutterstock*
Back cover photo: Lawrence Jackson, The Virginian-Pilot

Library of Congress Cataloging-in-Publication Data

Names: Brock, Macon, 1942- author. | Swift, Earl, 1958- author.
Title: One buck at a time : an insider's account of how Dollar Tree remade
    American retail / by Macon Brock, with Earl Swift.
Description: Winston-Salem, North Carolina : John F. Blair, Publisher, [2016]
    | Includes bibliographical references and index.
Identifiers: LCCN 2016032344 (print) | LCCN 2016038177 (ebook) | ISBN
    9780895876812 (hardcover : alk. paper) | ISBN 9780895876829 (ebook)
Subjects: LCSH: Dollar Tree (Firm) | Variety stores--United States. |
    Discount houses (Retail trade)--United States. | Retail trade--United
    States.
Classification: LCC HF5465.U64 D6537 2016 (print) | LCC HF5465.U64 (ebook) |
    DDC 381/.14906573--dc23
LC record available at https://lccn.loc.gov/2016032344

10 9 8 7 6 5 4 3 2 1

For Joan

Contents

Introduction

―――――――

This is the story of a great American company and the people who made it.

It is a company that has grown into a behemoth over the past few years and today boasts a presence throughout the contiguous United States and Canada. It offers something for everyone—man or woman, young or old, rich or poor, urban or rural—at a price that simply can't be beaten. Few American towns of decent size are untouched by its existence. Those that are won't be for long.

From more than six thousand storefronts, it provides millions of people a day with essential household fare, stationery, gifts for their friends and loved ones, toys and clothing for their children. Those goods, piled together over the course of a year, would dwarf the Great Pyramid. The retail space in its stores totals more than 45 million square feet, an area significantly bigger than New York's Central Park. Its work force has more than doubled in five years, to upwards of ninety thousand people—a population equal to that of Asheville, North Carolina, or Fargo, North Dakota, and bigger than that of several countries. Seriously, it's more than twice the size of Lichtenstein.

A surprising number of the tractor-trailers on the interstates carry its goods. Just one of its eleven warehouses moves a million cartons of merchandise per week, and in each of those cartons are up to five dozen items that will wind up on the shelves, and are almost sure to move off them quickly. In 2014, the company posted nearly $8.6 billion in sales, which is to say that it sold 8.6 billion pieces of merchandise—an easy piece of math, because each and every one of its products sells for no more than a buck.

Not bad for a business that started as an experiment, and one that precious few experts thought would work.

Now, this company, Dollar Tree, is putting the finishing touches on a corporate merger that promises to make all this success look pretty pale. By the time you read this, it will have more than fourteen thousand stores and pull in $20 billion in sales. That would make it significantly bigger than Eli Lilly or Southwest Airlines or Kraft Foods.

It'll be exciting to see what happens. Regardless of the outcome, though, this is less a story about a company rising steadily through the Fortune 500 than it is one of humble beginnings, because that's the real miracle of Dollar Tree: not how big and successful it is today, but how unlikely its good fortune seemed just a few years ago.

It's the story of an unassuming man from the North Carolina sticks who came to a city—Norfolk, Virginia—to learn how to cut hair and stuck around to open a barbershop. It's the story of how he parlayed that shop into a busy little knot of enterprises after World War II, among them an old Ben Franklin variety store. It's the story of how he enlisted his family into the business, and then a cadre of loyal staff—many of whom were in high school when they signed on, and most of whom didn't have a lick of college credit—and how, together, they worked long days against long odds to build something out of next to nothing.

It's a story I know well, because I was part of it. That barber was my father-in-law. Today, I'm the chairman of Dollar Tree's board of directors. For many years, I served as the company's president and chief executive officer. I was its public face as we demonstrated, year after year, that the idea at the heart of the business—that we could price quality merchandise that consistently surprised and delighted customers at just one dollar, and hold to that price no matter what—wasn't as crazy as it first seemed.

Which is one of the reasons it's important to me to tell this story now. Because I was Dollar Tree's spokesman in the press and its face to the public, I got much of the credit for the company's success. Dollar Tree and Macon Brock became synonymous in a lot of people's minds. And that's not how it was.

I'm no genius. I didn't come up with the dollar-store idea and can't claim any flashes of brilliance that transformed one tiny store into a national chain.

I worked hard—hell, I worked my ass off—but so did the people around me. Trite though it sounds, I was part of a team. It was a small team early on, and a bigger one later, but always a real team. Every member was essential to what we created, and everyone lived and worked by principles that we came to value together. *Do your best. Do the right thing. When in doubt, choose the solution that works best for the long term.*

Being the boss, or one of the bosses, was only so important. What made the difference, and made the company, was collective effort. We all—from buyers to warehouse workers, store managers to computer whizzes, accountants to payroll clerks—were the creators of Dollar Tree. We shared a sense of mission. We embarked on an adventure that we weren't sure would end the way we wanted it to, but we were united in giving it our best shot. In the process, we became closer than most families.

So before my memory starts to slip, I want to assign the credit for our success to the people who made it happen. I'll narrate the proceedings, and in the course of doing so I'll share my own meandering journey to and from that Ben Franklin store that started it all. But make no mistake, this is our story, not just mine.

I have a second, related motive. Today, with the company grown beyond our wildest imaginings, most of us are retired or have moved on to new ventures; only a few members of the team still go to work every day in Dollar Tree's offices. And while I have nothing but admiration for the many ways that our successors have built on what we started, not to mention the spectacular results they've achieved, I worry that the excitement and drama and sheer improbability of the early days will be forgotten once the last of us leaves.

I don't want that to happen. A company is more than an engine for delivering bags of cash to its stockholders. In America especially, it's among the most important building blocks of society. We each might go to work every day because we have to pay the rent, but we also—if we work at a good company—share a sense of purpose with our coworkers.

Building and sustaining that sense of purpose, that culture, requires an awareness of history. You can understand yourself only so much if you know nothing of your parents, the circumstances of your birth, your early childhood. Traditions mean little if you don't understand where they came from, and why it's important that you stick to them or challenge them and start new ones.

So in sharing the tale of Dollar Tree's creation and its long prehistory, I hope to offer up a corporate genealogy, if you will. I figure that explaining where this mercantile juggernaut came from, and how and why it turned out to be a winner, will be instructive to those ninety thousand people now working at the company, who will leap in number in the next few years. As for folks who have no connection to Dollar Tree and no intention of getting into the dollar-store business themselves, well, I hope they'll find something useful in the lessons we learned along the way.

Most of all, though, I don't want the early days forgotten because they make for a good story. Because if anybody tells you they saw this coming, they're telling you a tale.

1

Up from the Tobacco Fields

L et me take you on a tour of a Dollar Tree, so you'll better understand just how remarkable this company is. We'll walk through the doors of a store in Albemarle County, Virginia, north of Charlottesville, a pretty typical example. It occupies 10,781 square feet in a strip shopping center anchored by a Kroger supermarket, a Dick's Sporting Goods, and a T.J. Maxx.

The first thing we see, just inside, is a table marked "Item of the Week," on which are little solar-powered plastic animals—owls, pandas, and monkeys— that wave and dance when exposed to light. They stand maybe four inches tall. They're cute. They'd look at home on a kitchen window sill, say, or a child's dresser. They seem quite a deal at a dollar apiece.

Here's how good a deal they really are: If you were to log onto eBay, you'd find the same owls, pandas, and monkeys selling as a set for $10.49. Another seller is offering them for $9.00. You'd find the monkey alone going for $4.95 and the owl for $4.00 or more. In other words, shopping online for the same items costs three or more times as much. And that's before shipping.

We'll head down the aisle along the right wall of the store. Bounty Basic paper towels for a dollar. You can find them on Amazon at twelve for $12.95— not quite as good a deal, even without the $5.49 shipping charge. Here's a display of plastic clothes hangers, six for a dollar. The closest that one of the country's discount giants can come to that is eighteen for $14.99—five times as much.

It's springtime, so we enter an array of seasonal displays. Seed packets of flower and vegetable varieties, four packs for a dollar. Easter baskets and packages of fake grass for them. Saint Patrick's Day party supplies—banners, door posters, window clings, all at a fraction of what you'd pay elsewhere.

Along the store's back wall is a huge assortment of gift bags, wrapping paper, ribbons, and bows. It's first-rate stuff. The bags are heavily constructed and sharply printed (many with foil or glitter accents), and all come with an attached gift tag. I defy you to find a better bag for three, four, or even five times the price. As for the paper, I bought some last Christmas that was reversible, and was actually noticed and praised by people who got presents in it. It might be possible to find fancier paper elsewhere, with a velveteen finish or slightly heavier stock. But it'll run many, many times the dollar this paper costs.

We turn up the second aisle, lined with greeting cards by American Greetings and Forget Me Not. These are not cheapie knockoffs—the prices printed on the cards by their manufacturers run from $1.95 to $3.89. Many of them have those upscale bond-paper inserts. Beyond the cards is a long display of Easter candy—Russell Stover white chocolate bunnies, Reese's Pieces in mini milk cartons, Peeps in packages of twelve, Starburst chews in 3.5-ounce boxes, at a price you can come close to matching online, but only if you buy in bulk.

We swing down the third aisle, passing a slew of household supplies—spray cleaners, dish and laundry detergents, drain openers. An example of the deals on display: Ajax Triple-Action dishwashing liquid, fourteen-ounce bottle. I found the same product in a twenty-eight-ounce bottle at a nearby grocery store. The price was $2.89—twice as much soap for nearly three times the money.

Now, we're moving up the fourth aisle, much of which is devoted to toys—stuffed animals, fairy wings, bubble liquid, toy pompoms, dinosaur masks, packs of plastic soldiers. Try to find a better price anywhere for jigsaw puzzles and chess sets. And try to find Matchbox cars elsewhere for a dollar each. I've found packs of five for $5.49 at Toys "R" Us, but even that sale price (reduced from the usual $6.99) is 10 percent higher than Dollar Tree's—and you have to buy five cars to get it.

On the next aisle are hardback books by such best-selling authors as Dennis Lehane and Tom Wolfe. Dictionaries and Bibles—and not little pocket versions either, but the full-sized varieties. Beyond, in the stationery section, wait deals that seem almost crazy. Calculators in a variety of models and sizes—

including a scientific model with fifty-six functions—all for a dollar. Staplers. Two-roll packs of Scotch brand transparent tape. Gel pens. Poster-sized foam board, which our competition sells at twice the price or more. Padded manila envelopes, two for a buck—again, half the price you'll find elsewhere. Mailing boxes. Mead security envelopes, forty to a box; compare that to the office-supply aisle at the Harris Teeter a few miles away, where the same product in an eighty-count box goes for $2.79.

Incredible deals keep presenting themselves aisle after aisle. Movie-theater boxes of candy. Aluminum foil, forty square feet to the roll. Zipper-seal sandwich bags. Brake fluid. Two-stroke oil. Utz potato chips in bags marked $1.59. Sunny D in forty-ounce jugs. Sporty water bottles, for which other retailers charge six, eight, even ten times as much.

We're now on the left side of the store, where the back wall consists of a cooler filled with refrigerated and frozen items—four-packs of Luigi's Real Italian Ice cups, single slices of Edward's pies, Banquet TV dinners in three varieties. Fresh eggs by the half-dozen. Sliced bologna. Frozen waffles. Frozen blueberries. Sliced cheese.

The store's leftmost aisles are stuffed with groceries, all of them priced at a dollar: Frank's Red Hot sauce, which went for $1.59 at Harris Teeter the night I visited; Ro-Tel sliced tomatoes and green chilies and Hunt's ketchup, which up the street cost $1.25 and $1.89, respectively; three-packs of Nissin ramen cups, sold singly for fifty-nine cents at the other place.

Such are the deals that Dollar Tree provides its customers every day. They defy credulity. They seem to defy common sense. Yet the company's stores maintain one of the highest profit margins in the business.

We'll finish our tour back near the front doors, where we find a table stacked with stoneware plates and a couple dozen stoneware mugs, both in a variety of solid colors. There's nothing cheap about them. These are heavy, ridged pieces with even, smooth glazing. They're microwave and dishwasher safe, and good looking, too—they bring to mind the classic Fiesta dinnerware that's been around since the 1930s, and that so many people collect.

In fact, you could mistake them for the famous brand except that the Fiesta costs nineteen dollars for a single plate at Macy's or Kohl's. With the Dollar Tree plates, which have fancy-looking stamps on their bottoms reading "Royal Norfolk," you could set a table for your extended family and spend less than the Fiesta costs for one plate.

I'm willing to concede there might be something about the Fiesta that makes it superior, but I can't see it myself. And really, can it be nineteen times better than the Royal Norfolk?

I don't think so, and I'm not alone. People on the web seem to feel the Royal Norfolk dinnerware is good stuff. On eBay, I found one seller offering eight of these plates for $64.99, and another charging $72.99 for the same thing. Three bowls were going for $28.95. A website devoted to replacing broken dishes charged $10.00 to $16.00 a plate. So it's not like this is second-rate. It's viewed by other merchants as a quality product.

Now, I'll let you in on a little secret: Royal Norfolk is a house brand. Dollar Tree, and only Dollar Tree, imports these dishes under that name—a name we chose because our company started in Norfolk, Virginia. So when you go on eBay and find Royal Norfolk for sale, be advised that the seller bought it at the local Dollar Tree and is attempting to flip it at a much higher price. Chances are he'll get away with it, because nothing about the Royal Norfolk plates suggests they could possibly sell for a dollar. In fact, they're probably not a bad buy at $72.99 for a set of eight.

Here's the most amazing thing: These plates aren't what the retail industry calls "loss leaders," on which we make little or no profit in order to get customers in the door to buy other things. We double our money on every one we sell. Fifty cents' profit on each plate, multiplied by the millions we sell, adds up to a tidy sum.

That's the key to the company's success. We can absolutely floor our customers with the prices we offer and still generate a tremendous income. We don't have to make a killing on each item, just a healthy margin.

Which is another way of saying we didn't get here by being greedy.

We got here by being smart.

■ ■ ■

How all this came to be started with two families, both of which settled in the tobacco country of eastern North Carolina in the nineteenth century and saw sons and daughters venture north to Norfolk in the 1920s and 1930s. One of those families was mine.

I was raised in a comfortable home—not one of privilege, but not poor, either. As a matter of fact, the Brocks were of some means for a couple of generations before I came along. My father's father, Furnifold Brock, was born into tobacco farming in 1873 and farmed the weed for all of his life on a spread that grew to be right big. But he was also an entrepreneur in a great many other lines of work. He went to college for engineering and spent most of his twenties working as a surveyor, then moved to the nearest town, Trenton, where he was elected the county register of deeds. He also bought a gristmill.

The mill, which was turned by the water from a spring-fed pond, produced flour, cornmeal, and cracked corn for chicken feed and powered a saw and a cotton-ginning gear, all of which gave my grandfather a pretty fair income on top of what his farm earned. That must have come in handy when he married a local girl, Myrtle Foscue, and the couple had eight children in rapid succession. My father was born in the middle of the pack, in 1904.

Twelve years later, when my grandfather was chairman of the county's board of supervisors, he won a franchise to supply Trenton with electricity. He rigged a turbine generator to the mill and ran wires into town, and Brock Electrical Company lit the place from sundown to midnight. As a local newspaper later recalled, he "had a unique way of warning his customers that the midnight hour was approaching: At 11:45 P.M. he flickered the lights once or twice, and the residents would either secure for the night or hurry to light their kerosene lamps."

In 1917, a year into his pioneering career in public utilities, my grandfather was elected to the state senate. He held the seat for twelve years. After leaving politics, he opened a Ford dealership. It's still in business today, run by my cousin Charles Jones and his sons.

All of which is to say that Furnifold Brock was an admired and respected leader of his community, and the Brocks one of Trenton's first families. Even so, he remained a farmer who worked his fields. And when his children weren't in school, they worked alongside him. My dad, Macon Foscue Brock, hated those long days in the tobacco, and in particular the hornworms that grew fat and green and four inches long in the leaves. He dreaded a lifetime on the family land. As he moved through his teens, he mulled an escape.

In time, he found one, in a career completely removed from farming. He went off to Trinity College, his father's alma mater, which changed its name to Duke University while he was there; he was a member of its first graduating class, in 1925. That in itself wasn't unusual, because my grandfather sent all my aunts to college as well. They became teachers.

But my father convinced his father to invest serious money in his schooling and send him on to medical school. He graduated from the Medical College of Virginia, in Richmond, in 1930, then took an internship at St. Vincent

DePaul Hospital in Norfolk, which is how I came to be born on the Virginia coast. It was at DePaul that he met a pretty young nurse named Clara Augusta Prichard—a bright-eyed, adventuresome brunette with a mischievous sense of humor who'd come to Norfolk herself from Elizabeth City, North Carolina, about an hour to the south. They hit it off, courted, and eventually got married.

So mine isn't a rags-to-riches tale. I'm the son of a doctor, and as such enjoyed a pretty easygoing childhood, in a household that didn't suffer the financial worries of so many at the time. My father didn't earn as fat a paycheck as many doctors, however, because he devoted the first half of his career to public service. His first job out of school, a post he held for twenty years, was as chief doctor at Norfolk's Charles R. Grandy Sanatorium for the Treatment of Tuberculosis. At the time, tuberculosis killed more Americans than any other infectious disease. At the turn of the last century, it accounted for a third of all deaths of Americans aged fifteen to forty-five—more than accidents or acts of violence or the myriad other things that killed people in the days before modern medicine. More people died of it in four years—1904 to 1907—than died in the Civil War.

People called it "the white plague." A sneeze could spread it. So could eating the meat or drinking the milk of an infected animal. It was indiscriminate as well as deadly; its victims came from all walks of life, though the poor, and especially poor blacks, were its most common victims. You can still see signs of the disease in the United States today. Many cities have laws on the books against spitting in public, and the reason is tuberculosis; the paper Dixie Cup came along at about the same time, for pretty much the same reason.

Eventually, penicillin would halt the scourge, but when my father got to the Grandy campus in 1932, antibiotics weren't yet on the scene, and the only effective remedy for TB—and it was only so effective—was a "rest cure" at a sanatorium. Hundreds of these places sprang up around the United States before and after World War I. They provided patients with fresh air, nutritious meals, and close medical care, and cities with a way to keep the sick quarantined from the general population.

My earliest memories are of the sanatorium. My parents' three children were all born while the family lived in a house on the property—my sister Patricia in 1936, my sister Sally in 1939, and me in April 1942. Besides our place, Grandy consisted of three main buildings, where my father treated not only TB patients but those with polio, and nine cottages, where patients in relatively good shape passed their days resting in hopes of slowing the destruction of their lungs. It was a bucolic setting. The buildings were nestled in a forest of Virginia pines, maples, and loblollies miles beyond the noise of the city, overlooking a lake and farm fields that stretched an all but unbroken ten miles east to the Atlantic. Our neighbors were a work farm for petty criminals and what we kids called an "old folks' home." A little two-lane road, dirt when my dad started his tenure, linked this outpost to civilization, passing through a knot of houses at a road junction just to our west.

Nowadays, you'd scarcely recognize the area. Lake Taylor High School sprawls across acreage that I remember seeing planted with alfalfa, and a large rehab and end-care hospital has blotted out any trace of the TB compound. The little farm road is a bustling artery, and traffic rumbles by on elevated Interstate 64 a short way off. Subdivisions press in on all sides. About all that's left is the lake.

But I remember our almost rural life out there, and spending my days playing outside. And most especially, I can summon up snapshots of my parents in their youth.

I bear a striking resemblance to my father. He stood a lean and wiry five foot eight, his muscles hardened by daily exercise—push-ups, sit-ups, and aerobics in the house, decades before that became common. He ran on a mini trampoline. He knew that physical activity was key to his health, so he did a lot of it. Like any kid, I didn't always follow his advice or example, but his dedication to fitness is something I embraced from early on. He was a kind man with a nurturing bedside manner and was adored by his patients. It was commonplace that, after putting in a long day tending to the sick at the sanatorium, he'd make house calls on poor navy families living in government housing a few miles away.

Mom did the day-to-day child rearing. She was the boss. My two older sisters drew much of her worry and hands-on parenting; Pat and Sally have long insisted that I had it easy, being a boy and the last born, and there's probably some truth to it. Mom could be firm at times, but her most obvious attribute—the one I most often saw, anyway—was that spunky *joie de vivre* that had caught my dad's attention back at DePaul.

When I was ten, my father finished his twentieth year on the job and decided to retire from city service and go into full-time family practice. He set up his office in downtown Norfolk, and we moved to town, into a big, rambling, old house on a main drag, Cottage Toll Road. Out front were four lanes of traffic whizzing between the business district and the tip of Willoughby Spit, up on the Chesapeake Bay, where the road ended at a ferry terminal—the link to the cities across the mile-wide harbor.

At the time, I didn't pay much attention to the road or where it went, because out back was the Lafayette River—glassy, tidal, fringed in marsh and mud flat, and so wide in places that it seemed more a lake. It was crowded with fish and blue crabs. It was glorious. And off to the north, out the front door and to the left across the yard, was a street into a neighborhood called Roland Park, which was crowded with boys my age. That was even more glorious.

Until then, I'd always been surrounded by my sisters and their friends. Now, I spent my days on my bike, swimming in the river, and digging in the mud with a gang of new friends from Roland Park. One of the first and longest lasting of those friendships was with a kid named Harris Attaway, whose dad ran a store at Wards Corner, the region's first and biggest suburban shopping area, built around a crossroads a couple of miles from our house. In June 1953, not long into my alliance with Harris, his dad, Barr Attaway, just forty-one years old, was killed in a car crash while on a trip to Baltimore. I remember how it devastated Harris, and that his mother, suddenly without an income, decided she'd have to sell Mr. Attaway's business to keep the family afloat.

She found a taker in Kenneth R. Perry, who ran a barbershop a few storefronts down from Mr. Attaway's place. It was a modest transaction: Mr. Perry paid Mrs. Attaway forty-two thousand dollars in cash and financed the sixty-two-thousand-dollar balance. But in that deal was the seed of what would eventually grow into Dollar Tree.

■ ■ ■

If there's a hero in this story, a Horatio Alger figure born to humble circumstance who, through hard work and pluck, made something good of himself, it's Kenneth Redding Perry. Like my father, he came from North Carolina—from Louisburg, a little ways northeast of Raleigh—and like my father, he grew up on a tobacco farm and resolved to get as far from that line of work as he could.

Unlike my father, he didn't come from a family with the means to finance his escape. He was one of thirteen children, and the farm's budget was tight. So he decided he'd learn a trade, save money for school, and eventually go to Wake Forest University to study engineering. That's what brought him to Norfolk in 1934, when he was seventeen. His older brother Abner was already living in the city, so K. R.—as Mr. Perry would be known throughout his career—had a place to stay while he attended Vaughn's Barber School on Main Street.

Only his life didn't unfold according to plan. On graduating, he found he could earn twenty-five dollars a week, a good deal more than the eighty to eighty-five a month that college-trained engineers made at the time, so he stuck with cutting hair, working a chair at the Sanitary Barber Shop in downtown Norfolk for eight years, saving every penny he could. "When I made eighteen dollars a week, I saved five," he later said. "When I made twenty-five, I saved ten." He moved out of Abner's place but kept his expenses low—just twenty-six dollars a month covered his room, board, and laundry.

By 1942, he'd saved enough to go into business for himself. He spent thirty-two hundred dollars to open Perry's Suburban Barber Shop, a two-chair storefront at Wards Corner, which was built around the intersection of two major arteries: Granby Street, the main north-south boulevard, which stretched about a dozen miles from downtown to the city's Chesapeake Bay beachfront; and Little Creek Road, which ran across the city's middle and linked two huge military complexes—the world's biggest naval base, to the west, and a fast-growing amphibious base and army post, to the east.

Norfolk had long been recognized as the country's biggest navy town, but during World War II it exploded in size on the way to becoming the East Coast's headquarters for the fight against Germany. Warships and troop transports steamed continuously to and from the naval base's piers. New destroyers, cruisers, and armed freighters rose from the shipyard ways. Emergency housing flew up on every available lot. And most memorably, sailors swarmed by the thousands to downtown bars, the beaches, and the Ocean View Amusement Park, up on the bay.

It wasn't necessarily a good time to be a civilian in Norfolk. Venturing into the bar district on Main Street just a block from the barber college was a good way to invite a bloody scrape with sailors wanting to know why the hell you weren't in uniform. Beery gangs of wolf-whistling tars hit on high school girls and picked fights with their boyfriends. Many a homeowner woke to find our boys in blue passed out in the petunias. The streetcars smelled of stale beer.

But this hell-raising, raw-knuckled, oversexed town was a great place to be a barber, because every one of those sailors needed a haircut at least once a week. And K. R. could not have picked a better location for his first shop, because Wards Corner was convenient to the bases, a transfer point for streetcar lines, and the first outpost of department stores venturing into the suburbs. Everyone in town had a reason to go there.

The district was so bustling that locals didn't laugh when it started billing itself as "the Times Square of the South," though the physical resemblance was iffy. All four corners were dominated by strip shopping centers, the tallest of which rose in its middle to three stories. K. R.'s shop was located amidships in the strip on the southeast corner.

It did so well that in no time he was able to open a second barbershop, on Hampton Boulevard, outside the naval base's gates on the west side of town. He split his time between the two until he was called up by the army in early 1945. By the time he mustered out, he also owned four beauty parlors.

He was married by now, to the former Kathryn Louise Saunders, a small, dainty, pretty young woman born in Edenton, North Carolina. Her father had been a farmer down that way but had moved the family north when Kathryn was in high school to find work as a carpenter. They'd settled first at downtown's fringe, then moved out to a house just behind the shopping center where K. R. cut hair.

Kitty, as she was known to her friends, was a straight-arrow Southern Baptist who didn't drink and didn't much care for those who did. She could be forceful. But she was also magnetic, one of those people to whom others were drawn, no matter whether they had much in common. She and the quiet but friendly K. R. made a great couple.

Not long after came an episode that K. R. would recount to the end of his days. Sometime in the late forties, one of his customers, an old and experienced banker, warned him that the Norfolk economy was poised to crash. The country was paring down its military. A smart man would get out and go back to Carolina.

K. R. considered the advice and discussed it with Kitty, but after many sleepless nights decided that no matter what happened, Norfolk was now home, that they'd make a stand there. Instead of divesting, he started buying houses and lots all over town, in established neighborhoods and new G.I. Bill suburbs, and proved savvy at flipping them for profit. In one typical case, he bought a house for eleven thousand dollars, kept it for two years, and sold it for thirty-two thousand.

So in 1953 when Barr Attaway's widow approached him about buying Mr. Attaway's business, K. R. was flush. He was also ready to hang up his scissors. Though he'd remain the owner of barbershops into the 1970s, he found the new store far more interesting, and left haircutting to others.

That was how K. R. Perry came to own a Ben Franklin variety store a couple doors down from his barbershop at Wards Corner. I remember visiting the store as a kid, at about the time he bought the place. A candy counter

K. R. Perry poses with Kitty and their children shortly before he bought the Ben Franklin franchise at Wards Corner. All three kids—Joan, Kenny, and, at far right, Doug—would play important roles in the evolving family business.

COURTESY OF BROCK FAMILY

Aerial view of Norfolk's Wards Corner shopping district in 1964, when the busy crossroads was improbably marketed as "the Times Square of the South." K. R. owned the entire quadrant at upper right.

USED BY PERMISSION OF VIRGINIAN-PILOT

and popcorn machine stood just inside the front door. A lunch counter serving burgers, hot dogs, barbecue sandwiches, and fries ran down the left wall. Elsewhere, a little of everything filled shelves and glass display cases—children's clothes, knickknacks, inexpensive pots and pans, sewing gear, sunglasses, costume jewelry, hats and gloves, headache remedies, toys, even parakeets and goldfish. It was the quintessential five-and-dime. And like most Ben Franklin stores, it was a franchise. Mr. Perry was supplied with all his wares by the parent company. All he had to do was sell them.

Which he did very well. Retail suited K. R., who had worked his way through high school selling his family's castoffs from the roadside in front of their farmhouse. He was a bright, unassuming guy who loved contact with people, who could make small talk with anyone.

He might have stuck with this comfortable life, running the Ben Franklin and overseeing his small empire in real estate and hair care, and no doubt he'd have been able to look back on his career with satisfaction. But K. R., not yet forty, was an ambitious man. In 1955, he partnered with his brother Leon, still living down in Carolina, to buy the strip center in which the store was housed—the entire southeast quadrant of Wards Corner.

The Suburban Shopping Center, as the strip mall was called, cost $1.25 million—the largest single real-estate transaction in the city to that date, the newspapers said. In thirteen years, he'd gone from a two-chair barbershop to owning a complex that was home to twenty-six stores, a movie theater, a restaurant, and numerous offices, along with owning a beauty parlor and assorted properties scattered around town.

Within a year, he added to the center by erecting a two-story brick building beside it, situated at a right angle to the original and fitted for storefronts below and offices above. He moved his barbershop into a huge space in this new Perry Building. The shop's rather prosaic name was 15 Barbers, which advertised its number of chairs. It was said to be the biggest barbershop in the South.

K. R. and Kathryn had three children by then. Now among the city's true entrepreneurial success stories, the family moved into a new brick rambler on the Lafayette River south of Wards Corner, a couple of river bends and maybe an overland mile from my family's house on Cottage Toll Road.

2

The Rewards of a Contrary Nature

G rowing up the son of a doctor in the 1950s brought with it certain expectations, because doctors were gods—they had brains, they had money, and if they had kids, it was assumed that those kids were extraordinary. They'd succeed without question; the intelligence and tenacity necessary to a successful medical career would be passed genetically to succeeding generations. A doctor's kid would have a facility for science, and devour books for pleasure, and find satisfaction in the lonely focus of deep study.

I put those assumptions to the test.

As an eighth-grader at Granby High School in 1955, I established a pattern that endured through my graduation five years later. I was not a serious student. I had the ability to do well, but I didn't bust my hump on the work, didn't pay attention to assignments or study the way I should have. I wasn't a bad kid—I didn't play hooky or descend into serious delinquency—but I was much more interested in having a good time than in cracking the books. My classmates were sweating their grades, worried about college; I skated along with Bs and Cs, not a care in the world, enjoying myself thoroughly.

Everyone knows kids who peaked in high school, who were the stars of their class but found that afterward they could never regain that status, or who were smart, positioned themselves that way, then went off to college only to discover they weren't quite the geniuses they imagined themselves to be, and disappeared. I was never in danger of either fate. I considered myself dumber than the next guy. I wasn't a class leader. I strove to operate in the middle of the pack, not at the head or the tail. If I had any particular gifts, I didn't know it.

Now, I can see that I did have a few, though they weren't necessarily the sort that pleased my parents. I aced socializing. I enjoyed other people's company, laughed often, took delight in cutting up. I was quick on my feet and a little daring. I was apparently fun to be around. I had a lot of friends.

They came from all walks, though the ones who hewed closest to my own attitude were probably the River Rats, a group of boys who lived across the Lafayette in Norfolk's Riverview neighborhood. They had several boats among them and spent time on the water or cruising around town in the "Ratmobile," an early-fifties Sears Allstate (a Kaiser Henry J sedan rebadged for sale by Sears, Roebuck) that served more as a getaway car than anything else.

They could be a rowdy bunch. The River Rats were known to pile into the Ratmobile's trunk to sneak into drive-in movies, and to peel off in the Ratmobile after snatching watermelons from out front of grocery stores. They'd invade a little strip of river-front beach for midsummer parties that were guaranteed to disturb the peace of the surrounding neighborhood. They'd waste away afternoons lounging at each other's houses. They crafted fake IDs and scored drinks in the basement of the officers' club at the amphibious base.

I was the first outsider invited to join this exclusive club. My initiation was to chug an overheated can of Country Club malt liquor, the sole remaining soldier of a six-pack the guys had found discarded at the roadside. One sip and I understood why it had been abandoned. Getting to the bottom of that can was a gruesome experience, and had I been less stalwart, it might have put me off beer for good.

I met some of the River Rats at my first job, which I got with my father's help. From writing prescriptions, he knew the folks at Frazier's Pharmacy, a small, family-run business on Thirty-fifth Street a couple of miles from the house. At sixteen, I was working the soda fountain, running the cash register, stocking shelves, unloading trucks, and helping check in the various medicines as they arrived. I enjoyed it. I got to borrow the family car, a '55 Cadillac Coupe de Ville, after school and on weekends to drive to the pharmacy, and once on the clock I was often sent out in the company truck to deliver prescriptions to customers. I savored my time behind the wheel and got a kick out of running the register and talking to people. I found that I was a good fit for retail. It required only that I listen to people, respond to their needs, try to put myself in their place, and think as they did.

But a big reason I took to the pharmacy was that many of my fellow clerks were guys my own age—some were my classmates at Granby, while some attended our rival, Maury High—and we became fast friends. We River Rats water-skied the six-foot, humpbacked wakes of oceangoing ships out on the Elizabeth River, raced boats on the Lafayette, and convened in a shack in my backyard to play the bongos and drink beer on the sly. We hung out together, along with all of Granby's students, at a burger joint, Burroughs' Drive-In, just across the river on Granby Street. Almost despite ourselves, we avoided getting into serious trouble.

It was at Granby that I had my first serious girlfriend. Her name was Judy Melchor, and she was a tall, slim, pretty, and stylish brunette who was, at least on paper, as different from me as she could be. Judy was a cheerleader, marched on the drill team, was involved with student government and the French Club, and served as chair of our class's prom committee. She was a student leader, the sort whose picture appeared on every other page of the yearbook.

By comparison, my résumé looked pretty thin. My water-skiing skills notwithstanding, I was no athlete. I belonged to few clubs and led none of them. I joined a high school fraternity—such things existed back then—but wouldn't put up with the hazing and walked out. I spent time in DeMolay, a Masonic youth organization, but didn't catch fire for it. I ended my membership in the Boy Scouts well below Eagle. About the only consistent post I held was altar boy at Saint Paul's Episcopal Church, an eighteenth-century landmark in downtown Norfolk. My folks were faithful churchgoers, and I served Communion and went to Sunday school there for years.

Still, I got along with just about everyone, and Judy and I clicked. Her friends tended to be other student leaders, the school's "A-Team," and when I wasn't with the River Rats or my Roland Park buddies I spent my time with them. Mind you, there was overlap between these groups—they were by no means mutually exclusive—but as I progressed through high school I became a key member of the go-getter circle, and those kids became some of my closest friends.

One of Judy's tightest pals was a petite blonde who happened to be in my homeroom. Her name was Joan Perry—as in K. R. Perry, as in the oldest of the three Perry kids. Joan was an overachiever, by which I mean she made even Judy look lazy. She was the secretary of our freshman class and president of our junior class. She was elected "Miss Sophomore 1957." She was a big wheel in student government, a varsity cheerleader, a member of the French Club, president of the Tri-Hi-Y Christian Fellowship, and a princess on the homecoming court. She traveled out of town to student leadership conferences. She also pulled down grades good enough to earn honors. She was a force to be reckoned with.

Joan became a friend of mine, a pal, one of the gang. We'd all congregate now and then at her house, which was a good-looking place with a slate roof and a cupola over the garage and a big, grassy backyard that ended at the water. I was vaguely aware that her dad owned the Ben Franklin store up at Wards Corner.

She was fun, and it was impossible to ignore her. She was perky and cute, with enough wattage in her smile to light Norfolk and its suburbs. And besides that, she seemed to be everywhere at once. But she didn't turn my head. I already had a steady. I was unstirred.

That feeling, I was to learn, was not mutual.

. . .

At several points in my admittedly mediocre high school career, my parents signaled they were worried about me. An early example came when I got into trouble in homeroom, which wasn't even a class, but merely an assembly point. I didn't care for my homeroom teacher and he didn't care for me, and one morning he gave me a pink conduct slip, which I had to get my parents to sign. Then, within a short while, he gave me another.

Two pink slips. My normally quiet father let me know he was mighty upset about my behavior, then segued into a filibuster about my chronically lackluster performance, then threatened to send me to Norfolk Academy. As an adult, I recognize that Norfolk Academy is one of the finest private schools in Virginia, but at the time it seemed a fate worse than death, a desert island next to the with-it, highly social Granby. I grudgingly settled down.

But my grades remained average at best. My parents implored me to get serious about my classes, begged me to turn things around. And when that didn't work, I sensed their hopes for me began to sag.

Until then, there'd never been any question that all of their children would go to college. Their daughters had only strengthened that expectation. Pat had been a straight-A student and valedictorian of her class at Granby, had majored in chemistry, and by now was working as a teacher. Sally, no slouch either, was off at college and commanding her coursework.

But my grades already excluded me from the most prestigious schools of the day and promised to kill my chances at the rest. My performance wasn't boosted by the strange drama that colored my junior year. That fall of 1958, Granby was one of several Norfolk schools that shut down rather than integrate, as part of Virginia's misguided Massive Resistance program. At first, my reaction was unbridled joy—no school! But as the closure dragged on, we realized (or, more accurately, our parents realized) that we'd be left behind unless some remedy emerged.

Some of my classmates transferred to schools in neighboring counties. Some signed on at Norfolk Academy. And dozens of us—including Judy, Joan Perry, and I—enrolled in private tutoring groups that re-created the Granby curriculum off campus. My sister Pat, for instance, taught chemistry in the basement of our parents' house. Other classes, taught by the same teachers we had at Granby, convened at Temple Israel and Talbot Park Baptist Church or at students' homes in the neighborhoods ringing the high school. All that fall, whoever had a car would pick up his friends in the morning and taxi them from one class to the next, back and forth across central Norfolk.

Early in 1959, the state called a halt to its insanity, and the schools reopened that February. But the distractions of this patchwork junior year did me no favors, and as my senior year began back at Granby my parents' worries about my college prospects dimmed next to other, more basic concerns: What if I amounted to absolutely nothing? What if I couldn't support even myself, let alone a family?

They never shared this in so many words, but they didn't have to. They knew someone who was a harbor pilot, and they approached him about perhaps taking me on. They sat me down to talk about it. Pilots made good money, they said. This would be a career, not just a job. What I took away from the conversation wasn't that piloting was a viable option (which it wasn't, actually, because the rare job openings almost always went to family), but that my parents were in a panic. They were casting about for something, anything, to head off my impending failure.

And with that, something funny happened. Their doubts—heck, their certainty that I was destined to fall flat—ignited a contrary resolve in me. I can't point to any particular moment when I became aware of this course correction, but I can say that once it took hold, a determination grew inside me until it became a consuming fire. It was as if a switch had been thrown inside my head. I was going to make it. I would succeed. I had no idea what I'd do with myself, but whatever it was, I would be good at it. I would prove to myself—and to my parents, and to the world—that I was more than a goof-off.

I wonder if I would have had the drive that marked my adult life had my parents and teachers not had such doubts about me. It could be that I needed to do poorly early on to fuel my efforts to do well later. Had I been a whiz kid in high school, I might have amounted to a lackadaisical performer in life, might have been prone to kicking back and waiting for things to come to me, rather than pursuing them. I reckon that success rides on attitude and a certain amount of intelligence, but the biggest ingredient by far has to be desire. That's what fuels drive: wanting something badly and being willing to do the work to get it.

So it was a kick in the pants that got me into gear—that and a couple of positive influences who came along in the form of my sisters' boyfriends.

While I was in high school, much my family's leisure time was centered on the Outer Banks of North Carolina. In the 1940s, my folks had bought a lot and built a cottage there. A couple hours' drive on two-lane roads would take us from Norfolk south through black-water swamps and tidal marshes on the edge of Currituck Sound, then over a bridge to the long, narrow chain of sand spits and barrier islands that juts off the coast into the Atlantic. Once there, we'd turn north on the beach road to a knot of houses dubbed Southern Shores.

The place is almost unrecognizable today, as busy and crowded as it has become, but at that time the beaches were wind-swept and barren and bungalows were widely scattered behind the dunes. Anything we needed, we had to haul with us; one or two nearby shops stocked a few staples, but buying anything beyond the minimum necessary for survival meant driving twenty miles south to Nags Head.

Duck, which now is wall-to-wall condos and oceanfront mansions, was a small fishing village just north of our cottage, and beyond it, past the point where blacktop gave way to packed sand, the navy operated a bombing range. Corsairs would fly out from Oceana Naval Air Station in Virginia Beach to drop practice bombs, and observers in towers along the dune line would tell the pilots whether or not they hit their targets. As a kid, I was fascinated by that.

Anyway, I spent time at the cottage as a teenager, and my sisters would bring their boyfriends down for visits. I looked up to them. They were older and sure of themselves and seemed the epitome of worldliness. My sister Pat married a fellow named Frank Robertson while I was still in my teens. Sally's beau was Hal White. Both attended Randolph-Macon College, an all-men's school in Ashland, north of Richmond. Frank's brother was the college's registrar.

Throughout my high school years, any insight I gleaned into college life came through these two older guys and involved that one school. I was aware of other colleges; one, the Norfolk Division of the College of William and Mary—today's Old Dominion University—was no more than three or four miles from our house. But when it came time to consider where I might apply, I decided there was really just one choice.

It was only because Frank's brother was an administrator that I had a prayer of getting in, and even so it was dicey. Before I could be accepted, I was told I'd have to prove I could do college work, because Randolph-Macon was no cakewalk. I'd have to go to summer school and tackle two college courses. Frank's brother steered me to the Norfolk Division to attempt the task.

My graduation from Granby High was thus somewhat anticlimactic, because almost as soon as I closed my last book I found myself back in a classroom across town. A glance through the Granby yearbook reveals my smiling face in a couple of places, but not among the class of 1960's stars—unlike Joan Perry, who was voted Best All-Around, which was sort of like Cutest, Smartest, Most Popular, and Most Likely to Succeed all rolled into one.

By then, I might have sensed that Joan wasn't as indifferent to me as I'd been to her. Back in those dark days before Facebook, kids came up with a clever analog way to share their likes and dislikes with each other. They'd pass a notebook among their friends, each page bearing a name. Everyone involved would write notes—not necessarily signed—such as "Really hot" or "I like him" about a person under his or her name. It was an important way to communicate socially without risk; you didn't have to come out and tell a girl you liked her. I remember getting the book and reading what my classmates had written about me and thinking, *Whoa! I seem to be kind of popular.* And I recall that I recognized Joan's handwriting in some of the compliments about me. She'd been giving me the eye for quite some time—since the first time she saw me leaning against a locker outside homeroom, in fact—but I was oblivious to it. And even on sussing out that she might be interested, I didn't reciprocate. I was still going steady with her close friend Judy.

I was busy anyway. I went to the Norfolk Division that summer, telling myself, *You've got to prove you can do college work. Prove you can do it, damn it.* And I did. I got the grades I needed and that fall arrived at Randolph-Macon, which consisted of seven hundred students, give or take, and occupied a leafy, rolling campus of red-brick halls dating to just after the Civil War. I took to it immediately. I found it easy to concentrate there and to use my time effectively. And to the great surprise of my parents, I made the dean's list.

Once I had that first taste of academic success, I wanted more. I earned all

As and Bs majoring in Latin, of all things. And I still had fun. Because my sisters' boyfriends (by now my brothers-in-law) had been members of Phi Delta Theta, I joined that fraternity. The Phi Delts were my social world, and fraternity life, then as now, involved a yen for partying. But six nights a week, I was serious and disciplined. I wish I had taken more math; if I had to do it over again, I'd take accounting and business math. But at the time, I didn't anticipate the career I would have and didn't earn a single credit in anything that directly applied to running a big organization.

My new determination to succeed manifested itself in another way that I have to credit to one of my brothers-in-law: I decided to earn a commission as an officer in the service. I was not answering a family tradition in this. I'd never been encouraged to consider a career in uniform. But the draft was in place, and while I could delay service while in college, I would be expected to serve afterward. That obligation loomed. I figured that as long as I had to go in, I might as well go in as an officer—I'd make more money, have a leadership role, get better training, and so on.

I had little interest in the navy, to which I'd been overexposed in Norfolk. I'd seen townspeople treat sailors badly, calling them "goat-heads" and "squids." And to be candid, I'd seen sailors earn some of the disrespect. I couldn't see joining the army, which seemed oversized and featureless to me. But the Marine Corps! Everything about the marines—from their dress blue uniforms to the swashbuckling image they cultivated (they carried *swords*, for God's sake!) to John Wayne's portrayals of tough, fearless "gyrenes" in the movies—called to me. I figured the Marine Corps was the most demanding of the services and would be the greatest test of my newfound discipline, a particularly effective proof of worth. Besides, Pat's husband, Frank, who was six years my senior, had joined the marines after college, and the family had gone down to Camp Lejeune for his graduation. I'd been awed by the pomp and flourish of the ceremony and by the sight of him in uniform. That memory had stayed with me.

The marines had a program called Platoon Leaders Class, or PLC, which was a means for a young person to join the Corps as an undergraduate, train while in college, and enter the service after graduation as an officer. PLC was built around two summertime visits to the marine base at Quantico, Virginia, each of them six weeks long. The first came between freshman and sophomore years, the second between junior and senior. Together, they provided three months of basic training.

In the first session, in the summer of 1961, I found myself at Quantico's

Camp Upshur. We woke in the predawn dark to the sound of a Coke bottle rattling against the inside of a steel trash can, mustered outside within two minutes, and started the day with a three-mile run. We had to maintain our places in the formation during the run, and I swear it was all uphill. If you fell out, the drill instructors would be on your ass, and if you couldn't make it, they'd throw you out. You were done.

After the run, we'd make our bunks, get into uniform, go to chow, and for the rest of the day race to complete tasks in too little time and under constant harassment. I did my best not to be noticed. A few of my fellow boots were the sons of generals or admirals, and they attracted huge helpings of abuse. I maintained a place in the middle of the pack and managed to avoid being singled out.

The point of all the physical challenges, the screaming, and the sleeplessness was to weed out candidates the Corps judged to be physically or mentally weak. If you made it, though, you were close to joining the team, and clearing that hurdle was a new well of confidence for me. When I got back to Randolph-Macon, I found I was even less interested in cutting up. My first summer of boot camp instilled pride of country and uniform in me, hammered the Corps' values into me, transformed me from the first day I was there.

The second round was almost as physically tough but focused more on leadership training and programs that tested our capacity to think and lead under pressure. We had to perform with our mates while the instructors judged us. I earned a high IQ rating, which was news to me, and gratifying to learn, and a boost to my confidence—and which I hope didn't surprise too many of my friends back home.

My task now was to graduate from college with a solid grade-point average, after which I'd be commissioned as a second lieutenant. And once an official marine, I'd be off to Basic School, a six-month, intensive course in infantry leadership that all marine officers must complete. Every officer in the Marine Corps, no matter his or her eventual specialty, is trained first as an infantry officer. If you're a pilot, you do Basic School first, learn how to lead marines on the ground, then go on to flight school. Even the United States Naval Academy graduates who choose the Corps have to go to Basic School. It's something all marine officers have in common.

I was looking forward to that. I was eager to start my time as a marine. It would be, I reckoned, another chance to prove myself. I was starting to enjoy those opportunities.

■ ■ ■

I was getting ready to go off to my second summer boot camp, in 1963, when one of my fraternity brothers, Johnny Crumpler, asked me to be in his wedding in Norfolk. As an usher for the ceremony, I escorted women to their seats in the church, and who should wind up on my arm but Joan Perry.

Judy had given me the heave-ho a couple of years before, and while I'd dated in the time since, nothing serious had developed. Joan, likewise, had dated while at Longwood College in Farmville, Virginia, which at the time was a state teachers' college and just a handful of miles from an all-male college, Hampden-Sydney; like me, she'd not found true love. She was just back in town after six weeks in Europe and was attending the wedding with her mother.

It was at the reception at the Norfolk Yacht and Country Club that we got a chance to talk, and I learned that she'd been, predictably, a star at Longwood—president of her class, high grades, perhaps even more energetic than at Granby. And to my own surprise, I found that this girl I'd overlooked back in high school had my complete and undivided attention.

It wasn't until much later that I discovered Joan had spotted me in the church before I saw her, and had engineered her place in line at the door so I'd be the usher who walked her in. She says she was certain back in high school that I was a good fit for her, and that the three years since we'd gone our separate ways hadn't cooled her opinion of me. She confesses to being aggressive. I suppose I was operating at a disadvantage, because she was a math major. She knew how to calculate.

The hunter and prey got tougher to distinguish after that, however. Back at Randolph-Macon after my second PLC boot camp, I began to see Joan regularly. Our schools were roughly seventy miles apart, and as neither of us had a car we relied on Greyhound for weekend visits all that fall and the following spring. It was another age in terms of dating, almost an extension of the Victorian era. When I traveled to Longwood, I had to sign Joan out of her dormitory and have her back at a respectable (and rigidly enforced) hour. When she came up my way, she'd take the bus to Richmond and I'd borrow a car to pick her up. She'd stay with a family just off campus, several of whom made extra money by putting up girls who came to Ashland for functions at the college. The understanding was that I'd have her back to her room by an agreed-upon time.

Neither of us tested the rules. Our courtship had more in common with those of our parents than with those that came just a short while later—after JFK's assassination, which occurred late that fall, at which point we seemed to lose our innocence as a society, and after which came Vietnam, the pain and

Vacationing with my parents at about the time I began my socially stellar but otherwise shaky stint at Granby High. Mom and Dad already look worried.

violence of the civil-rights movement, student disruptions, riots, more assassinations. The world went crazy.

Still, even in those prim and proper circumstances, we got to know each other well enough to see that our pairing was good, that it had the potential to last, that it was serious. We had much in common—a dedication to hard work and a commitment to support each other in bad times as well as good. Before long, our dates deepened into an abiding love and admiration for one another. She was smart and funny and held herself to a high ethical standard. I was proud of who she was and proud to be with her. And it certainly didn't hurt that since high school this cute girl had become a beautiful woman.

We got to know one another's families, too, well enough to recognize that we came from completely different households. My folks were avid readers; Joan's rarely cracked a book, though it was clear both of them were smart and savvy people. My folks weren't much for fraternal organizations; Mr. Perry was a Mason and a Lions Club officer who hadn't missed a club meeting in decades. My parents' friends were doctors and other professionals; Joan's folks socialized with friends from church, not professional but hardworking and successful people.

Mr. Perry was fairly quiet, perhaps even a little shy, an unassuming fellow who offered no clue in conversation that he was the impresario of a large and growing assortment of businesses. He did not pretend to have answers to the big questions of the day; in fact, he was unlikely to ask those questions. He loved to laugh and rarely ruined a pleasant chat with a serious subject. I took a liking to him right from the start. He seemed to think pretty highly of me, too.

Kitty Perry was a tougher sell. Fact was, she didn't care for me one bit—didn't approve of my wild high school days or my fondness for beer in college. The Baptist teetotaler in her sized me up as unworthy of her daughter. She didn't keep the opinion a secret. One example: Both sets of parents were at our graduations in June 1964. I was in Joan's dorm room with a group of her friends when the Perrys arrived for the Longwood ceremony. Mrs. Perry greeted everyone in the room but me with a hug or handshake. I shook it off. I figured I just had something new to prove.

And by then, it was clear I would have to prove it, because on one of Joan's visits to the Phi Delt house that spring of 1964, I'd asked her to marry me.

Of all the things I've done in my life, proposing to Joan was the best. Everything good since—our life together, our children, our success with family and business—grew out of that moment. Or, more accurately, the moment after, when she said yes. At the time, I had no idea what I'd do with my life—didn't know whether I'd make a career of the service or find some job after a stint in uniform—but I was young, confident, soon to be a marine officer, and excited at beginning an adventure that, with Joan at my side, promised to be remarkable.

I graduated from Randolph-Macon with a three-point-something average. By then, my parents' doubts about my making it had subsided a little, but they were euphoric just the same. My graduation present was their help in buying my first car: I borrowed half the money, my father gave me half, and I bought a new '64 Ford Galaxie 500 convertible from my cousin Charles at Brock Motor Company in Trenton, North Carolina. It was baby blue and about half a block long and boasted a sporty floor shifter.

I received my commission at graduation and had roughly a month before reporting to Quantico for Basic School. Joan and I spent much of it together, then parted ways. She landed a job teaching tenth-grade geometry and algebra at John Randolph Tucker High School in Richmond and got a room in a house with five or six other young women. I headed north to Quantico in my new convertible.

3

A Cog in
the Machine

B asic School was nothing like the boot camps I'd attended. On arriving for those summer sessions, I'd had drill instructors busting my chops from the second I stepped off the train, calling me a maggot and ordering me to do push-ups and in general shitting on me like a raw recruit at Parris Island.

But now I was a lieutenant with gold "butter bars" on my collar. This was more like graduate school. I'd proven myself in those earlier boot camps and by holding down good grades in college. I was treated with respect.

We learned the philosophies that guided the movement of marines under arms, the decision-making processes and tactics that might spell the difference between life and death on a battlefield. We were inculcated with Marine Corps culture—the service's history, its jargon, the measures by which all of us new officers would be judged. We took up marksmanship. I was a good shot, felt easy around weapons, and enjoyed that quite a bit.

At the time, I probably didn't appreciate the effect this training had on me, but I certainly do now. It remade me—how I related to people, how I made decisions, how I handled the unexpected, both good and bad. My style as a leader is based on the principles I learned there. Many of today's top American business executives are Basic School graduates. That's no accident. It changes you. You come out of Quantico with conviction. You know what you have to do, and you know how to get it done. Looking back, it occurs to me that college didn't teach me anything about life, just how to learn. Basic School taught me how to live.

During my weekend breaks, I dashed down to Richmond to see Joan. Her house was crowded, noisy, and hot. She and her roommates were shoehorned into three bedrooms and, worse, shared one and a half baths. And none of the rooms was air conditioned. Nowadays, officials cancel school if something goes wrong with the air conditioning, but at that time climate control was a real luxury. I slept on a sofa in a sweltering spare room. On Sunday nights, I raced back to Quantico in time to get squared away for the coming week.

So it went through my first five months at Basic School—until, at Thanksgiving, we were married at her family's church, Talbot Park Baptist in Norfolk. We had no time for a honeymoon; I still had a few weeks to go before my graduation. I drove back to Quantico a day into married life. But we managed our time together with extreme efficiency, as befitted a young Marine Corps couple. Even before I graduated that December, Joan was expecting.

At Basic School, I had the opportunity to request what kind of work I'd do in the Corps—what my military occupational specialty, or MOS, would be. I requested a job in Marine Corps aviation rather than with ground troops, and got my wish. I was slotted into "airfield launch and recovery."

Marine aviators exist to support marines on the ground—that's the only reason the service has its own attack planes, such as the F/A-18 Hornet. These jets are not kept around to fight other planes, as navy and air force fighters do, or to bomb enemy targets in faraway cities; instead, they swoop in when needed, guns blazing and missiles at the ready, to eliminate any entrenched bad guys resisting the marines down below.

At the time, the top brass were exploring ways to get our planes as close to the action as possible, so as to cut their response time. Among their experiments was this notion of airfield launch and recovery, which called on marine jets to take off and land on short airfields cut into the jungle in the same way they did on aircraft carriers, with catapults assisting them into the air and a wire on which they'd tail-hook to land. I trained in the system at the naval air station in Lakehurst, New Jersey, though the whole idea of a carrier deck on terra firma never really caught on; everyone realized that the navy could park a carrier plenty close enough to accomplish the same thing. Any airfield management I might perform would more likely involve helicopters than attack planes.

My first duty station, where I reported in January 1965, was Beaufort, South Carolina, a city the marines dominated the same way the navy did Norfolk. Just to the south and across a narrow estuary was Parris Island, the sprawling marine boot camp. To the north lay the air station, one of the Corps' biggest and busiest. A big naval hospital was planted right in the middle of town.

I worked at the air station. Joan took a job teaching eighth-grade math at Beaufort Junior High School. No base housing was available for us when we arrived, but an officer in my unit knew of a place in town I'd be able to afford with my $110 monthly housing allowance, and we took it—the main floor of a three-level house on Craven Street, a lovely, shaded lane in the town's center, lined with deep front porches and draped in Spanish moss. The landlady lived upstairs; another couple, who became our friends, rented the basement. Our digs consisted of the house's living room, dining room, and kitchen, with our bed in the dining room and a clothes rack in the foyer. It was makeshift, for sure, but our first home as a couple was a happy one. In our spare time, we'd drive out to one of the Sea Islands off the Atlantic coast, Fripp Island, which is all golf courses and luxury homes now but was barren and wild at the time. We'd sit on the beach among driftwood and stranded horseshoe crabs, sprayed by the surf, convinced we had it made.

That summer, the housing at the air station loosened up, and we moved into a three-bedroom, two-bath house on base. At about the same time, our first daughter, Kathryn, was born at the naval hospital.

■ ■ ■

It's quite possible I had never heard of Vietnam when I entered Randolph-Macon, but by now I knew quite a bit about it. My awareness of the place and the trouble there grew in stages. It had come up first during my classes at Basic School; advisors had been on the ground in Southeast Asia for a decade by then, and they'd run up against some challenges that became teaching points.

The marines made up a relatively small share of those advisors in 1964—eight hundred or so out of a total force of twenty thousand, most of them stationed in and around Saigon, the South Vietnamese capital. But then came the infamous Gulf of Tonkin incident, in which North Vietnamese torpedo boats were said to have attacked a couple of our warships, and things heated up fast.

By the time I arrived in Beaufort, serious debate was under way about committing American combat troops to defending our interests in the south against the communist North Vietnamese. Within weeks, the North Vietnamese were actively attacking American advisors, and it was clear that the United States faced the choice of quitting the place altogether or increasing its presence. The

Joan and I pose with our Galaxie convertible on the Outer Banks in 1964, not long before I reported to my first Marine Corps post. Within eighteen months, I'd be keeping far less agreeable company, in far less agreeable surroundings.

COURTESY OF BROCK FAMILY

first combat units to enter the country were marines, whose landing craft hit the beach at Danang in early March 1965.

Vietnam dominated conversation at the air station as spring gave way to summer, and even more so as summer turned to fall. It was clear that a real shooting war had started. Some of my colleagues at Beaufort shipped over. Some marines I'd gone to college with did, too. One of them was a buddy of mine, Bill Wester, who wrote me about his life there. It didn't much sound like fun.

A few months into 1966, I figured I'd probably luck out and remain stateside, since my hitch ran only through the middle of 1967. I had less than thirteen months remaining, unless I re-upped—and thirteen months was the standard deployment to Vietnam. I kept my mind on my job and on helping Joan with the baby.

Evidently, I underestimated my importance to the war effort; that summer, with just about a year left in my service obligation, I got orders to join the fight. I was unhappy about it. I was worried not only about getting myself killed but about leaving Joan alone to shoulder a job, run the house, and care for an infant. But mostly, I was surprised. I wrote to Bill Wester: "I'm coming to see you."

We decided right off that it made sense for Joan to go home to Norfolk with

Kathryn. I helped set her up in her parents' house and told Mr. Perry I'd pay rent to him for the duration of her stay. It seemed only right to do that. It was my responsibility to take care of my family, and even if I couldn't be with Joan I intended to fulfill that obligation. He accepted my proposal. He respected it.

We had a week's leave together before Joan started a teaching job in Norfolk, at Northside Middle School, and I got on an airplane. I flew first to San Francisco, then Okinawa, then Vietnam, my surroundings bleaker with each stop. I landed in Danang in a C-130, a fat-bellied, prop-driven cargo plane, and stepped into the swirling red dust, withering heat, and relentlessly intense sun of a Vietnamese summer day. Folks in Virginia and Carolina take a perverse pride in the sticky discomfort of their summers, but nothing at home had prepared me for the tropical furnace of the China Sea coast. It was so hot and humid that my clothes were soaked through the moment I stepped off the plane, and they stayed that way until I got back on a plane to fly home.

I was hustled aboard a helicopter and flown a few miles to the south, toward the big fixed-wing air base at Chu Lai. Just above it along the coast was the marine chopper base at Ky Ha—pronounced Kee-Haw, usually with a bit of a whoop, as in Yeehaw! My ride touched down there, and I checked into my new unit: Marine Aviation Squadron 36.

Ky Ha occupied most of a peninsula jutting into the South China Sea, ringed by white-sand beaches, and under other circumstances it might have been a beautiful place. As it was, it had that despoiled look of most front-line military installations. The quarters for the marines stationed there were plywood hooches built on tiers carved into a hillside. They overlooked a huge steel mat on which the helicopters parked—old, slow, fat-nosed H-34 Choctaws, which by this time only the marines were using, the other services having abandoned them for comparatively sleek and fast replacements; early versions of the UH-1 Huey, which would prove the most durable of the newer choppers and could be outfitted for every duty from air ambulance to gunship; twin-rotor CH-46 birds for hauling cargo and troops; and the occasional Sikorsky Skycrane, which could lift a tank off the ground and created so much downdraft it would blow over the base's latrines.

I was assigned to a hooch that slept ten to twelve. A buddy from the States, Steve Kirkpatrick, was already living there and showed me around. Plywood walls. Plywood floor. No plumbing. Not much in the way of privacy. Dark, hot as hell, poorly ventilated. You get a dozen guys in a confined space like that, sweating in the equatorial heat, and it doesn't take long for the air to turn creamy with stink. The first time I walked into my new home, the smell hit me like a baseball bat across the face. But as with all things, I got used to it. Before long, I couldn't even detect the reek.

The latrines were housed in separate plywood shacks, to which we'd dash when we got the call. We shaved with cold water, and showered in hot on those occasions when everything worked as it should. My office was built of plywood, too. Like everything on base, it was makeshift and utilitarian. This was field living, a temporary setup. The whole place was task oriented; comfort and good looks were not among Ky Ha's priorities.

Don't think for a second that I'm complaining. I had it as good as it got in Vietnam. Next to most assignments in country, mine was gravy. I wasn't flying low and slow over the jungle every day, getting shot at; my job was to support the guys who *were* getting shot at. I was an administrative officer, part of the squadron's command structure that kept operations running smoothly. I rarely had reason to leave the base. I never laid eyes on a bona fide Viet Cong insurgent or a North Vietnamese soldier. I never had to duck a bullet or grenade. My days were long and my duties oftentimes complex, but they kept me on station, on de facto American soil.

So no hero, I. I was merely a cog in the machine. I got up early, worked all day and into the night, and sacked out in my cot. I enjoyed a cold beer now and then, ate hot food every day, and got my mail from home more or less reliably. Most of the guys sleeping in the cots around me were administrative officers, too—one, I recall, was a dentist. The pilots and their crews slept elsewhere, and I can only imagine that their sleep didn't come as easily or as regularly as mine. I flew out on one mission and got enough of a taste for what those guys saw every day that I was, and remain, mighty thankful I didn't do it as a regular part of my job.

My work was interesting enough, thank you. I spent my first several months in country as a personnel officer, writing up citations for medals earned by the air group's marines. Then, as the more senior officers rotated home, I was promoted to first lieutenant and quickly to captain and was assigned the more difficult duties of running the base's messes, supervising its sanitation protocols—in other words, getting the latrines emptied—and overseeing its stores of jet fuel and our firefighting teams. Among the important lessons I learned was that effective leaders knew when to get out of the way. I trusted my sergeants to do their jobs, and they didn't let me down. In the marines, as in the business world, micromanagement is a waste of time and talent.

It wasn't obvious at the time, but perhaps the luckiest break I got at Ky Ha

Captain Brock deploying a marine-issue scowl at Ky Ha, a once-idyllic stretch of Vietnamese beach transformed into a sprawling helicopter base. This picture captures me late in my deployment and military career.

COURTESY OF BROCK FAMILY

was that I was there early in the war. I arrived just as the first marines in country were leaving, and eighteen months before the Tet Offensive, when everything started to turn bad. In 1966, we were still winning every fight we picked, and the sound of gunfire rarely reached us.

We were mindful that it could, of course. Outside the hooches, we built sandbagged bunkers in case trouble came our way. The base was targeted by rocket attacks once in a while and came under mortar fire a few times, and we'd hightail it into the bunkers, where anything but a direct hit stood little chance of doing us harm.

But on most days, my biggest complaint was that I had too much to do in too little time. And then, all of a sudden, my enlistment was up.

I don't mean to suggest that time passed quickly, because while I was there it didn't seem that way at all; on the contrary, it crawled by. Loneliness was a constant. I spoke to Joan only once during my tour. But in looking back, I faced the decision of staying or quitting the marines while I was still a relative newbie.

Re-upping was a temptation. I was proud to be a member of the Corps. I liked being useful to my fellow marines. And were I to stay in uniform and return to Vietnam for a second tour, I reckoned I'd most likely get another administrative job, though that was no certainty regardless of my specialty. But it would certainly mean more time away from my family, and I missed Joan, missed baby Kathryn, and felt as if my time overseas had placed them in hardship. The fastest way out of the country was to get out of the marines. So I got out. I came home.

I've been back to Ky Ha, by the way. In the late nineties, Joan and I were headed to Hong Kong on a buying trip for Dollar Tree, and we invited along a buddy from my hooch, Steve Kirkpatrick. We caught a flight from Hong Kong to Hanoi, traveled on to Danang, and set out in a van to find the old base, armed with pictures of what the place looked like thirty years before.

We found a road branching off Highway 1 that I thought I remembered, so we took it. And through a combination of dead reckoning and wandering around lost, we stumbled on the old installation's gates. We weren't authorized to be there, and no sooner had we reached this point than we were surrounded by army officers, who seemed pretty damn displeased to find foreigners snooping around.

Vietnamese soldiers have a lot of stars on their uniforms, so that all of them down to the lowliest teenage grunts look like generals. They were confrontational. If it hadn't been so tense a moment, I might have laughed; a year at this place during an actual war had been less hazardous than our peacetime tourist drive-by. But Joan and I displayed my old photos, and our driver explained why we were there, and the officers took an interest. They climbed into the van with us and showed us around.

Our old base was barely recognizable. A cemetery filled the hillside where the hooches had stood. The tarmac on which the helicopters parked was still there, though broken and weedy. The perforated steel Marsden matting the marines had laid as a temporary airstrip was rusty and twisted by trees that had punched their way through to stand fat and tall. It was a strange sensation, both exhilarating and bittersweet, to visit such a ghost from my past. I'd been intimately familiar with this piece of territory once upon a time—familiar enough to curse it and to count the days before I could escape it. Here, I had worked hard, pined for my wife and daughter, missed home and all I'd left there. Here, I had agonized over my career and what the future held for us. Now, just the slightest vestige, a whisper, of those intense days remained.

After we dropped off our escorts and left the property, we swung through An Ha, a little village outside the gates. Then we drove back to Danang, to a five-star resort on the site of the old American base at China Beach, to eat like kings.

. . .

I've always said it's better to be lucky than smart, and I was certainly lucky to leave Vietnam when I did. I arrived back in Norfolk that summer of 1967, and thus watched Tet unfold on TV, along with its aftermath—the immense American troop buildup; the increase in the size, boldness, and capabilities of the opposition; the rising casualties; the disintegration of the whole affair. I signed up for a stint in the Marine Corps Reserves on my return, joined a unit on the naval base, and put in time on weekends and for two weeks each summer. But as a practical matter, I was through with the military. I wasn't destined for a marine career.

What I was better suited to was a mystery to me. I still had a strong desire to succeed at something but had no clue what that might be. What I needed, however—and fast—was an income. I had a family to support. I went to an agency that specialized in placing naval officers in civilian jobs and applied to a number of different places. While I job-hunted, Joan and I bounced between our parents' homes—two weeks with the Brocks, two weeks with the Perrys, and so forth—because we didn't want to overstay our welcome in either place.

In time, I got an offer from Kaiser Aluminum to work at its plant in Ravenswood, West Virginia, as a foreman. I knew nothing about aluminum or factories in general. I knew nothing of civilian management either. In fact, the list of things I didn't know was pretty impressive, and the list of what I knew was a little alarming. But Kaiser offered good pay, and the company was encouraging. Come on out there, it said, and it would get me up to speed. I took the job.

Ravenswood is between Parkersburg and Charleston on the Ohio River. It's a tiny place in the back of beyond. It dates to 1810, but at the time I drove out with much of our household loaded into a truck, Kaiser had been running its huge smelter and rolling mill there for ten years, and Ravenswood had become a company town. One of its nicknames—which I did not know when I took the job—was "Gateway to Hell." I am not kidding.

I went to work at this enormous factory and encountered trouble almost straight off. It was a union plant, its workers represented by the United Steel Workers. I'd never been exposed to unions before. I was used to the Marine Corps. If I told someone to do something, I expected him to do it. That didn't fly in Ravenswood.

Every shift brought some little bullshit confrontation. I couldn't pick up a hammer—just holding a tool constituted labor, and was therefore outside the duties of management. If I stepped over that line, no matter how minor the step, I'd have somebody in my face yelling, "I need a shop steward over here!" Too many days brought a tense faceoff with the union. And if the workers didn't get their way, they'd screw things up to slow or halt production.

Heck, one day, I saw a piece of paper on the floor and bent over to pick it up and got into a skirmish. I couldn't understand it. It seemed mindless. The union's stance wasn't just anti-management, it was anti-accomplishment—it seemed to be, "Everything for *me*, and nothing for the mission." In fact, the mission shared by many workers seemed to be to screw the mission. Even if I hadn't just mustered out of the marines, I think I'd have balked at my new surroundings. The plant was supposed to operate efficiently and make money. That's why we were there, all of us. That's why Kaiser paid us.

My bosses in management stuck by me, but my confusion and discomfort at the job were amplified by the crazy hours the post required. I was on shift work—seven days of graveyard, seven days of swing, and seven days of day shift, then back to graveyard. My life was turned completely upside down. I couldn't get into the rhythm, so I didn't sleep much.

Joan, meanwhile, was struggling to take care of both Kathryn and her sleep-deprived, miserable husband. And on top of that, she learned she was expecting another baby. She went home for Christmas, and I couldn't join her—I had to work—and in her absence I plunged into deep melancholy. I wasn't happy. She wasn't happy. As a family, we weren't happy.

So I went into the office and quit. I didn't give Joan a heads-up before I did it, which I felt bad about, but it was clear that Ravenswood didn't offer the life we sought. We'd made some friends there, and the approach of our second child suggested we'd enjoyed some good times, but otherwise our brief adventure in West Virginia served only to inform us about what to avoid later in life.

By that, I mean that we don't have unions at Dollar Tree. Not one. We have had unions make runs on our warehouses, but our answer has been to address our workers' needs as best we can, so they're not spurred to organize. I've found that if we pay people well, treat them with respect, and recognize that their contributions are key, they'll be eager to pocket what they would have spent on union dues.

It could be that, had I given the job more time or been exposed to unions earlier—if I'd grown up in a union household, say—I would have reacted differently. I'm sure those organizations have been essential in some industries at some points in time. I imagine that good things can come of them. But it's hard for me to picture myself having to put up with the sort of nonsense I endured at Kaiser.

. . .

I returned to Norfolk, again unemployed and without direction.

Among the jobs I'd applied for at the same time I put my name in with Kaiser was a government post that required lengthy background checks—so thorough and time consuming that they weren't completed until after we moved to West Virginia. Now, I called the Office of Naval Intelligence and asked if I could resubmit my application. The people there said I could and pushed through the paperwork, and in I went.

The ONI had two branches, one criminal and the other investigative. The criminal side tackled the sort of stuff you see in the television show *NCIS*, though in truth it wasn't much like that at all. I was assigned to the investigative side, putting together background investigations.

A candidate would apply for a government job that required security clearance, and we'd dig into his or her past—the more sensitive the job, the deeper the digging. A candidate for a White House post or a position at the National Security Agency—any work that involved top-secret stuff—got a lot of attention from the ONI.

We agents traveled to wherever the candidate had lived, checking out every address he'd listed, every reference. We talked to his bosses, his coworkers, his neighbors, his coaches and teachers and friends, and we did it in person, knocking on doors and interviewing people. If we got one derogatory comment, we had to get at least three or four positives to discount it. The questions we asked were mostly behavioral: Did this person drink? Did he fight? Did he gamble? Was he a big spender? Was he in a stable, healthy relationship? That was a big one.

We investigated the person's sex life for anything the navy might consider abnormal or deviant. Of course, you know what Winston Churchill said about his own country's navy—that its traditions were "rum, sodomy, and the lash." Even so, we were to pay close attention to anything out of the sexual norm, and in 1968 that included homosexuality. The fear was that being gay made a person a target for blackmail, because to be exposed back then was disastrous to career, family, the works. If the candidate's behavior suggested he was gay, the navy feared he could be leveraged to cough up the government's secrets. Sounds crazy, I know, but that's how it was.

Finances were also a big target of inquiry. A fellow who was deep in debt could be enticed to violate secrecy with the promise of money.

Any whiff of a problem had to be checked out. A candidate would step off a ship at the pier, and I'd be sitting with another agent in a car, watching and waiting. We'd follow him wherever he went. Once the fact gathering was done, I went to the office and wrote a report about whom I'd talked with, what each said, how he or she said it. We gauged how much credibility the witnesses had. Had they known the subject for two years, three years? How well had they known him?

My reports had to be written according to strict navy protocol. There was a path to doing them, and I learned to stay true to it. I'd better not misspell a word, and I'd better make sure my punctuation was right, and I'd better be certain my grammar was good. I'd turn a report in, and it would come back covered with red marks, which I'd correct in a do-over. Eventually, the higher-ups would approve the report and pass it on.

A couple of times, the criminal side needed help, and I got to try some cloak-and-dagger stuff, chasing some character around the city. I enjoyed my life as an agent. I found it stimulating. I wore a badge and had a gun, which appealed to me. I looked forward to going to work, because I had a purpose. I looked forward to going home at day's end, because I enjoyed my family.

Which was growing: Joan gave birth to another daughter, Christy, so now we had a toddler and an infant to care for. After another round of bouncing between our parents' homes, we found a house—a little two-bedroom Cape Cod on a quiet street that dead-ended on the Lafayette just a few blocks from the Perrys' place.

So as 1968 drew near its end, I held a job that I could consider a career, that offered security, decent pay, and opportunity for advancement. We owned our first home. We had two healthy kids. Joan and I had been married for more than three years, and our bond was strong and getting stronger. For the first time since Beaufort, I felt somewhat at ease about the future.

Then, one evening, Joan's father dropped by our house, saying he wanted to talk with me. Just me. We sat down in the living room, and Mr. Perry asked if I'd consider going to work for him at the five-and-ten.

4

Asking Alice

‾‾‾‾‾

At first blush, the offer didn't much appeal to me. I knew the store well. I'd stop at the lunch counter some weekdays and chat with Joan's brother Kenny, who was often there at the same time, and I always enjoyed those visits. But afterward, I'd go back to my job as an agent, which seemed far more glamorous. I wore a suit. I carried a badge. I had authority. All of that conferred a certain status—I was a young guy who had a *career*.

Mr. Perry was asking me to trade that for a job as a schlep in a five-and-ten-cent store. It was hard to see it as anything but a comedown. I remember thinking, *I've got status, and he wants me to be a glorified stock clerk?* Not only that, he wouldn't match my navy salary. I'd take a pay cut and get a crappy job out of the bargain.

We talked only about a job at the store itself, nothing more. Mr. Perry made no mention of my someday having a shot at owning the business. If he was thinking about succession as he advanced through middle age, about grooming his replacement, he kept it to himself.

I asked about his two sons, Kenny and Doug. How would they feel about my moving in on the family turf? They had rightful claims to the job, while I was an in-law, a ways down the pecking order. He told me he didn't think they were interested, but that I could talk with them if I liked. I asked him to let me think about it. He agreed, we shook hands, and he left.

So I thought about it. I thought about nothing else for a couple of days. And with all that thought, and many conversations with Joan, my perception of the offer began to shift.

Here was my thinking: I had a job I liked. My career path was clear. If I stuck with Naval Intelligence and performed well, I'd advance through the government's civilian ranks to GS-whatever, the top of the bureaucracy. I could make a pretty good living. I was well suited to the work. I understood the military and its rules, thanks to my years in the marines. I'd be happy and relaxed.

But everything good about the job had a flip side. I'd always be able to imagine my future. There was nothing wrong with that—after my experience in West Virginia, a little job security was mighty attractive—but it was limiting. Where would I wind up if things went perfectly? There were only so many possibilities. Top agent in Norfolk? Top agent in D.C.? Once I was as good as I could get, I'd plateau. I'd have no further opportunity to advance.

Some agents moved on to the FBI or the Secret Service, which I thought might be interesting. But even then, I'd remain an agent of the government, working within a framework that was rigid and predictable and capped with a bulletproof ceiling.

Mr. Perry's offer, on the other hand, represented the unknown. I might prove to be a terrible assistant manager. Then again, I might not. I might turn out to be some sort of retail whiz. If I succeeded, it seemed to me, there were few limits to how far I could go. My income wouldn't be preset by a policy written by someone else. If K. R. didn't offer me bigger challenges over time, and with them bigger opportunities and rewards, then I could take my track record elsewhere. I would command my own destiny.

And there was this: I might learn something. Mr. Perry was a self-made businessman. He'd pulled himself up without the benefit of college business courses, a benefactor, any help at all. Working with him would amount to an education in achieving success, taught by a whip-smart guy who had his hands in several different businesses. I had nothing but respect for the man. I admired his work ethic and honesty, his humility, his basic goodness. I was part of a big club in that regard; a year later, the mayor of Norfolk, Roy Martin, convinced K. R. to run for city council on the mayor's ticket, and although he didn't win, the invitation testified to how liked and respected he was.

Besides all that, Joan pointed out, I'd enjoyed dealing with customers during my days at Frazier's Pharmacy. I seemed to have a knack for it. And the store offered a chance for creativity that I probably wouldn't have at ONI. I might be able to come up with ways to make it better, to boost sales. That sort of challenge might be fun—and ultimately more satisfying than investigating the bad habits of job applicants.

I talked first with Kenny, who was a couple of years younger than me, and Doug, who was five years my junior. Their dad made me this offer, I told them. What did they think about it? Kenny, who'd graduated from Virginia Tech with a degree in accounting, said he had no interest in the job. Doug was likewise unexcited about a career in his dad's store, where he'd worked part-time all through high school. Be my guest, he told me.

With that, much to my own surprise, I took Mr. Perry up on his offer.

Late in 1968, I turned in my badge and became the new assistant manager of a dime store.

■ ■ ■

I don't want to get off on a long side story about how such stores came to be, but it's worth sharing just a little bit of history, because they represent one of the most enduring business models in retail. Many of the principles that guide the business today date back a century or more—to one man, really, whose name is known to just about every American of a certain age: Frank W. Woolworth.

Woolworth didn't invent the idea of a store that sold a little of everything. General stores were serving customers in even the smallest American towns of the late nineteenth century. In fact, he got his first paying job as a clerk in one of them, in Watertown, New York, in the mid-1870s. And he didn't exactly dream up the idea behind the five-and-ten either. The inspiration for that came to him from a traveling salesman who visited the Watertown store in 1878, when Woolworth was twenty-six and the store was overstocked with merchandise and teetering on the brink of failure. Up in Michigan, the salesman said, stores had been experimenting with "Everything's a Nickel" tables, and they'd done right well with them.

Woolworth, so the story goes, convinced his boss to set up such a table in Watertown. The store ordered a hundred dollars' worth of pins, pens, wash basins, buttonhooks, thimbles, and soaps and displayed them alongside wares that hadn't moved in months under a sign reading, "Any Article on This Table 5¢." As Woolworth later told it, "The goods vanished like snow in April."

Woolworth figured that if a table could draw that kind of business, a whole store selling stuff for a nickel might do even better. After a false start in Upstate New York, he opened a five-cent store in the center of Lancaster, Pennsylvania, in 1879. Inside of a month, his inventory turned over three times. Within a short time, he boosted Lancaster's top price to ten cents, creating the first five-and-dime. He opened his second permanent location, in Reading, Pennsylvania, in 1884, and by century's end—when Woolworth stores were moving fast into the big cities of the East—he had close to one hundred, their shelves filled with an incredible range of goods, from ice skates to ladies' gloves to umbrellas to driving goggles, all of much higher quality than a shopper might expect for so little money.

He recognized early on that, while wholesalers could supply most of the goods he sought, better and more interesting deals waited overseas. He was a smart merchandiser who understood what his customers wanted, even if they didn't yet know they had to have it. One example: he found glass Christmas tree ornaments in Germany, brought them home by the millions, and made them an American holiday staple.

Joining forces with five friendly rivals made the company a juggernaut. It built the world's tallest building as its headquarters. It became the largest department-store chain on earth, and its lunch counters one of the planet's biggest suppliers of prepared food. Woolworth's aim was to have a store in every town of more than ten thousand people, and he damn near achieved it; by the mid-1950s, the chain had 2,850 "red fronts" in prime downtown locations throughout the United States, Canada, and Europe.

Naturally, this success attracted competitors. S. S. Kresge opened for business in 1897, and others followed, among them McCrory's, S. H. Kress & Co., and, starting in 1927, Ben Franklin.

Unlike the Woolworth stores, which were company owned, most Ben Franklins were franchises, much like modern fast-food joints. The company maintained central control of purchasing, prices, signage, store layout. The operator ordered his merchandise from the company, which kept him in supply in exchange for a hefty chunk of the sales and a periodic franchise fee. The stores tended to be snugger than Woolworth locations, suited to modest shopping centers and small towns. It was as a Ben Franklin franchisee in tiny Bentonville, Arkansas, that Sam Walton got his start before opening his own discount operation, Walmart, in 1962.

K. R. had operated as a franchisee at Wards Corner for a decade before breaking his ties with the mother ship. Chafed by its claustrophobic policies on pretty much everything he did, and by his realization that he could buy his merchandise for less money elsewhere (and thereby increase his income), he'd gone independent in 1963. Now, he ordered his goods through a variety wholesaler in Atlanta and had rebannered his store K&K Five and Ten, short for Kenneth and Kathryn.

Still, when I reported for my first day as assistant manager, the store hewed pretty close to the Ben Franklin model and looked much as it had when I'd gone in as a kid. Spinning stools at the lunch counter. A square of wooden counters just inside the door, topped with glass cases full of bulk candy and a popcorn machine. Aisles formed by wooden gondolas—that's industry jargon for shelf assemblies—running to the rear wall, about 150 feet back. Birds and fishtanks back there, and a toy department—large for a store of that size, which was right about 10,000 square feet. Through a door in the back wall was a large stockroom, and beyond that was a small warehouse.

That was my new domain. Inside of two years, I'd gone from war-torn Vietnam to a factory floor in Appalachia to wearing a badge to this humble storefront in the middle of Norfolk.

. . .

When I showed up for work that first day, I met two important players in the operation. The first was my boss, the store's manager, and he'd been there for years. He was a nice enough fellow, and certainly knew how to manage people and inventory well, but it did not take long to see he wasn't exactly a ball of fire in drumming up ways to make the place more inviting or useful or fun for our customers. He was like a great many mid-level managers—competent but uninspired, dutiful but not particularly motivated.

The second was a force of nature, and among the most memorable people I've ever met. Back in the day, the label some men might have used to describe Alice Parlett was *broad*, though they'd have been taking their lives in their hands to use it to her face. She was a wide-shouldered, big-boned, two-fisted drill sergeant of an assistant manager, a bulldog who wore her hair stretched back in a severe bun, had a mouthful of teeth that looked like a freeway pileup, and growled her way through the workday. The high school girls who worked part-time in the store were scared to death of her, and for good reason: Alice never addressed any of them by name—they were "dummy" or "ugly"—and raised hell about the way they dressed—"Your mama let you out of the house like *that*?" They never worked hard enough or well enough to suit her.

One of those high school girls, Debbie Sorensen, applied for a job at the store when she was fifteen, and Alice shook her so badly while growling and

Alice Parlett in the former Ben Franklin store, which she ruled with an iron fist. This photo was taken twenty years after she served as my mentor, but it captures the severe personal style that struck fear in the hearts of her charges.

barking her way through the interview that Debbie actually forgot her own name. That was in 1976. Debbie's now the most senior employee at Dollar Tree.

Alice didn't think much of me when I walked through the doors. I reckon she had me pegged as a silver-spoon hire and wasn't expecting me to work hard. I surprised her. I threw myself into the job. I unloaded trucks, stocked shelves, priced the inventory, helped customers, mopped, and swept. I never took a break. I worked longer and harder than anyone there, and what's more, I enjoyed it. I found it fun. And within a few days, I think Alice came around in her opinion of me, which was a good thing, because soon enough I needed her help.

I hadn't realized when Mr. Perry offered me the job how little a role he played in the store's day-to-day operation. Fact was, he played next to none. He ate lunch at the counter every afternoon, and he conferred with my boss now and then in the office, and he loved visiting with customers he knew, but he was busy with his other enterprises and entrusted most of the actual work to the people he hired.

Another thing about K. R.: he disliked confrontation. Unassuming and humble as he was, he went to extremes to avoid coming to personal loggerheads with anyone. Shortly after joining the store, I realized my hiring happened to coincide with his having grown exasperated with the store manager. For whatever reason, K. R. had recently decided, years into having this gentleman run the business without incident, that the fellow wasn't who he wanted for the job. Now, the two weren't getting along, in the way people don't when one of them won't say what's eating at him, and can't put it into words even if he wants to speak up.

The poor manager must have seen the future when the boss's son-in-law showed up as his assistant, and he didn't mull his options for long. After three or four weeks, he quit. Mr. Perry came to me and announced, "Okay, you're the new manager."

I said, "Excuse me? *What*?"

All these years later, I understand his thinking, and might have made the same decision. You can always teach someone a business. It's a lot harder to teach smarts or drive or honesty. The old manager knew the business and was certainly honest, but he didn't have the most important ingredient—he didn't have desire, the hunger to make of the place something bigger and better. I still nursed an unfocused but strong desire to succeed. Plus, though I didn't know the business at all, I shared a strong work ethic with my father-in-law. I've always believed that hard, honest work is its own reward, and that it almost always pays dividends in time.

When I balked at the news, K. R. was reassuring. He'd help me, he said, and Alice would help me. I'd figure things out.

He was right: Alice did help me. For the next several months, I was manager in name alone; what I was, really, was a student of the business, with Alice as my tutor. She wasn't a patient mentor, exactly—Alice wasn't user-friendly, not some sweet, old grandmother type—but evidently she decided I deserved the effort, and she schooled me in all aspects of running the place.

Retail is not complicated. Those who do it well do it through people. I had been a Marine Corps officer and knew how to run people. And really, I could have had no better instructor to help me adjust those skills to the variety business, at least in how the store had operated to that point. Alice had started there at eighteen. She dated back to Barr Attaway's first days as owner. She understood the Ben Franklin system of accounting and inventory control, which K. R. had stuck with even after dissolving his franchise.

Everything about that system was low-tech. Our accounting and inventory control were performed by hand, with pencil and paper. We filled out every invoice in longhand. We wrote checks to our vendors the same way. We used ledgers to keep track of how much we paid, how much we charged, and how much of each item we had on hand. We used the same approach to ride herd on shrinkage, the merchandise that went out the door but wasn't sold, through giveaways and, more often, theft. We used a "profit wheel," made of cardboard, to figure the prices we'd sell each item for, based on what we paid for it. We'd want a markup of 40 percent in some cases, 50 percent in others, maybe as little as a third in a few.

It was Retail 101. Years later, when we started Dollar Tree, I drew on what I'd learned back at that little five-and-dime at Wards Corner. Those days with Alice were the basis for much of my thinking. But of course, that future was unimaginable in 1969, through the months of my asking, "Alice, what comes next?" and her telling me what to do.

By late in the year, I no longer had to ask. By then, I'd started to think about ways we might make the business better. And it was at about that point, just before Christmas, that Joan's brother Doug came aboard.

■ ■ ■

Doug Perry went to Granby High, as Joan and I had, graduating five years behind us. All through his teens, he worked every summer and Christmas at the five-and-ten, stocking shelves and unloading trucks. That had cured him of any plan to run the store someday. Instead, he'd gone to college at Chowan, in North Carolina, and later at Old Dominion, and had amassed about ninety hours toward a degree. He'd also operated his own store for a while, a skinny storefront around the corner from K&K that sold incense, black lights, and rock-and-roll posters.

Now, at twenty-two years old, he gave up both to join the family business, in what I'm sure he viewed as a temporary arrangement. I knew him mostly as the little brother who'd hung around when I visited Joan's house in high school, but now I saw he was his own man, in some ways like K. R. and in other ways his father's opposite. Doug was among the most outgoing people I'd ever met; he seemed incapable of encountering a stranger without engaging him in conversation, and came across as genuinely interested in what others had to say. He was a hard worker but liked to play. Doug was a river bum who loved afternoons boating on the Lafayette, relished his time on the beach, enjoyed the company of friends having a good time. He was smart—very smart—but like K. R. not a bookish sort. He put on no airs.

So Alice, Doug, and I ran the store. I was officially the boss and Alice and

Doug my assistants, but anyone watching probably wouldn't have been able to see that most days, because we all did whatever needed doing. We behaved as equals. Doug and I also discussed how we might improve things, and discovered we thought alike on a couple of big changes.

First, the store desperately needed a freshening. What with the ancient wooden gondolas that crowded most of the floor, it looked like something from before World War II. So we set about remodeling it. We tore the old counters down, installed modern shelving, brightened the whole experience for customers.

K. R. was all for it. He was a change artist in his quiet way, never stuck in the past, always ready and eager to embrace new ideas. With its new look, the K&K Five and Ten erased much of its leftover resemblance to the old Ben Franklin chain and was a much more appropriate presence at Wards Corner, which was probably at its height of popularity. Our neighbors were fashionable restaurants, two big department stores, a men's clothier, a bowling alley, two supermarkets, a massive all-night drugstore, and the flagship location of a regional shoe-store chain, Hofheimer's, which featured a monkey in a glass cage.

The second, even bigger change was to expand our already large toy department. We emptied the stockroom, cleaned it up, and filled it with toys, doubling the department's size. In the days before stand-alone toy stores, this was a distinction customers noticed; we were now, in effect, a toy retailer attached to a variety store, and business picked up almost immediately. We even had a separate entrance into the toy department from the parking lot out back.

We encountered a few kinks in the new operation. Initially, we set up the toy department's cash register just inside the back door, and one night somebody snatched the machine from the counter and took off with it. We rearranged the room, moving the register away from the door, and instituted a new rule: because the room couldn't be seen from the front of the store, the clerk on duty back there couldn't leave without first being relieved by another clerk.

The girls who held most of those jobs knew to take the rule seriously, because doing otherwise would provoke Alice. One night, a man in a trench coat wandered in, loitered among the toys for a while, then flashed the girl at the register. He didn't seem in a hurry to leave afterward—he just stood there, staring at her. The girl, whose name was Robin Jernigan, wouldn't budge. She was more afraid of Alice than of the flasher.

Robin Jernigan West is still with the company, by the way.

Such minor foibles aside, the new department performed better than we hoped. We started advertising, and business became ever more brisk.

We offered layaways, which was unusual at the time. We traded on great merchandise at great prices, and by the following Christmas we were the go-to destination in Norfolk for families buying for their kids.

Business was good enough that we were already thinking bigger. A few miles to the southeast, a new venue for retail was under construction—the region's first enclosed mall, Military Circle. A variety store specializing in toys would make a killing there, we figured, and it would give Doug a store of his own to oversee.

When we approached the developers leasing the mall, however, we found they weren't nearly as enthusiastic as we were. They saw no future for a smallish local variety store in their stylish new cathedral to retail, especially seeing as how they already had a Woolworth penciled in at a prime location. In retrospect, they did us a tremendous favor, because at the time other variety retailers were planning huge new stores in the area—S. S. Kresge, the old Woolworth competitor, was building Kmarts all over the place, and McCrory's was set to open a store on the mall's edge. We'd have been eaten alive.

So Doug, who found he was comfortable in the wheeling and dealing of lease negotiation, went back to the mall people with a new plan: what if, instead of a variety store that specialized in toys, we ditched the variety component and just opened a toy store? The leasing agents liked the idea—this was late 1970, and stand-alone toy stores were rarities—but now the mall's grand opening wasn't far off, and they had no space left for us. They did have a storefront already committed to Plum Tree, a Philadelphia-based gift-store chain, so for a brief while we considered making our second store a Plum Tree franchise. Doug even flew to Philadelphia to talk to the company.

But some elements of the franchise deal struck us as unreasonable. Plum Tree wanted us to outfit the store with gear the company would supply—everything from cash registers to shelving—and the price wasn't cheap. After discussing the matter with K. R., who had severed his ties to Ben Franklin over the same sorts of rules, we bagged the idea.

Then a break came our way. Plum Tree pulled out. The mall found itself with a vacancy. And we swooped in with a plan for the first K&K Toys.

5

When We
Got Eyes

When we opened that first toy store, Doug and I had a sense that it would do well, but it was just that—a sense. We had practically no empirical data on hand to predict how a store selling only toys would do in a new suburban mall, and we heard from more than a few people that it wouldn't work, that we were bound to go broke.

Up to that point, Americans bought most of their toys at department stores, which did the great bulk of their trade in toys at Christmas; during the holidays, their toy departments would double or triple in size. Catalog sales were big, too. Remember the *Sears Wish Book*? It came out in August or September every year for sixty years, and a great many kids found inspiration in its pages when it came time to make their Christmas lists.

But we felt we could succeed. We'd seen the toy department at Wards Corner grow in reputation and customer traffic, and that told us that devoting a whole store to toys, and locating it along a big, busy thoroughfare of a new, clean, air-conditioned mall, would generate business not only at Christmas but throughout the year. As K. R. put it, we "went into it with the idea that every child will have a birthday between now and next December. Most will have a party with about twelve kids, and each kid will bring a gift." They'd buy a good percentage of those gifts from us.

Even so, we underestimated just how big a hit the Military Circle store would be. From the first day, we were mobbed. The volume was insane. We were buying our merchandise from three jobbers, or wholesalers—a couple of

The K&K Toys store at Military Circle, our first venture into both stand-alone toy sales and mall retailing. This bustling Christmas scene testifies to the experiment's success.

companies in Norfolk and another in Richmond—and they couldn't keep up with our orders. Doug couldn't get the toys on the shelves fast enough. That first Christmas, we might have sold three dozen Monopoly games at the variety store. At Military Circle, Doug sold a gross. It was that way with virtually everything he stocked; he sold four, five, six times the number we moved at Wards Corner.

Bear in mind, this was before the malling of America. In the early seventies, you might find one big regional mall in a metropolitan area, and all the mall-bound shoppers now spread among five or six of them were squeezed into that one very finite space. With that many people herded onto the mall's indoor avenues, it was a cinch that some would peel off into our store. Sure, the rent was high, but the traffic made up for it many times over.

It was so clear we had a winner that Doug and I almost immediately contemplated a second store. We found a promising location in Landover, Maryland, a suburb of Washington, D.C., where a new mall was set to open. Doug moved up there to run it, while I ran the two Norfolk stores. And soon after that, we opened our third store, at Crabtree Valley Mall in Raleigh, North Carolina. We put a guy named Lewis Mitchell into the manager's chair there.

Lewis's story is a good illustration of how seat-of-the-pants the operation was at the time. Every day, K. R. would stroll into the five-and-dime at Wards Corner to pick up the cash receipts, then deposit them next door at Virginia National Bank. In the teller line one day, he got to talking to a navy enlisted man who was there making deposits for his command. K. R. was impressed by the sailor and told him that when he left the service he should come by to see about a job. Which Lewis did. We put him to work at the variety store and later moved him down to Raleigh.

Our corporate structure was almost naively simple. K. R. was at the top and owned just over half of the company. He handled all the money. Below him were Doug and me, in charge of two stores each, and each with a fifth of the ownership pie; we held pretty much the same jobs, both of us buying from vendors and overseeing store operations, our domains defined not by specialization but by geography.

We kept separate books—and checkbooks—for each store. When merchandise shipped from our warehouse to a store, the warehouse invoiced the store for the shipment, and we paid the bill with that store's checkbook. Such was our internal accounting system. Again, we did all of this by hand—the ordering, invoicing, bill payment, payroll, you name it. We didn't have a computer. Heck, we barely used calculators.

The warehouse, out back of the five-and-dime, was every bit as unsophisticated as the office. Trucks were loaded and unloaded by hand. Merchandise was shelved the same way.

It became apparent as we prepared to open our fifth and sixth stores, however, that this tiny enterprise might grow pretty quickly, so K. R. started a separate firm to handle the payroll. He opened an office—K&K Management—in the Perry Building and tapped Joan to run it. She had plenty of insight into how the stores operated and was expert at juggling the paperwork—all through high school, while she was excelling in class and all but running Granby High, she'd also walked down to her father's store two afternoons a week to keep the books and work the cardboard profit wheel. Now, she became an important back-room player in our rapidly expanding toy business. By overseeing payroll in a separate company, she ensured that the wages we paid to our people stayed private. And because she was in the loop on everything that went on throughout K&K, she was indispensable as a trusted advisor and sounding board.

Meanwhile, changes were coming to our personal lives. Joan gave birth to our third child, Macon III, in 1971. That same year, having outgrown our little house, we traded up for a bigger place not far from Wards Corner. And Doug hired a high school kid as a stock boy at the Military Circle store and learned that the boy's big sister was a beauty he'd much admired in high school. One thing led to another. He married Pat in July 1972.

■ ■ ■

One strange feature of the toy business—and I don't know of another business that is quite so odd in this respect—was that we did half the year's trade in the few weeks between Thanksgiving and Christmas. Those weeks were close to sleepless for me. We worked seven days a week and late into every night.

After Christmas, our workload remained heavy, but it wasn't quite so frenetic. We planned for the coming year. We spruced up the stores. A retail chain is always rethinking, reorganizing, redoing. We had to set up the new toys for the spring, put up new displays in time for the little bump in business at Valentine's Day, followed by the much bigger bump at Easter. Then we remade the stores again, this time for summer, when people trooped in for hot-weather toys—squirt guns, Slip 'N Slides, Water Wiggles, lawn darts, croquet sets. In the fall came another spike in activity in the weeks leading up to Halloween. And as soon as we recovered from that, the Christmas onslaught was again upon us.

I never minded the work. I enjoyed selling toys. Some parts of the business were murderous, but the products themselves could be a whole lot of fun. I liked the idea that we helped make kids smile. A toy store was by definition a happy place. We sold good times.

I also found I had a feel for what made a successful toy. I understood "play value"—whether or not a toy had the features a kid would return to time and again. A toy lacking play value was a waste of money for both the retailer and his customer; it was the toy abandoned after less than an hour of use, never to be retrieved from the toy chest. With three children under my own roof, I saw a few cases of insufficient play value up close. Kathryn, Christy, and Macon got a first look at just about every toy that came along in the seventies and eighties, and their reactions helped me identify the dogs.

The enduring toys of that period were those that called on a kid to use his or her imagination. Barbie and G.I. Joe were great examples. The store supplied the doll, but it was up to the kid to supply the action, the narrative, of any play involving the doll. Hot Wheels cars worked the same way. The toys themselves were inert until they were made part of a story by the kid playing with them.

Every stuffed animal has a distinct personality bestowed by the child hugging it, who imagines that the animal loves back. Paints, colored markers, Play-Doh, and sidewalk chalk are tools for creative thinking, and that kind of thinking happens to be fun. You always hear about kids forsaking play with some fancy new toy in favor of messing with the cardboard box it came in. Imagination is key.

Any toy that fostered interaction among kids generally succeeded over time, too. Again, Barbie scored high in that regard, because little girls loved to play Barbie with their friends. Likewise for board games, balls, anything kids could do better, or have a better time doing, with others. We opened K&K Toys at perhaps the best moment for toys in American history. I am thankful our venture didn't come fifteen or, God forbid, twenty years later, because toys changed. I doubt I'd find much satisfaction in the merchandise today.

What changed the toy business was the introduction of electronics, starting with Atari and Pong and the small, early gadget games that relied on just buttons and blinking lights. In the few years between those pioneering electronic toys and modern Nintendo games, kids themselves changed. What attracted them to an electronic toy was not the imagination it spawned, not the play they could make up with its help, but a turnkey experience. They now played games that were all figured out by someone else. They weren't called on to do anything but perform certain moves in a certain order, dictated by a computer programmer they'd never met and with whom they might have zero in common. They were along for a ride, rather than inventing the ride and deciding its course themselves.

Playing Madden football on your Nintendo is fun, but not the same kind of fun as pretending your G.I. Joe is your favorite NFL running back, and moving him along the living-room carpet toward an imaginary goal line, and simulating crowd noise with your voice as he gets close. We are shortchanging imagination for prepackaged experience.

Kids now are quickly bored—and part of the reason, I'm sure, is that they're not called on to tap into their mind's eye. I see it with my own grandkids. I buy them an elaborate game covered in buttons and flashing lights, capable of making all kinds of sound effects, and they're done with it in ten minutes. They push the buttons and see what it does, and they've run its course. *"Next!"*

The old-school toys still sell, but to ever-younger kids. Barbies used to appeal to girls in their early teens, and it wasn't unusual for a girl of the mid-sixties to break out her collection now and then well into high school. By the mid-eighties, Barbies were aimed at girls five years younger. Now, they seem to appeal to preschool girls and to lose their magic at age ten or so. Because kids are growing out of traditional toys at a much earlier age than they once did, the toy companies are developing new electronic games aimed at those younger kids. At the rate we're going, kids will soon outgrow traditional toys before they can walk.

Even some old-school toys have changed in subtle but revealing ways. Construction toys—Lincoln Logs, Erector Sets, and such—have always been a mainstay of the business. The biggest construction toy of all is Lego. In fact, it's now the largest-grossing toy company in the world. But Lego is no longer just a box of simple blocks that kids can shape into anything. Now, it comes in sets that call on kids to build specific things—a spaceship, a vehicle, the Eiffel Tower. Lego makes itty-bitty plastic parts specialized to just that one item. And what happens when kids build it? They're done.

If I sound like an old fogy on a rant, so be it. Point is, we got into the business at a point when selling toys brought satisfaction and fun. I had a blast.

■ ■ ■

By locating in the big, new regional malls, we were participating in a national trend. All across America, specialty toy stores became standards in shopping centers' retail mix. So we set ourselves apart by giving the stores a little British flavor, featuring giant Nutcracker-style toy soldiers standing sentry at the entrance and high-end European toys among the board games, stuffed animals, and other playthings on the shelves. We refashioned the two Ks in our name into marching toy soldiers, too.

In late 1972, as Christmas approached, we had our first real crisis. One night, a fire broke out in the supermarket a few doors down from the Wards Corner five-and-ten, and it quickly spread. It spared our store but gutted our warehouse out back—which was stuffed with merchandise waiting to ship to the stores for Christmas.

We had insurance, but that didn't solve our biggest dilemma: half of the year's income depended on having toys for the Christmas rush, and now we had precious few to sell. We managed to place emergency orders in time to limp through the season, but the close call convinced us we had to get more serious about our warehouse operations.

That led us to move K&K Toys into its first freestanding headquarters. By modern standards, it was a tiny place—about twenty-three hundred square feet of office attached to a fifteen-thousand-square-foot warehouse—but it was lavish compared to the cramped offices and jerry-rigged storage we'd used to that point. The company's new home was in an industrial park in Virginia Beach, a sprawling suburb of Norfolk, and just minutes from the airport and Interstate 64. Doug and I worked in adjoining offices separated by an accordion door. We left it open most of the time so we could holler back and forth to each other between phone calls.

From this humble new home, we managed what we figured at the time was pretty explosive growth. By the end of 1973, we had ten stores in Virginia, North Carolina, and Maryland. In 1974, we opened three more stores, followed by another four in 1975. We had to expand our headquarters to keep up, more than doubling the warehouse's size to thirty-one thousand square feet. By March 1978, we had twenty-two stores, including five in southeastern Virginia. Our business was growing by 12 to 13 percent per year. It promised to get only bigger and better from there.

And the new offices soon filled with new people, some of whom became key players in what was to come.

The first was Kenny Perry, the middle of K. R. and Kathryn's three children. He was a smart, capable guy who'd wrestled in high school and come close to winning the state championship for Granby, which was a wrestling powerhouse with a national reputation. This despite being diagnosed with type 1 diabetes as a teenager.

After graduating from Virginia Tech in 1966, he'd found work in the insurance industry. In the early seventies, he partnered with K. R. in the boss's mortgage business, watching our early attempts to expand our little chain of toy stores, and decided he wanted in. Doug and I were fine with that, bringing him aboard to open a new store in Frederick, Maryland. In time, he oversaw all of the company's Maryland operations and owned 5 percent of K&K.

Another was a kid just out of high school who would prove himself an important ingredient in our success in both the toy business and Dollar Tree. Toward the end of my career, I was fond of saying we were "ordinary people doing extraordinary things," and there was probably no better example of that slogan than Bryan Bagwell.

Bryan was born in Nassawadox on Virginia's Eastern Shore and raised in Virginia Beach just a shout from our headquarters. In 1977, when he was a day out of high school and about to turn eighteen, at which point K&K consisted of nineteen stores, he walked into our warehouse looking for a summer job. We put him to work pulling orders, unloading trucks, and stacking freight.

The warehouse was busy early in the week but a bit slow before the weekend, so on Fridays I got in the habit of asking this kid to take my car and Doug's to a nearby car wash. He had smarts aplenty, but I was even more impressed by his people skills. Bryan was outgoing, friendly, and able to put just about anyone at ease. He also had a lot of hustle and proved capable at every task we assigned him. After a year in the back, he was hungry for greater challenges. Doug and I pulled him into the office to do some administrative work for the warehouse, then suggested he try working in a store, where he'd have a clear path for advancement—to store manager, then district manager overseeing several stores, maybe even into the upper-management ranks.

He transferred to the Military Circle store as an assistant manager. It didn't suit him. He was bored stiff by the slower pace and didn't care for the late hours. I caught wind that he was looking for another job, that he'd taken the civil service exam and was thinking about following his father and older brother into work for the government. So one night, I dropped in on the store and talked to him.

The company's growth was accelerating now; we were opening six or more stores per year. A smart, personable guy could make something of himself in such an environment, I told Bryan. Leaving just when we were getting big would be about the worst mistake he could make, especially seeing as how he'd be nothing in a government job but a small gear in a big machine. It wasn't so long before that I'd done that kind of work myself.

He agreed to stick around. We moved him back into the office and put him in charge of handling the orders from all the stores each week. He thrived, so we gave him more responsibility. He mastered that. He eventually rose to the top echelon of the company, becoming the senior vice president for merchandising of Dollar Tree, in charge of selecting and buying all the goods sold in the stores.

Another key hire was Kay Waters, who was twenty-five years old, fresh out of the army, and all muscles and short hair when she came to work in the warehouse. After she spent a couple of years back there, we moved her into the office to take orders from the stores, then promoted her to purchasing assistant. She was to make many overseas buying trips with Joan, Bryan, and me and to demonstrate a real panache for selecting merchandise for Dollar Tree.

And I should mention Alan Wood, whom we hired out of high school to work as a stock boy at Military Circle, promoted to manager of the Landover store in Maryland, then brought back down to handle some of our purchasing—and eventually to head up a little sideline project that became Dollar Tree. Didn't have a single college class behind him.

Like I said, ordinary people doing extraordinary things. Regarding management style, I believe you should hire people who are smart and driven to succeed, then empower those people. Trust them to achieve. Trust that they're honest. They're usually worth it, and if they're not, you'll figure it out soon enough.

We were building this company, Doug and I, with no firmer idea of how to succeed than most of the people we hired to help us. They'd ask me questions, and I'd tell them, "Don't ask me how to do it. I've never done it either. Just go do it, and I have your back. We'll figure it out."

And we did—mostly because we hired well.

■ ■ ■

As we grew, the financial management of the company became more of a burden. We were still keeping separate books and checkbooks for each store, and it was clear we could not continue that old Ben Franklin style of doing business. At the time, we used the services of a small father-and-son accounting firm, and it so happened that among the son's neighbors was a financial whiz who, he suggested, might be interested in a new opportunity.

Ray Compton was thirty-six years old when he came by the office to talk to Doug, Kenny, and me in 1979. He was a country boy, born in Pittsylvania County, Virginia, where he grew up on a 250-acre tobacco farm his family had owned for five generations, and still owns today. Don't feel bad if you haven't heard of Pittsylvania County. It probably won't help to know that the nearest town to the farm was Gretna.

He went to business college and in 1962 began working as an accounting clerk in the Lynchburg offices of the F. S. Royster Guano Company, a big fertilizer manufacturer based in Norfolk. After a brief stint in the army, he moved to Royster's Baltimore sales office, then to its outpost in Seaford, Delaware. He moved into corporate accounting in Norfolk in 1971.

It was a family-oriented business, a great place to work. After eight years in Norfolk, he rose to manager of Royster's general accounting department, reporting to the vice president of finance. He was happy there. He didn't realize he was ready for a change—not until our accountant asked him if he'd consider something new. That got him thinking. If he was ever going to jump, now was probably the time to do it.

So it was that an accident of geography changed the face of our enterprise: had Ray not lived next door to that accountant, we never would have asked him to an early-evening sit-down at our office. Ray walked in to find that the receptionist had already gone home. The place seemed deserted. He stood around for a few minutes until a gangly kid appeared and asked if he needed help. That was Bryan Bagwell, working late. Bryan tracked us down and brought us together.

We got along immediately. Ray seemed a natural fit with Doug's personality and my own, and his strengths dovetailed with ours, which were more intuitive and market oriented and not fixed on the details of managing the business. He was, in short, a professional, expertly prepared by his seventeen years at Royster to reinvent our front-office procedures and inject a new level of competence into our entire operation.

The move involved some risk for him; he had a secure job and a wife and two little boys. But it also seemed he'd accomplished as much as he could at Royster and was excited by K&K's skyward trajectory. We talked over the course of a couple of months, made him an offer, sealed the deal with a handshake, and brought him aboard in May 1979.

It would be easy to say, all these years later, that we knew then that Ray Compton would change everything about K&K, or that we recognized our later success would be impossible without him. But the fact is, we were simply trying to fix a problem. We couldn't have foretold the synergy his presence would bring, the calmness at the center of our collective culture. He came along eleven years after I started at the five-and-dime and eight years after we opened our first toy store, but Ray Compton was as much a founder of what would become Dollar Tree as Doug or me.

In his first two years at K&K, he completely revamped our system. No longer did the individual stores write checks to the warehouse. No longer did we maintain handwritten ledgers. We were up to thirty-odd stores now, and that old Ben Franklin plan was unwieldy. It was everything we could do just to keep track of where the money was moving.

Ray simplified all that, so that now we bought merchandise, put our retail price on it, and shipped it to the stores, and when the stores sold it, the cash came back to the corporation, and the corporation paid the vendor. So straightforward. Ray will say that he did nothing brilliant, but that it worked. It sure

Ray Compton's arrival in 1979 remade K&K's administration and laid the groundwork for our success in toys and beyond.
Photo by Tamara Voninski, used by permission of *Virginian-Pilot*

looked brilliant to me. He created a system that enabled us to see the forest, rather than a bunch of individual trees. On our balance sheet, thirty stores appeared as one entity. It gave us an uncluttered, much sharper view of what was and wasn't working across the whole company.

We hadn't realized just how blind we were until we got eyes.

■ ■ ■

The period immediately after Ray's arrival saw a tremendous amount of change at K&K, some of which would not have happened without him. He was not simply a good number cruncher or an organizational genius, though he was certainly both; he was also a heck of a leader and a font of methodical common sense for Doug and me. He was a balance, a ballast, to our sometimes breakneck ambitions.

And he got to know the toy business. Ray's attitude was that everything he did in terms of keeping the books and managing the company's growth was a byproduct of what Doug and I did, so it behooved him to understand exactly what that was. He joined us on buying trips, listened in on negotiations with the big toy manufacturers, took part in every discussion, every pitch.

Among the first people Ray hired was a woman in her twenties named Darcy Stephan. Darcy had come to Norfolk from Ohio with her high school sweetheart, a sailor, and learned to operate and program computers while working for a big furniture outfit in Virginia Beach. She brought that expertise to K&K at a point when we had needed it for years.

Darcy arrived two weeks before the delivery of our first bona fide computer, a big IBM System/36. Once she programmed it—which involved the painstaking process of writing code and melding existing software with our needs, tasks that required such long hours that on some nights she slept on the floor of her office—we entered the digital age. Goodbye, handwritten ledgers.

With our administration streamlined and automated, we now had the means to ride herd on a bigger network of stores. We expanded into South Carolina, then into Georgia, then north into Pennsylvania, then into West Virginia. We leased a fleet of tractors that we hooked to company-owned trailers and sent out on multiple-store runs from our warehouse.

We grew so big, so fast that even with Ray's improvements and Darcy's computer, distribution got to be a handful as we topped fifty stores. Doug and I were trying to manage the warehouse at the same time we bought merchandise, leased store space, and attended to the details of everyday operations. And it wasn't as easy to do as it had been with half as many stores.

The solution lay in bringing Kenny back down from Maryland and putting him in charge of our warehouse and distribution. He did exactly what we needed: he brought the beast under control.

Which was good timing, because the beast got bigger. In late 1983, we bought a six-and-a-quarter-acre piece of open land in Norfolk Commerce Park, not far from our headquarters, and built a big, new complex there—more than ten thousand square feet of office space and an eighty-four-thousand-square-foot warehouse.

It seemed immense, but we filled it up. We had sixty-four stores when we bought the land. We had ninety by the time we moved in.

6

Toys Aren't
Kid Stuff

W hile Ray handled the finances and Kenny our logistics, Doug and I
were running everything else in duplicate. We had the company's
stores divided geographically between us—he was the northern boss and I the
southern—but we went on buying trips together, negotiated leases together,
showed up for meetings side by side. Most of K&K's operations were overseen by two guys of equal stature and with what amounted to identical job
descriptions.

Obviously, this was not an efficient arrangement. I suppose it grew out of
having K. R. at the top of the company but without a strong day-to-day role
in actually running it; he was a symbolic leader, the conscience of the enterprise, more than a traditional boss. With neither Doug nor I his clear second-
in-command, we both filled the job. And our mutual drive for equal footing
produced twins.

That we managed to make it work for years testified that we had comple-
mentary strengths and together were pretty formidable. We had similar helpings of brains but were wired differently. I tended to be better talking on my
feet than he was, and more comfortable in front of a roomful of people. He was
perhaps more introspective, adept at turning an idea over in his head to see it
from all sides. I was probably more attuned to merchandising, to the products

that would excite our customers. Doug understood real estate far better than I did and was especially sensitive to keeping the goodwill of our workers.

We had enough in common that we got along well. He was, and is, a stand-up guy in addition to being smart—a faithful husband and father who follows a strong moral code, believes in treating people fairly, takes the long-term view on decisions. I think he sees me the same way. We had just the right mix of difference and similarity to hit on ideas and solutions that neither of us would have found on his own.

Still, it was a tremendous waste of time and effort for us to show up as a pair for every product purchase, every real-estate convention. So we decided to further divvy up what needed doing. Our first split into areas of specialization came in toy buying.

Let me explain how the process worked. In the early days, we got our merchandise from wholesalers, who bought the stuff from the manufacturers. The toymakers might have dealt directly with some of the really big retailers, such as Sears or Kmart, but rarely did they bother with comparatively small outfits like K&K. It was much easier for them, far less complicated, to deal with jobbers that supplied several retail customers.

But jobbers were middlemen and marked up any goods that passed through their hands. We saw the need, as we grew, to knock down our purchase costs. On top of that, we found that our wholesalers were having trouble keeping up with our demands. So Doug and I started going to New York every year to talk to the toy companies, to try to get their direct business, to convince them we were worth the effort.

The bigger we got and the stronger our buying power, the easier it was to make this pitch stick. It might seem strange that we had to sell the manufacturers on the idea of working with us to sell their products, but that's how it was—we'd plead with them to "open us up," as it was called, as direct accounts.

Eventually, we got them all to work with us, but it took several trips and a lot of begging. Our meetings typically came at Toy Fair, a trade show that was held each February in the Toy Building, a fourteen-story office block at 200 Fifth Avenue in New York City's Flatiron District. All the factories had showrooms in the place, some big, some small, depending on the size of the company. And in the case of the big companies, the showrooms could be almost crazily elaborate. We'd make appointments with each, and Doug and I would wander the halls from showroom to showroom to inspect the new products in the works for the coming year.

The toy business was vibrant in those days, with plenty of manufacturers and a fast-growing roster of independent toy retailers. It was exciting to be there. Mattel had the most extravagant showrooms of anyone, and it would put on these enormous presentations to coax orders from us. We'd be met at the door by our account rep, who showed off the goods, took our order, and was the guy we'd call with questions about shipping or the details of our account. Many of the reps and most of our fellow merchants were Yankees, and here we were, a pair of Southerners trying to navigate this strange northeastern world, striving to conduct ourselves in such a way that we'd be considered mensches.

We learned quickly how to do that. The key was to be honest and decent, to behave in a respectful, businesslike fashion. We had to *be* good, we saw, to be viewed as a good account—had to pay our bills on time, play straight with people, be polite and friendly to everyone. Say no nicely. Never let our egos get in the way of business.

Which isn't to say Toy Fair was all smiles and good cheer. An ongoing challenge in dealing with the big vendors was that they always tried to dictate what we'd buy from their lines, and if we didn't go along with their wishes, they could squeeze us by denying us perks—discounts, say, or advertising allowances, or letting us delay payment on the whole year's order until early December, when we had plenty of cash on hand.

They might refuse us the products they knew we wanted until we agreed to buy those we didn't. In our dealings with Mattel, for instance, we always wanted Barbie. She was a franchise. Barbie almost always sold. Our account rep would present the new Barbie line, and we'd be ready and able to buy, but then he'd show off another toy line—I'll call it XYZ—that perhaps we didn't like so much. We could get all the Barbie we wanted, he might say, but only if we supported XYZ at such-and-such a level.

The vendors' goal was to load us up with as much product as possible. The pressure was always on to buy more. If we did $1 million worth of sales one year, they wanted us to do $1.2 million the next. They'd want all the orders as early as possible, and we, naturally, wanted to wait as long as possible to place them. The whole process was an ongoing tussle over what we needed for our business to stay healthy versus what they needed to promote their lines and maximize orders.

It wasn't bitter negotiation. It was business dealing. But a lot rode on it. Getting stuck with dud merchandise was no fun. We could, if we got really hung one year, use that experience in our negotiations the next, and try to win a discount on new lines—"get some help," as the industry put it—but it was no sure thing. It all depended on how good at negotiating we were.

This back-and-forth took time and required a certain amount of expertise, so Doug and I decided we'd split the buying pie to create more time to meet with the really big vendors, which we'd continue to do as a team. I specialized in games and boys' toys, Doug in preschool and girls' toys. We started taking Bryan Bagwell along as an assistant to both of us and to handle the purchases of batteries and other small items.

Doug was a first-class negotiator but over several trips to Toy Fair began to find the process less satisfying than haggling over real estate, which alongside buying was the most important thing we did; our existence depended on getting good locations at reasonable rents in well-performing malls, during a period of growing competition from other, bigger toy-store chains gunning for the same spaces.

So we agreed to a more substantial division of labor. Doug would handle everything related to locating, leasing, and opening our stores—he'd go to real-estate conventions, meet with mall developers, negotiate leases, build out the spaces, handle everything right up to the point that the first customer walked in.

If a mall developer wanted two toy stores under his roof, it was Doug's job to talk him out of it. If he tried to get another store to bid against us for a space, jacking up the rent, it was on Doug to convince him that we'd make the better tenant and to knock the rate back down. If the landlord wanted to put us in some dead-end corner of the mall, Doug's task was to get us moved to the center of the action. He oversaw store design and kept build-out costs down. Seeing as how we were now opening stores at a frantic rate, this all amounted to enough work for several executives.

I, meanwhile, would handle all of K&K's buying. Which was to say that once Doug opened a store, it was up to me to make it fly.

■ ■ ■

Toys are a fashion business. It's all about what's in, what isn't. In the early days of the industry, most products were basics—dolls, balls, cap guns, standard toys that stayed around for a long time—but as television grew ubiquitous, commercials became a huge factor in creating demand. Spots sandwiched among the Saturday-morning cartoons were especially important.

So a manufacturer's plans for TV advertising were a big factor in how much of a particular toy line we were willing to order. Toys aren't like the book business—you can't return your unsold merchandise to your supplier. If you buy a mountain-high pile of toys you expect to be hot, and they're not, you still have to cough up the dough for them and figure out what to do with all the surplus you have sitting on the shelves. You can lose a ton of money on one bad buy. You can go belly-up.

Much of our conversation at Toy Fair thus centered on marketing. We'd have a chance to handle the toys and eye the ads. There was always some back-and-forth over whether kids would respond to a commercial, whether it would create demand, but the decision on how big an order to place often came down to whether or not we believed what the manufacturer said about its plans for advertising—whether or not all that big talk about buying tons of commercial time would really happen.

We could have assumed it would, had we lived in New York City—it was a big market, and worth it to toymakers to foot the expense of booking commercials. But our stores were in smaller cities mostly in the South, and it wasn't a sure bet that toymakers would push their products in our markets to the same degree. We had to do a little handicapping over whether or not a television-promoted item would really get a push in our neck of the woods.

As we continued to grow, the big toy manufacturers starting inviting us to private presentations, usually in the fall preceding Toy Fair. They'd set up at some cool location—a resort in Arizona, say—and foot the bill for us to come out. They wanted our attention on their products without distraction, and they were willing to spend money to get it. They'd have us there for two days, maybe, and we'd sit down with our account rep and talk business, have a wonderful dinner, enjoy some drinks by the pool. They were fun to attend. And they worked—we couldn't help being favorably impressed, because they put on a show.

As time went on, these pre–Toy Fair meetings fell earlier and earlier in the fall, because the toymakers couldn't afford to wait until February to get orders from their big accounts; they had to have some commitment before they could take the gamble of putting a toy line into production, because the lead time needed to build it was immense. The bigger the account, the earlier we met with them.

Sometimes, a toy we saw at these getaways was so new that the manufacturer itself wasn't yet fully committed to it. The meeting served as a test balloon; the manufacturer studied our reaction, sought feedback, and gauged our excitement by the size of our order. If it didn't get the necessary commitment, it could theoretically can the idea, but if a new toy had made it that far, the manufacturer was probably going to give it a try. The question was, again, how much support it would give the toy, how much advertising. If a toy was in trouble, that would be the first thing to go, regardless of what we'd been promised.

■ ■ ■

We couldn't go into a buying season with a blank checkbook. We had to have a plan.

We got pretty skilled at planning. We'd develop an annual sales budget, which company-wide would amount to x millions of dollars, and we'd have a margin we'd want to aim for on those sales. Subtract the margin from sales, and we knew how many dollars we had available to spend—how much we were "open to buy."

One of my responsibilities was to figure out how we'd divide that amount among our vendors. That's where a merchant's touch, his intuition for what would sell, became critical—when it came down to saying, "I'll buy this item, but I won't buy that one."

But it wasn't a simple matter of picking winners from the lineup of new toys each year. The big toymakers had retailers they preferred to work with, and we were pretty far down the list. The reason: Advertising cut both ways. We relied on the toymakers to back their wares with ad blitzes; they relied on local advertising from their retailers. And while K&K advertised, we didn't do it on nearly the scale of Target, Kmart, or Sears, who were our biggest competitors throughout the seventies.

The toy companies knew those big stores would carpet-bomb their markets with ads, and thus ensure that their toys would sell. In effect, our competitors paid twice for the merchandise—they paid for the toys, then invested more in pushing the toys on the public. So when it came to hot toys, which were always in short supply, those big boys got what they wanted, and outfits such as K&K got the leftovers. There was a pecking order.

The toymakers knew that the big boys would set a low price on their toys, too, and thus move a lot of units. The manufacturers got paid the same no matter what the retail price was, so they were all for discounts. Discount department stores treated toys as loss leaders, knowing that if they could lure customers in the door with a discounted price on a hot toy, they'd make up for the loss in the other stuff people bought while they were there.

So they'd sell a fifteen-dollar hot toy for twelve dollars and advertise the hell out of it. Shoppers would flock in. Customers responded to the advertising—and to the advertised price—long past the point that the big store ran out of stock. That put pressure on us. If we slapped a 30 percent markup on an item—which was not high—we'd look foolish because we sold that same item for fifteen dollars. We'd look like crooks. So while they were advertising, our price couldn't exceed theirs by much.

Our relationship with the big toy companies was thus a weird one. We needed their hot toys, because we had to have them to get shoppers in the door. But we could get only a fraction of the hot items we wanted, because our money was worth less than the competition's. And on those hot toys we did get, the marketplace sliced our profit margin.

Come spring, the Sears stores and Kmarts would shrink their toy departments and use the space for garden supplies, backyard grills, and such. Nine months later, the cycle started anew. All the while, we kept plugging along.

Hot toys were not the product of advertising alone; movies and TV shows were big creators of must-have buzz as well. Starting in the late seventies, whenever a kid-friendly movie hit the theaters, a line of toys related to that film would crop up. The first movie toys to score really big were *Star Wars* action figures and spaceships. The demand was tremendous. It changed the whole industry.

After a while, the manufacturers would come to Toy Fair selling both a movie and the toys that went with it, which put me in the position of having to judge not only if the toys were good but if the movie would be. I remember that one movie, *Tron*—about some electronic character—was a dog. It didn't sell toys at all. On the other hand, I was pulled into a side showroom and shown a clip from *E.T.* before the movie came out, and thought to myself, *That's going to be a huge hit.* The manufacturer had one *E.T.* doll, the title character, which was way overpriced, in my view. We didn't buy a lot of it because we thought it was too expensive. Big mistake. The doll was hot as hell, and we ended up chasing it and never did get what we needed. But we had to trust our gut.

Batman, the first Tim Burton version, was one we saw coming and that we knew was going to be hot. *Ghostbusters* was another. *Power Rangers*, too—the TV show aired five days a week after school, which so saturated households with the characters that they couldn't help being popular.

Some years, the manufacturers would tart up their presentations with visits by the stars of the shows. Lee Majors attended Toy Fair when Kenner introduced its *Six Million Dollar Man* action figure, and the *Charlie's Angels* cast turned out, too. Even Evel Knievel made an appearance. But a TV show didn't always produce a hit toy, especially if the show itself was lacking. We flew out one fall to a meeting with Mattel in Arizona and were introduced to BraveStarr, a space cowboy character who lived on a planet called New Texas and battled an assortment of villains (including a pig dressed in a Union army uniform) with the help of human and alien pals. Mattel was releasing a line of BraveStarr action figures to partner with a planned TV cartoon. The toys were pretty interesting, but the show was a mess. Both sank.

On occasion, it was hard to tell whether a show helped a toy or the reverse. One year, we met with reps from Playmates Toys Inc., a California company that specialized in making baby dolls. That was pretty much all it made; when we went to see Playmates, we knew we were going to be looking at dolls.

Not this time. It showed us a line of action figures, which surprised us—it had attempted nothing like that before. Even more surprising, it was calling these figures the Teenage Mutant Ninja Turtles. At the time, the cartoon hadn't debuted, and the movies were years away. *TMNT* existed only as a comic book, and a rather obscure one at that. We'd never heard of it. The whole concept seemed so preposterous, the name so crazy, and Playmates such an unlikely source for this kind of toy that for a moment we thought the company might be putting us on. But the salesman, whom we knew, told us no, it was for real, and that Playmates was excited about it.

We left laughing and shaking our heads, asking ourselves, *What in the world are those guys thinking?* Investing in such a toy was a gamble, because we had only so much money to spend, and the market was loaded with much surer bets. How could we decide if it was worth the risk?

Well, we typically relied on the company's track record, which in this case worked against Playmates. It had no experience with this kind of product. Going up against G.I. Joe and Masters of the Universe was way outside its comfort zone. We looked at its marketing plan. This wasn't always reliable, because we were in smallish markets, and besides, if a product didn't sell as expected, its manufacturer would often pare back its marketing budget.

But in this case, the whole idea was so goofy that it stood out to us. It seemed a toy that people would remember. And we were further convinced by the deal Playmates offered. Its dolls were all made in China, and it was willing to let us buy the Turtles freight-on-board from the factory—meaning they wouldn't be shipped to the Playmates warehouse but directly to us. That saved money for both K&K and Playmates, enabling it to lower the price and us to boost our margin on sales.

So we went for it. We bought a bunch. It was a good Christmas.

Not all toys needed a boost. Some, as with some fashions, became hot without help, seemed to spawn national crazes almost by magic. Pet Rocks were one. Beanie Babies were another. At one point, there was almost a tulip mania around those small beanbag animals. People cashed in their savings to snatch them up, betting they'd grow in value over time. Needless to say, they didn't. They're practically worthless today.

My daughter Christy was the first kid at Independence Middle School to have a Rubik's Cube. She took it to class, and all her friends were frantic to have one. Advertising didn't sell that toy; it spread through human contact, like a virus.

And of course, there was the hottest toy of all time, which I recognized as a hit when I first saw it at Toy Fair. The manufacturer wasn't one of the majors, but on this occasion it had put together a showroom that was particularly elaborate. It was set up like a hospital delivery room, staffed by actors dressed as doctors and nurses, even wearing stethoscopes. In the room's center was a giant fake cabbage, and from among its leaves the "medical" personnel were easing fat, chubby-cheeked dolls into the world, using the movements and lingo real doctors would while delivering real babies.

That was my first glimpse of the Cabbage Patch Kids. I remember we looked at each other and said, "Holy cow, this is going to be off the charts." We ordered piles of them and soon discovered we'd aimed low. We could never get enough Cabbage Patch Kids. We could have ordered three times as many and it wouldn't have satisfied the demand. We got more calls for that toy than any other. People chased our trucks on the street, hoping to buy the dolls from the drivers.

A craze is fueled by scarcity. Every little girl in America wanted those dolls, and the tougher they became to find, the more the kids—and their parents—had to have them. And unlike so many hot toys, the Cabbage Patch Kids were in heavy demand not for just a single Christmas season but year after year.

One Christmas Eve, Ray got a call from a woman down on North Carolina's Outer Banks, on the hunt for a Cabbage Patch. We had exactly one on hand: a doll on layaway and never picked up at one of our stores in Virginia Beach. That woman drove something like fifty miles and Ray a good thirty to make the handoff at the state line.

• • •

Such heartwarming moments aside, the displeasures of the business mounted as we got bigger. Competitive pressures grew. The toy companies remained difficult to work with. Kay Waters, who overheard some of my phone conversations with vendors, says that at times I pounded my desk, stamped my feet, and cussed like a sailor. As she tells it, I tried to explain myself after one such tirade. "Kay," I told her, "sometimes you have to get mean. And sometimes you have to use profane language." At which point, Joan, across the office, hollered, "No, you don't!"

The big toymakers became so difficult to deal with, so demanding in their requirements of what and how much we ordered—always more than the year before, no matter what—that something had to give eventually. One year, we went to Mattel having not sold the expected volume of Barbie the previous year—a rare occurrence but a real problem, because we couldn't take on a big pile of new Barbie stuff when our shelves were already filled with unsold merchandise we'd carried over. Mattel came into the conversation expecting us to ratchet up our order. I explained our situation and told the reps we couldn't meet their targets. They wouldn't budge. If we wanted to order from the world's largest toymaker, we'd have to do it their way.

So I passed. I told them I wouldn't place the usual order for the year. A lot of "color" happened, with the salesmen and me going back and forth—"You're not going to do this" and "Oh, yes, I *am*." They were taken aback. Hell, they were scandalized. They figured they held all the cards and didn't realize they were overplaying their hand.

We lost our perk of paying Mattel in December and instead had to meet net thirty-day terms, which was just what it sounds like. But I made the point that I didn't think what the company demanded was right for our business. It wasn't good for us. I didn't need what it was selling, and I wasn't going to buy it.

We cleared all our inventory and made it through the year ordering the specific toys we needed when we wanted them, rather than hewing to Mattel's plan for us. Everything worked out just fine.

When it came time to meet the reps in Arizona that fall, we were in a much stronger position to negotiate. First, they knew we were willing to walk away

The K&K Toys leadership team, early 1980s. Clockwise from top left are me, Kenny Perry, Doug, K. R., Ray, and Joan.

COURTESY OF BROCK FAMILY

from the table. That shifted the balance of the exchange. And second, our business with Mattel had fallen substantially over the year, which reset the bar the reps expected us to exceed on our next order.

That was the only occasion on which our dealings with a big vendor came to a showdown. We needed each other. At its zenith, K&K had 136 stores scattered all across the Mid-Atlantic and the Southeast. We were hungry for product to sell, and the toy companies depended on us to sell it.

■ ■ ■

I want to share one more aspect of the sometimes surreal business of buying toys. From the salespeople's point of view, the whole process rested on getting to know us and posing as our friends. They'd take us to lunch or the occasional dinner, insist on picking up the check, and aim at being likable. Many of them were in fact very nice people—there were some I enjoyed meeting with and considered, if not friends exactly, at least friendly.

But I say they were posing because, at its core, the relationship was purely a business tactic. We interested them only so long as we carried "a big pencil"— which was to say we were in a position to buy their goods in quantity.

Doug had a saying he shared with Bryan: "Don't ever let salespeople get in your pocket." That was good advice, because it wasn't unheard of for account reps to offer something more extravagant than a meal while fishing for business, and we had to guard against it. They'd send lavish care packages at Christmas, filled with liquor, expensive cheeses, hams, and candy. A rep sent one of our buyers something really over the top—a ring or a fine fur coat, I don't recall which. Stories throughout the industry told of buyers being influenced by this sort of under-the-table trading, of being on the take—and doing harm to their employers by repaying vendors' favors with orders bigger than they should have been.

This sort of thing never influenced Doug and me. We owned the company, after all. We had a vested interest in keeping everything honest. And our culture at K&K was such that the buyers we hired to work with us, starting with Bryan, proved themselves as immune to temptation as we were. Small as our office remained through the seventies and eighties, there was a real feeling of shared mission among our team, a sense we were all in the venture together.

The best safeguard against inappropriate influence, I believed then and still do, was to have an up-front conversation about it with our people, so they'd recognize it when it came their way. Full disclosure. Talk about it. Sunlight is the best disinfectant.

Another thing we did involved the Christmas care packages, which usually came to the office. We'd have the buyer accept it, then divide up the contents among everyone in the office. As for what was delivered to people's homes, well, we could never be sure. But the buyer who got the ring or fur coat brought it into the office, as I remember, so we could get rid of the thing.

Any former buyer who no longer holds the pencil will tell you just how superficial the relationship with a seller can be. One year at Toy Fair, after Doug had phased himself out of buying and Bryan was taking over much of that duty, the two of them were approached by some salespeople who'd done business with Doug in the past. They completely ignored him while pitching to Bryan. A few years later, when Bryan left buying, he found that sales reps he'd considered friends would walk right past him without so much as a hello.

When people are blowing smoke, you may start believing how great you are. Well, lose your pencil and see what happens. Those same people won't take your phone calls. That's a reality check. To them, you're only as great as your next order.

7

The Eureka
Moment

I
f I were to identify a point at which the frustrations of the toy business began to outweigh the gains, a turning point in the K&K adventure, it would
have to be in 1980 or 1981, because at about that time we saw a pair of trends
assert themselves that spelled trouble for our fast-growing but still modest
company. One we recognized as a threat right off the bat. The other took a little
longer to see.

The obvious threat was that our competition stiffened in new and unpleasant ways. Until then, our chief rival was a company called KB Toys, which had
been around since 1922 and was a lot like us, since most of its stores were smallish and located in malls. KB used a different formula to lure its customers. It was
among the first major toy discounters in America, while we aimed at higher-
end buyers. It didn't trade in the fancy British brands—Corgi cars, Britains toy
soldiers—or the upscale European wooden toys we did. It didn't stock as many
expensive Madame Alexander dolls or first-rate train sets or Japanese plastic
models of planes and tanks. It stocked the hot toys of the moment and the
tried-and-true favorites and did a good job of keeping its prices low.

Despite the differences, KB was a pain in our necks, and especially in
Doug's, because it was gunning for the same space in malls that we were—and
we and the mall developers agreed that two toy retailers under the same roof

was one too many. The mall people solved this dilemma by encouraging us to bid against KB, and it against us, in the rent we were willing to pay in order to land the locations we sought.

This was bound to end unhappily, because K. R. was a pretty conservative guy when it came to rents, and mall rates were staggering. Back in his day, he could have rented a store for four to six dollars a square foot; now, the rate could run ten times that, and to K. R. that seemed terribly high. More often than any of us liked, he'd kill the deal, regardless of how long and hard Doug had worked to get it. We lost some opportunities to place stores in high-performing malls as a result. I know it frustrated Doug.

But then a couple of new players began to muscle their way onto our turf, and we saw that next to them KB was a relatively minor worry.

The more vexing was Toys "R" Us, a New Jersey–based retailer that operated out of enormous big-box stores, places larger than supermarkets. In its number of stores, it wasn't much bigger than we were in 1980. It had eighty-five locations, give or take, spread over a much larger area than our forty-five or fifty. But it was expanding rapidly—it planned to open fifteen more that year—and the amount of business it did out of each was mind boggling to us.

These stores were behemoths. When one set down in a metropolitan area, it seemed to almost exert its own gravitational pull. The stores advertised the heck out of their wares. They discounted hot toys to the quick. And shoppers flocked to them in every city where they set down. In 1979, the big-box toy stores, dominated by Toys "R" Us and a smaller rival, Circus World, accounted for 36 percent of all toy sales by unit in the United States. Department stores, our old nemeses, posted 13 percent. Stores like ours stood at 14 percent, and variety stores such as our Wards Corner location, which was still going strong with Alice at the helm, accounted for 11 percent. Those numbers were shifting in favor of the big-box retailers every year. The message was clear: in the eyes of the American shopper, bigger was better.

Toys "R" Us already had three stores in the suburbs ringing Washington, D.C., and another in Richmond—but none in southeastern Virginia—when we decided to try the big-box format ourselves. Doug, Kenny, and I formed a subsidiary of K&K, DMK Associates, to buy land in Chesapeake and Virginia Beach and build two giant Toy Castles for something like $1.25 million apiece, which represented a huge investment for us. Creating the subsidiary ensured that the experiment, should it fail, would leave the parent company without any bruises.

On the outside, the new stores were just as their name suggested—they took the form of medieval fortresses, with crenulated rooflines and Gothic arches over the doors. Inside, they were little more than warehouses, with linoleum floors laid over concrete and exposed ceilings, lights, and ductwork to keep construction and maintenance costs down.

The first opened in September 1980 to quite a lot of fanfare. The newspaper ran a substantial story on us, and what I told the reporter reflected our hopes for the new undertaking. "We aim to be a one-stop kid shop," I said. "We will carry a wide selection of radio-controlled toys, electronic games, juvenile furniture, sporting goods, crafts and hobbies, and infant care items.

"We recognize that there's a void in the market. There is no complete store that offers everything a child needs from day one. We're going to try to meet that need."

For a brief while, the stores performed well. They made money. But the vast inventory each required cut into our profits—the big stores didn't show the kind of return we got from our mall locations—and after years of positioning ourselves as purveyors of high-quality merchandise, we found the discount warehouse approach an uncomfortable fit. It wasn't our shtick.

Besides, it was less than a year later that Toys "R" Us pulled into town, with Circus World on its heels and Children's Palace not far behind. And to make a long story short, they crushed us.

We closed the doors and turned our full attention back to the malls. But now, the landscape was changing. The big-box retailers would be a major part of the shift, but in ways we didn't anticipate.

■ ■ ■

In August 1972, Magnavox, an American electronics company known for its TVs and stereos, introduced the Odyssey, the first home video-game console. It was a primitive battery-powered machine with a black-and-white video output to your TV, no sound, and a handful of simple games stored on circuit boards. The same year, another American company, Atari, introduced an arcade video game called Pong, which simulated table tennis on a black-and-white screen. Both the home and arcade machines were instant hits, and together they launched a video-game industry that was to remake the toy business.

You read that correctly, by the way: Atari was American.

At the time, neither development was of much interest to us at K&K. The

Magnavox consoles were sold at department stores for the most part, and the Atari machines were the province of arcades, bars, and bowling alleys. But that changed soon enough. Late in 1976, yet another American company, Fairchild Semiconductor, introduced its Video Entertainment System, a home game console that combined microprocessor-driven brains with read-only-memory game cartridges—the forerunner of modern video games.

Odds are, you don't remember the Fairchild. But just a few months later, Atari came out with a console using the same technology—its Video Computer System, later renamed the Atari 2600, which was easy to use, elegant in design, and almost single-handedly created a craze for video-game cartridges.

Over the next four years, game developers in the States and Japan hurried to meet the demand for new games, and did so with a string of hits that remain familiar to anyone alive at the time: Asteroids, Space Invaders, Pac-Man, and finally Donkey Kong, a game designed and marketed by a Japanese outfit called Nintendo.

By the fall of 1979, when we met with the big toy companies to order for Christmas 1980, game cartridges were becoming a toy-store staple. Problem was, a slew of companies was trying to repeat the Atari machine's success, so the market was suddenly flooded with consoles and the games to go with them. Remember Mattel's Intellivision? Or Coleco's Colecovision? We couldn't order just Atari and risk losing customers who owned one of those other machines— and there was no way of telling, in a market that was out of control, which machines might prove to be big hits. So we, like a lot of retailers, stocked a variety of consoles, along with their games. The whole toy industry went electronic that Christmas.

Now, I can look back and see that it's plain what had to happen. The country was mired in a recession. Money was tight. The consoles and games were expensive compared to traditional toys. And the market was split too many ways by too many players. A few games sold well—Space Invaders, for one— but most remained on the shelves late into the season, until the big retailers dumped their stock, slashing prices just to unload the stuff. The ripple effects of this dumping were brutal. Christmas was a disaster for toy stores from coast to coast.

So if you had asked me in early 1981 what I thought of the future of electronic games and toys, I would have told you they'd shown themselves to be a brief and expensive fad that ultimately flopped. I would have predicted a return to basic, traditional toys. I said as much at a Toy Fair round table that February. And if you'd flipped through the industry trade journals of the time, you'd have come away with the impression I was right. Articles and ads alike centered on a return to traditional toys.

I wish it had gone that way. We'd be a different and better country if it had. But I was wrong. The industry's electronics hangover was momentary. A lot of people, it turned out, bought the Atari 2600 and other machines at deeply discounted prices, and they wanted games for them. Manufacturers kept churning out new games and consoles until sales reached $3.2 billion in 1983.

Even more companies were making too many consoles by then, and for a brief while we tried to keep up. But it was tough. How much should we invest in game cartridges for each console? They sold for twenty to thirty dollars apiece, meaning they cost us plenty. We had a tremendous amount invested in inventory that didn't take up much space in the stores. And because the cartridges were small, they presented us with a real shoplifting problem.

Theft wasn't confined to the stores, either. When games went missing in our Norfolk warehouse, we built a cage in which we locked the most expensive merchandise, including the gaming stuff. Even so, we detected shortages in our inventory and launched an immediate search for the missing cartridges. We found a pile of them in the dumpster out back. Someone on the cleaning crew had thrown them away, anticipating he'd be able to come back at night and dumpster-dive for them.

That year, the market's oversaturation finally caught up with it, and the home video-game business suffered a collapse that all but killed it. Atari went belly-up. Coleco and Mattel took heavy hits. But at the same time, easy-to-use and affordable home computers appeared in force, led by the Commodore 64 and the Apple II, and the demand for games simply jumped platforms. Then, in 1985, Nintendo introduced its Entertainment System, or NES—and with that, a whole new generation of video games was born.

So was a new gorilla in the toy business.

■ ■ ■

Nintendo was by no means the first Asian manufacturer we'd traded with. The early eighties had seen us adopt the same tactics that F. W. Woolworth had nearly a century before, by venturing overseas to buy some of our toys directly from the sources, and that had meant dealing with the Chinese.

China had long produced most toys enjoyed by American kids. The package might have said Mattel or Ideal or Hasbro, but by the seventies most toys were stamped out and assembled in factories scattered across Taiwan, and a little later the People's Republic. So just after Christmas each year, we'd head to Hong Kong for the Chinese version of Toy Fair.

The vendors we met there were mostly small companies with showrooms scattered across the colony, most of them in Kowloon. We'd usually stay a week or so, crisscrossing the city to make three or four appointments a day to see the goods, which were basic toys—the perennial, year-round stuff that every kid played with, such as train sets, racecar sets, toy cars, plush animals, squirt guns, swim flippers, and other summer toys. Dolls.

This was not, in other words, merchandise with a familiar American name. Though Mattel might buy from the same factories, we were not buying Mattel-branded toys from the vendors.

Typically, we dealt with vendors who represented Chinese factories, rather than the factories themselves. These guys would display lines of goods produced by different manufacturers; they'd already done much of the legwork in identifying the products that might appeal to American kids. They'd present their lines to us, and we'd order from the menu. Payment was by letter of credit—all the money was up-front—but the prices were so much better than those back home that it was worth the hassle and risk. Plus, the toys were so affordable that we could double our money on an item and still sell it for an amount that most American shoppers would consider a bargain. Once our order was complete, the vendor would shepherd the goods from the various factories he represented and put them on a boat, and we'd see them in Norfolk three months later.

These trips to China in the eighties laid the groundwork for our success with Dollar Tree, because we grew accustomed to the rhythms and tones of doing business there and earned a reputation as stand-up operators. We also grew handy at getting around Hong Kong, which was no small thing.

Ah, but dealing with Nintendo and the Japanese was a different matter entirely. Nintendo had a hierarchy that was absolutely rigid—a down-from-the-top style of doing business that was unyielding. And the attitude apparent throughout the company's chain of command was that it didn't care whether it did business with us or not.

Nintendo had a handful of major retailers it supplied with all the product they wanted: Toys "R" Us, Walmart, Target, Kmart, Best Products—the merchants who accounted for the great bulk of the toy business, in terms of national sales. We and everybody else were afterthoughts. We could get only a tiny fraction of the consoles and game cartridges we wanted. How small a fraction? At Christmas, we'd sell out of our allotment in an afternoon.

And within just months of its introduction, the NES was like every hot toy that had come before it, combined. To get any customers into our stores, we had to have it. We had waiting lists for consoles and games, lists that grew by the day while we begged and cajoled the Nintendo people to ship us more product. It did no good.

The situation drove us crazy. We were a pretty big chain, opening new stores every year. We were growing the business. But we had more competition now, and that competition was getting Nintendo while we struggled to make do without it. It was akin to fighting with an arm tied behind our back. How could we survive, let alone expand, if we couldn't establish a supply chain? Our destiny seemed to be in the hands of others.

In short, it was much the same disadvantage we'd faced with the big American toy companies, only many times worse, because we never had the opportunity to forge a relationship with the Japanese. Instead of negotiation, we received an edict. They rarely let us order in the numbers we wanted, and when they did they simply failed to ship the stuff, and we got a fraction.

I remember just one Christmas when we received more than the usual pittance of machines and cartridges. One year, Nintendo had a shipment bound for Best Products, and the chain couldn't accept the order for financial reasons. It was maybe two or three days before Christmas when we got a call: would we take it? Heck, yes, we said. The shipment arrived at the Norfolk warehouse, and everyone at headquarters loaded consoles and cartridges into their cars, as well as the company's trucks, and raced them out to the stores. They disappeared off the shelves as quickly as we put them there.

Made no difference to Nintendo the following year. It simply didn't think much of us. It knew it would sell its stuff with or without our help.

It got to the point that I flew out to Redmond, Washington, where the company kept its American headquarters, to explain our situation face to face, to appeal to Nintendo's sense of fairness. We wanted it to sell to us on an equitable basis, based on our relative size. If we represented 1 percent of the toy business, I told them, all we asked for was 1 percent of the inventory. It seemed common sense.

I tried to appeal to the company's sense of compassion, too. If it didn't sell us product in reasonable numbers, I said, it would force us out of business—it was that simple. And that wouldn't be good for anyone. If it drove operations like K&K out of business, it would whittle down the number of outlets for its merchandise to an ever-smaller number of ever-larger, more powerful retailers, until it would eventually see the power dynamic shift to favor the buyer, rather than the seller. It would help create a monster that would eat it.

Competition, fair competition, is good for any company. It invigorates. It encourages good business practices.

I met with Nintendo's top sales honcho for the United States. He was polite. He heard me out, agreed that the situation wasn't fair, smiled. We shook hands.

It didn't change a thing.

． ． ．

In 1985, at just about the time Nintendo came on the American scene to drive us nuts, we suffered a major loss at K&K. Kenny Perry, who'd turned our warehouse and distribution system into a smooth operation, and who'd been running it since, died in his sleep at forty-one years old.

When Kenny was diagnosed with juvenile diabetes at age sixteen, the doctors had told the family he had a reasonable life expectancy of twenty-five additional years, and that's just what he got. He was a good man beloved throughout the company, from warehousemen and truckdrivers to the women in the office; his loss cast a pall over the place that took a long time to lift.

His death also changed the company's structure. He'd owned 5 percent of K&K, which now passed to his widow, Linda—who, after mulling her financial situation, decided she needed money more than company stock. We offered Ray an opportunity to buy into the ownership ranks and were able to work out a way for him to finance the purchase of Linda's shares.

Ray assumed oversight of our distribution. Combined with everything he was already doing, this would have overtaxed anyone, but he stuck with his expanded duties for years—nearly nine of them, in fact—before we brought in a bona fide logistics expert to relieve him.

We limped along. That's the best we could do in 1985 and 1986. Besides losing Kenny, we felt the heat of tightening competition with other toy retailers and faced sky-high rents in the malls, both of which stifled our attempts to find good locations for new stores. Toys were changing, and it was hard to keep up with the times—and depressing to witness the rapid abandonment of old-school products that had fostered imagination and creativity.

We couldn't get the merchandise we desperately needed from Nintendo. Some of the big American toymakers were going public, coming under stockholder pressure to increase profits, merging. Given time, this consolidation would leave us with just two or three stateside toy vendors, and the prospect for the same disregard we were getting from the Japanese; the landscape would feature huge toy companies selling to a handful of gargantuan retailers.

In short, the toy business as we'd known it was maturing, and selling toys wasn't so much fun anymore. We were still making money; in fact, our earnings were robust and growing. But continued growth was becoming an ever more doubtful proposition. And as the old saying goes, if you don't grow, you die.

So Doug, Ray, and I started talking about doing something different, or at the least finding a second type of store to open so we'd be more attractive to mall landlords. It would sweeten our appeal if we could offer them two specialty retailers instead of one.

But what kind of second store? We had no idea what we might do. We talked about the shoe business for a while. An old Norfolk-based chain, Hofheimer's, had forty or fifty stores around the Mid-Atlantic, one of which—the flagship—occupied a prominent spot at Wards Corner, directly across Granby Street from our original variety store. We knew the company's chief financial officer and thought he might hear us out.

But it was more a conversation among ourselves than a deep look, because we didn't need long to see that the shoe business was a lot like the toy business. Competition was fierce, and the industry was changing. Leather shoes were headed south. The athletic shoes that were replacing them, along with an influx of Chinese imports, meant the prospects for growth weren't good. Hofheimer's was probably struggling every bit as much as we were.

We decided we'd keep our eyes and ears open for an attractive opportunity and in the meantime make the best of K&K's situation. And we succeeded at that. Until now, we'd located our stores exclusively in enclosed malls, but we revisited the assumptions that had led us to that policy. The retail landscape had changed markedly in the fifteen years since we opened the Military Circle store. Many malls were surrounded by strip shopping centers anchored by department stores, big-box bookstores, or sporting-goods outlets, and they drew traffic. The strip centers anchored by Walmarts were especially busy.

We opened a few K&Ks in these shopping centers. They attracted as much business as our mall stores in some cases, and the rents were quite a bit cheaper; Doug didn't have to bid against KB for these storefronts, or agree that we'd pay the almost criminal maintenance fees the malls demanded.

. . .

It was part of Doug's routine to drop in on stores whenever he was in their neighborhood, to gauge how they looked to customers, to compare our front windows and customer service with those of the competition, and to sniff out any changes afoot in the malls' retail mix—in sum, to give the stores and their environs the once-over.

So one day in 1986, he was visiting Tower Mall in Portsmouth, across the Elizabeth River from Norfolk. After checking in with our K&K there, he wandered around the mall—and strolled through the doors of a small store labeled "Everything's A Dollar."

He'd been vaguely aware of the business. Everything's A Dollar had four locations in the greater Norfolk region, including three in local malls and another on the strip at the Virginia Beach oceanfront. And its owners, Boden Perry (no relation to our Perrys) and his childhood friend Michael Porter, had been the subject of a big write-up in the paper. Until this particular day, though, Doug had never paid the stores much mind and had never set foot in one.

By small, I mean the place was the size of a 7-Eleven at most. It was crowded with big plastic bins filled with a crazy assortment of closeout merchandise—small housewares, vases, costume jewelry, sweat socks, discontinued toys, candy. Some of it was crap—cheaply made or so utterly useless that no customer would want it, even for a buck—but some of it wasn't. What he found in a few of the bins really set him back on his heels, because it seemed a heck of a buy for a dollar.

In its array of merchandise, its lack of a unifying theme, Everything's A Dollar reminded Doug of an old-time variety store. But those bins, which forced customers to dig around for the items they sought, gave it the air of a treasure hunt, too. And people evidently enjoyed searching for unexpected bargains, because the little place was bustling with shoppers clawing through the bins and approaching the counter with multiple purchases.

Doug bought a sampling of items and lugged the pile back to the K&K

offices. I was out of town at the time—in Hong Kong, I think—so I did not witness the transformative scene that followed. He walked into Ray Compton's office and dumped the pile on his desk.

And he said, "We can do this."

8

Surprise
and Delight

=================

That scene in Ray's office is still talked about as our moment of epiphany at Dollar Tree. From that seemingly mundane act—Doug's dumping the contents of a shopping bag onto Ray's desk—started a series of events that, ever accelerating, is still unfolding today, and promises to keep doing so far into the future.

I got back from my trip to find Doug energized about the dollar-store concept, and his enthusiasm was contagious. One of his great strengths was that he, more than just about anyone in the company, could see opportunity from new and unexpected angles. He was our idea man. And he didn't need long to convince me he was onto something.

Doug never made it a big deal that Dollar Tree's first spark of life originated with him. That speaks to one of our key characteristics as an organization: our egos never did battle. We were always open to new ideas, new and better ways of doing things, and it didn't matter whether they were mine or Doug's or a truckdriver's. If they were good, they were good.

The three of us kicked this idea around and visited the Everything's A Dollar stores to give them a closer look. They were bright, cleverly lit, attractive. And they were mobbed.

The idea appealed for several reasons beyond the fact that Everything's A Dollar was hot. First, we'd be able to bring to bear our expertise in the variety-store business because, done right, a dollar store would be just that—a variant on the old Woolworth model, with a wide range of goods sold at a fixed price point. Second, we had a ready supply chain. We had relationships with variety-store suppliers in New York, as well as vendors in Hong Kong. We knew how to buy. Third, thanks to K&K, we had infrastructure in place: a fleet of leased tractors and company-owned trailers providing a link between our warehouse and a far-flung network of toy stores. That gave us the ability to locate dollar stores wherever we wanted, so long as they were inside the area we already traveled. Fourth, we'd completely control our destiny. We'd never have to beg for our lives to a Nintendo or Mattel. We'd buy what we wanted, based solely on whether or not we achieved a price we liked. If we didn't get that price, we could walk away and find something else. Next to the toy business, it promised to be an almost stress-free enterprise.

All of this added up to a single overarching thought: we could operate a chain of dollar stores better than the people already doing it. That is, our stores would be better, and we'd be better at running them. We had the experience, the knowledge, and (most importantly) the discipline to outperform Everything's A Dollar.

Not surprisingly, once we got started, the Everything's A Dollar folks were unhappy with us. They accused us of ripping off their idea. I can understand why they felt that way, but the charge was off the mark. We ripped off *what they wanted to be*. Not what they were.

Besides, they were not the pioneers of the dollar price point—it wasn't their idea any more than it was ours. The first one-dollar player in modern times was a Californian named Dave Gold, who founded his 99 Cents Only chain in Los Angeles in 1982. Working in his family's liquor store, Gold had observed over the years that an item priced at $1.02 would sit on the shelves, but that one priced just three cents cheaper would fly out of stock. So he used that as the basis for a fixed-price store selling everything for ninety-nine cents, and the idea took off.

Dave Gold was fond of stunts that made him something of a celebrity out there. At his stores' grand openings, he sold TVs for ninety-nine cents. At the end of the Los Angeles Dodgers' awful 1992 season, he took out an ad congratulating the team for losing ninety-nine games. Jay Leno did bits on the *Tonight Show* from his stores. By the time he sold the business, Gold had something like three hundred outlets in four Western states.

As Bo Perry told it, he came up with the idea for Everything's A Dollar on his own, and that very well may have been true; I couldn't say if he'd ever heard of Dave Gold or his stores. Perry went to Granby High, just as Joan, Doug, Kenny, and I had. In a pickup basketball game, he'd befriended Michael Porter, who went to a school across town—Lake Taylor High, built on the alfalfa fields across the street from the sanatorium where I spent my early childhood. In the summer of 1976, while both were in college, they went into business together in Newport, Rhode Island, renting some vacant lots and converting them to parking lots for tourists visiting the city's bicentennial celebration. They did well.

At summer's end, Porter returned to law school, while Perry opened an ivory-importing business. At some point after that, Perry told the Norfolk newspaper, he was in a casino in Las Vegas or Atlantic City and watched as gamblers fed dollars into the slot machines, getting nothing in return. "It got me thinking," he said. "There weren't many things left in this world that you could get for a buck. The dollar was becoming extinct. I mean, what can you buy for a dollar? Half a hot dog? I decided I was going to give people something for their dollar."

Perry opened his first dollar store in 1980 on the Virginia Beach oceanfront but couldn't make it work. He refined his business model and tried again four years later, this time achieving some traction. Reunited with Porter, he opened the Tower Mall store in the fall of 1985 and another two mall stores in early 1986.

When we entered the game, they were planning two more stores in the Norfolk area and another in Richmond. They had a good concept. But their buying was seat-of-the-pants and tended toward products they could get really cheaply and others with too thin a margin; they couldn't sell the former and made too little money on the latter. Their infrastructure was practically non-existent: they were expanding before they'd developed systems to keep their existing stores supplied. And they lacked the internal controls on spending that we had.

So we saw an opportunity. We hoped to occupy the same role in the dollar business that Henry Ford had in the car business. He didn't invent the automobile, but he made it available and affordable to the masses. We wanted to bring *scale* to the concept, which no one else had done.

We thought we could succeed by staying true to a philosophy: we wouldn't try to do all the business, just try to make a profit on the business we did. That was an approach that meant maintaining margin control, cost control, rent control. In a word, running a business with discipline.

The toy business had taught us a handful of other guiding principles: One, make shopping convenient and easy. Two, run clean, bright, inviting stores that exceeded customers' expectations. Three, choose our locations wisely. And four, strive for quality and high value in everything we sold, in hopes of pleasing and occasionally dumbfounding our customers.

If we did all that right, we'd get their business and their loyalty. Surprise them. Delight them. Change the inventory to keep them coming back. Make the experience impulsive. If we hewed to that approach, we'd shove aside any competition.

If that sounds cutthroat, so be it. Retail isn't for the faint of heart.

■ ■ ■

We decided we'd call ourselves Only $1.00. It was the concept pared down to its absolute essence; we couldn't find a name that used fewer, shorter words to get the idea across. Doug and I created a new corporation for the business, each of us taking 45 percent ownership and offering Ray an opportunity to own 10 percent in recognition of the profound impact he'd exerted on K&K and was sure to have in this new venture. We ponied up very little money to establish the new company's bank account; Doug and I each pitched in twenty-five thousand dollars, I think it was, and Ray a smaller amount. That was our entire initial investment.

At the start, we figured we'd remain mall retailers. Our thinking was that with two different types of stores to offer developers, we'd have better luck landing spots in the most desirable shopping centers. Mall developers were always looking for something new to draw customers. We reckoned they'd be excited about Only $1.00.

So in May 1986, at the annual International Council of Shopping Centers convention, we unveiled our plans for a chain of dollar stores, looking for space in malls. We brought storyboards with us, detailing how the stores would look, how we'd display merchandise—in bins, like Everything's A Dollar, or right in the boxes in which the items had shipped—and how easy the single price point would be for customers to embrace.

The mall developers gave us a listen, because we'd developed a reputation as good operators with K&K. Then they laughed in our faces. They thought the

Here's an early Only $1.00 store, though it's tough to pinpoint which, since they were all in malls, tiny, jumbled, and—as this view suggests—busy.

idea was crazy. "You're going to sell stuff for a lousy dollar?" they asked. "Forget about it. It's bound to be junk, and we don't want a junk store cluttering up our shiny new mall." Over and over, we heard variations on this theme, along with doubts that we could keep the concept going for more than a year or two. Inflation would destroy us, our audiences predicted. Customers would visit once, but the slim pickings of merchandise wouldn't keep them coming back.

Just one mall developer, a Chattanooga-based company called CBL, offered us a foothold. It owned centers in Dalton, Georgia, and Maryville, Tennessee, and was game to experimenting with Only $1.00 stores in both. We decided we could put another store in K. R.'s shopping center at Wards Corner. The small cinema there had shut down years before, and K. R. had repurposed the space into a tiny enclosed mall. Doug was also able to score space in another local shopping mecca, Chesapeake's Greenbrier Mall, and in a mall in Richmond.

These would be postage-stamp stores of roughly two thousand square feet, but when it's your job to fill them with merchandise you can buy cheaply enough to sell for a buck, that can seem a vast amount of space. All that summer, I scrambled to buy products that would work. We bought closeouts from toy companies—toys that had been released the previous year, or the year before that, or even further back. We went to variety retail shows in New York, which Alice and I had attended over the years on buying trips for the five-and-ten, looking for notions and sundries.

I appointed Alan Wood, who'd started out as a stock boy in our Military Circle toy store, as the head buyer for Only $1.00, and introduced him to vendors I'd known since my earliest days working for K. R. We had credibility with these people, because they knew our track record as retailers and knew we paid our bills.

I pulled Kay Waters out of the toy business, where she'd been working in purchasing, and made her Alan's assistant. The three of us scoured the East Coast, on the hunt. We'd walk into closeout shows and category trade shows, our hats in our hands, and explain what we were trying to do. They'd look at us and say, "What?"

They were baffled. They didn't want to talk to us. They didn't want to think about selling stuff for a dollar. They had money invested not only in their products but in packaging, shipping, advertising. What we were proposing seemed insane. "Look," we'd say, "we don't need to have fancy blister packaging, and we'll send our own trucks to your warehouse to pick up the goods. We'll pay you in thirty days, guaranteed, and if we sell your product we'll come back and buy more. The thing is, though, we have to sell it for a buck."

The whole business came down to that single fundamental idea. The rest of the retail world went out and bought a bunch of stuff to put on the shelves and figured out what to charge for it, based on what they'd spent. We did the opposite. We knew what we'd charge. We just had to find merchandise inexpensive enough to sell for that price.

From early on, we had three tests for merchandise. First, and most obviously, it had to sell for a dollar, so it had to have a "first cost" of considerably less—meaning sixty-five cents or so, tops, and as a rule considerably less than that, before tax, shipping, and such. Second, it had to have a perceived value of higher than a dollar, so anyone encountering it in our stores would be surprised it was priced so low. They'd reasonably expect to pay more. The third test was that it had to be of some quality, some value. It had to be something people would want. It couldn't be junk. Otherwise, we observed few rules. Random, serendipitous, whatever, we'd buy it, whatever it was, in any quantities we could: two dozen, a gross, five gross.

When we were unable to convince some vendors that our thinking was sound, we enlisted help in the form of Peter Ginsburg, a Holocaust survivor and old-school merchant who split his time between New York and Florida and had contacts in the retail trade going back decades. Peter was a persistent negotiator who managed to stay a real gentleman throughout the turns of a deal, and he helped us gain traction with merchandisers in both New York and Chicago. We relied on his help and advice for years.

In November 1986, we opened the first Only $1.00, in Dalton, Georgia. It was a shoestring operation. We didn't put price stickers on anything, instead just opening the cartons; stickers represented a labor cost. We didn't accept credit or debit cards, just cash and checks. The checks involved some risk, but we knew Southern customers expected our trust and would be riled if they didn't get it. We needed no fancy electronics at the checkout stand, because all our clerks had to do was count up a shopper's items and add the tax. We didn't advertise, figuring that word of mouth would be fast and sufficient. We even used closeout shopping bags, some of which had other stores' names on them—anything to hold our costs down.

Right from the first day, the Dalton store did a shocking volume of business. By New Year's, just a few weeks after it opened, we knew we had a winner. And the other four stores we opened just behind it were just as hot.

． ． ．

If you'd walked into that Only $1.00 in Dalton that Christmas season, you'd have found little in common with a Dollar Tree of today. In theory, we had categories of merchandise, but in practice we bought whatever we could get, so the place came off as something of a hodgepodge.

Customers didn't seem to mind. Every carton off the trucks brought a surprise. Every item they dug from a bin seemed a too-good deal. It didn't matter that they might not need the item—hell, in exchange for paying just a dollar for it, they'd invent a way to use it. And if they failed at that, who cared? They weren't out much.

Those first five stores—all of them modest operations by virtually any standard—set a pattern that has held for Dollar Tree ever since. Every store paid for itself within its first year of operation. In other words, it made enough money to cover all the costs of building out the space and filling it with inventory, and keeping the store full of merchandise, and paying everyone involved in opening and running the place. That meant that in its second year of operation, having already paid off all the opening-related debts that many businesses would have to amortize over several years, each of our stores made a serious profit.

And here's an even more remarkable fact: most of our stores did far better than simply pay for themselves in their first year. Some earned enough to damn near pay for a second store. Next to the toy business, the speed with which the dollar venture became profitable bordered on scary.

The numbers weren't as impressive at first glance, because we weren't selling twenty-dollar stuffed animals and forty-dollar video-game cartridges. A toy store's annual income was going to be higher. But we were spending fifty or sixty cents on the merchandise we sold for a dollar, and our operating costs were rock-bottom, so the net was impressive on the modest gross income produced by a dollar store.

If you'd walked into our headquarters at that point, you might have had some difficulty picking out the space devoted to our dollar-store operation. It was a couple of desks in a corner of the K&K offices, no more than twenty feet square—and I'm probably overestimating—occupied by three full-time employees: Alan and Kay and another woman, Laura Hoyle, whom we brought in as liaison to the store managers.

Most people in the building, in fact, didn't treat it as a separate company. A lot of our K&K employees referred to it as "the dollar department." The fact was, however, that although it often felt like an offshoot of the toy company, it was a completely separate corporation from its first day. Not one penny from K&K went toward starting our dollar stores. It had to be that way, because the ownership was different. K. R. was the majority owner of K&K, but he didn't have a piece of the dollar business. He welcomed the experiment, encouraged our success with it, but didn't invest in it, and in fairness to him it was vital that we keep the books separate and not have one company prosper at the expense of the other.

So when I say that we were able to take advantage of K&K's existing infrastructure to grow the dollar chain, I don't mean we did so without paying for it. We split the costs of our shared activities, billing a percentage to each company according to its share of our total business. That percentage changed from year to year—in Dollar Tree's early days, when K&K was the dominant partner, the toy operation probably covered 80 percent or more of the joint costs.

When a truck left our warehouse bound for Georgia, say, carrying merchandise for three toy stores and a dollar store, the cost of that shipment was carefully figured so each company paid its share. This split didn't stop at infrastructure. Those employees like me who worked for both saw each company charged a percentage of our salaries, based on the time we devoted to it. Many of us in the office did double duty. One minute, we might have our toy hat on, another our dollar hat. The same people opened both our toy stores and our dollar stores—built them and fitted them out—and their pay was financed in the same manner. The same went for our field management. Our regional managers and district managers were shared, as was the expense of keeping them.

This situation couldn't last once Dollar Tree reached a certain critical mass; a district manager had his hands full riding herd on only the dollar stores. As the number of Only $1.00 stores grew, we started hiring headquarters staff for just one company. Eventually, only a few activities—information systems, some of the accounting functions—remained joint. But in those first days with those first few stores, the Only $1.00 corner of the office was nothing much to look at. You'd have had no clue that this humble operation was fast creating a monster.

■ ■ ■

A few of us could see that's exactly what was happening. Still selling closeouts, castoffs, and an odd assortment of lucky buys, we added sixteen stores to the original five in 1987. All took off at a gallop. Just keeping them stocked with merchandise was a challenge.

One of our chief sources of merchandise was New York. Alan Wood, as Only $1.00's chief buyer, would travel up there with Bryan and me during Toy Fair. While the big show was under way at the Toy Building, another show of closeout wholesalers was taking place over at the Javits Convention Center. The sellers in this flea market sort of operation were wholesalers—Universal Sales out of Minnesota, Division Sales from Chicago, several New York companies, and one-man outfits from all over. They'd buy up last year's leftovers from retailers and stock from companies that had gone belly-up, as well as freight salvage—a train car derailed, and its contents, written off by an insurance company, wound up with these guys. They'd then try to sell it to mom-and-pop stores. They'd buy overproduced shampoos and conditioners from the manufacturer, pallets of unwanted canned goods, all sorts of stuff. Alan trolled through all these offerings, looking for deals.

As you might imagine, the surroundings were not as glamorous as those over at Toy Fair. Alan wasn't invited into any fancy showrooms. Bryan would go over to Javits to shop with Alan for some basics we needed at K&K. They'd walk through the place together, on the lookout for anything we could sell cheaply at one store and for a dollar at the other—Barbie clothes, crayons, batteries, coloring books. A lot of the stuff Alan bought was unpackaged; it came in bulk, in a pile, which was fine by us, since it went straight into a bin at Only $1.00. Some of the packaging we saw was so bad that we tore it off before dumping the goods inside into a bin.

Now, we took a second pass at the mall developers who'd laughed at us when we first proposed the stores, and found they were laughing no more. We started getting invitations into their lovely new shopping palaces. The people at Everything's A Dollar weren't laughing, either. They sued us for unfair business practices—namely, for ripping off their idea and having a name they believed was too similar to theirs. In federal court in Norfolk, we each presented our side, and Judge Robert Doumar decided it down the middle. We had every right to be in the dollar business, he said, but we had to change our name because it was confusing to consumers. We threw a bunch of names around—I think a lawyer, Tom McPhaul, came up with Dollar Tree—and went back to the judge, saying, "Your Honor, what about *this*?"

The new name wasn't a suggestion that everyone in the room instantly recognized as world-class. We didn't all turn to each other crying, "That's it!" Fact was, we liked our original name and had no intention of pulling it from most of our stores. The court's ruling required that we change our name only in those markets where Everything's A Dollar was established first—a half-dozen cities or so, most in Virginia. So we kept opening Only $1.00 stores except in those few markets.

But we quickly came to believe the Everything's A Dollar people had done us a favor by forcing us to come up with a new name, because the beauty of "Dollar Tree" was that it made no promises to the customer. Unlike "Only $1.00," which assured shoppers they could expect one price, and one price alone, the new name didn't mean anything, really. It simply played on the old saying about money growing on trees.

That lack of a promise was important to us, because we didn't know if we'd be able to stick to the dollar price point. I'm talking very early on here—the first year or two, when we were selling nothing but closeout merchandise out of baskets. Doug and I got to talking about the future one day and realized that if we did have to move off that price point, we'd need to rebrand all the stores that bore our original, promise-making name, which would be enormously disruptive, if not fatal, to our identity.

We decided we'd try a little experiment. On the next few stores we opened outside the six contested markets, we'd use the Dollar Tree brand and see if it made any difference in how shoppers responded.

It turned out that it made no difference at all. Shoppers referred to our stores as "the dollar store" no matter what we chose to call them. They still do. It's been only in the last few years, with Dollar Trees sprouting up almost wall to wall around the country, that anyone has used our actual name, and most still don't bother with it.

Owners get hung up on a name. But once your identity is established, your name is almost beside the point. Look at the Christmas Tree Shops in Boston, owned by Bed Bath & Beyond. They are *not* Christmas tree shops. They're big variety stores with outdoor furniture, pillows, bedspreads, and curtains bought at closeout. But everybody knows what they are, and customers flock in. They don't give much thought to the name.

Once we understood that it didn't matter what we called ourselves, we decided to drop Only $1.00 and rebrand everything as Dollar Tree. We phased the original name out as our leases expired. It took years to erase the name completely. No one cared.

■ ■ ■

Meanwhile, we continued to grow, and fast. By May 1988, we had thirty-five stores and plans to open another twenty by year's end. It was at about that point that we slipped past Everything's A Dollar in number of stores. It had thirty-three and hoped to open another seventeen in the coming months.

The ultimate outcome of our contest was pretty clear to us, if not them. One night, Ray drove past the Everything's A Dollar warehouse in Norfolk. Its loading-dock doors were open, and he saw that the warehouse floor was a scene of utter chaos—stuff piled all over, in no particular order. We, on the other hand, were operating out of the well-organized K&K warehouse, which we had spent years refining into an efficient operation. Everything's A Dollar spent a lot on freight; we supplied our Dollar Trees with trucks that were headed that way anyway.

As our competition heated up, Everything's A Dollar paid some crazy mall rents to get out in front of us. We refused to do so. In those early days, we were offering malls a toy store, too, so they were willing to work with us on rents. Before we signed a lease, we made sure the numbers worked for the long term. We didn't open stores willy-nilly; we controlled our growth. One rock-steady rule was that we wouldn't outrun our infrastructure. The other guys played a looser, faster game. They actually opened a store in *Hong Kong*, for goodness' sake. Why on earth would they do that?

With years behind us in the variety business, we had a pretty good sense of what people would buy and what they would not, even for a dollar. Sure, we bought closeouts and made whatever random deals we could, but that didn't mean we bought just anything. We turned down a lot. Everything's A Dollar didn't follow suit as often as it should have. At one point, it bought a pile of those weighted rings you slide over baseball bats for batting practice. Now, I ask, how many of those was it going to sell?

In sum, what the other guys lacked was discipline, and it proved their undoing. They were driven at times by their egos, by bravado, rather than by good financial management. They didn't pay attention to the mundane but essential details of growing a business. In October 1989, by which time we had a hundred stores and they had sixty-one, Everything's A Dollar sold out to Wisconsin Toy Company Inc. of Milwaukee. A few years later, our competitor's parent company filed for bankruptcy.

Everything's A Dollar had wanted us to buy it, at one point before the end. We weren't interested. Instead, in an irony of ironies, we bought its name after it went under. We paid the bankruptcy court twenty-five thousand dollars for the marquee, as it was called.

Today, we use it on our internal signage and occasionally on our storefronts, to back up our own name—"Dollar Tree, where everything's a dollar."

9

Saving the Dollar, Changing the World

O f all the questions I've been asked about Dollar Tree over the years, the most persistent by far is, "How long do you think you'll be able to keep the price point at a dollar?" Even now, with the company's thirtieth anniversary behind us, people can't believe we can stick with it indefinitely.

I can understand that, because we weren't confident about it at the start either. The conventional wisdom held that it would prove impossible. How could we adjust for inflation with our price locked at a dollar? How could we maintain a decent margin if the dollar fluctuated versus the Chinese yuan or the Thai baht?

Our concerns were exacerbated by the pressure we felt from vendors, who pushed hard to get us off a fixed price. If we charged *two* dollars, they said, imagine what wonderful things they'd be able to sell us! Our customers would barely notice the price change, but, my, how they'd love the range of stuff they could find in our stores! Besides, they argued, it was just a matter of time before circumstances forced us to make such a change—so why not take charge and do it ourselves?

Don't believe that kind of talk didn't get us thinking. There was quite a bit of it inside the company, even without the vendors' contribution. We debated in the office about whether or not ditching the price point was, in fact, inevitable. Those who believed it so advocated experimenting with multiple price points. We should give it a try, some said. Open a couple of stores at a $1.29 price point, for instance, and see what happened.

When I say there was debate, I don't mean yelling or serious disagreement. Perhaps discussion is a better way to describe it. Conversation, even. It was low-key and collegial. But even so, the price point was clearly a subject on people's minds, and few subjects were more important to the nature of our business than that.

Personally, I viewed the dollar-only concept as sacred. It was everything. Without it, we'd be just another discount retailer, a small fry among bigger, hungry fish. How could we compete against Family Dollar and Dollar General, variety-store chains already ensconced in thousands of small towns across the American South? How could we avoid being crushed by Walmart, which would always be able to undersell us on general merchandise?

Ditch the dollar, I believed, and we'd surrender our niche. We'd also damage our negotiating position with the very vendors who were bitching about our price point, because as things stood they knew what price they had to meet before we would or could buy from them. They knew we had no wiggle room. Take away that hard ceiling on any conversation about the price of their products and I was sure their products would suddenly get more expensive. The dollar price point helped us negotiate low rents, too. Prospective landlords knew we could pay only so much, because we sold everything for a dollar. It was clear to everyone on both sides of the negotiating table that we had real limits on what we could afford.

Most importantly, we'd lose the element of surprise we had over our customers, who would not be quite as amazed at the goods we sold if they were priced even twenty-nine cents higher.

On top of all that, I was confident that the merchandise we'd sell at $1.29, or two bucks, or even three, would not be appreciably better than what we were already offering for one. I devised an experiment to test my thinking. I sent Alan Wood to New York with instructions to buy merchandise we could sell for one dollar, for two dollars, for three and five, and to bring back a sampling of goods at each level. He returned, and we spread all the booty on a table and asked people in the office to pick out which items should go in each pile.

They couldn't do it. Everyone was shocked. Even I was shocked, and I'd come up with the experiment. It was impossible to tell the difference between

Doug and I sit for an interview with Norfolk's Virginian-Pilot *in 1987, as our experiment in fixed-price retail began to attract attention.*
PHOTO BY JIM WALKER, USED BY PERMISSION OF *VIRGINIAN-PILOT*

an item we could sell for a buck and others we might charge three or even five times as much for. So how could a customer tell when she got a good buy on something? She couldn't—and she couldn't tell when she paid too much either.

That told us that the magic of our business model was having everything priced at a dollar, so a customer had no doubt, none at all, that she was getting a bargain. At a dollar for everything, the thought never occurred to her that an item might be overpriced. How could it be?

Another piece of magic that the dollar price point brought was that when a customer walked into our store, she could shut off her brain. She didn't have to think, didn't have to calculate how much she was spending. All she had to do was count—"One, two, three, four, five, six. I have six items, and I have six dollars. I can buy this." Whether or not she was on a limited budget, it made the transaction as easy as spending money can be.

That little experiment made up our minds that we had to stick with a dollar. If someday we were forced by circumstance to shift it, we'd do so, we decided.

But unless and until that happened, we'd stand firm on price. And as inflation and supply and exchange rates changed, we'd instead alter the merchandise we offered.

Which we could do, see, because we weren't beholden to selling any particular product. Think about that for a moment. We were a dollar store. The only thing customers expected, on walking through the doors, was that everything inside would sell for a dollar. If they found motor oil on the shelves one week—and believe it or not, in the company's early days, they did find quarts of top-grade oil at Dollar Tree—they wouldn't start thinking of us as their go-to supplier for motor oil or auto supplies. They'd recognize that they got lucky once. Maybe, but not necessarily, they'd get lucky again and find oil for sale on their next visit.

So when we could no longer buy oil at a price that enabled us to sell it for a dollar and dropped it from our stores, no tears would be shed. We'd replace the oil with something else that we *could* get at the price we sought, and which packed a surprising value of its own. We sold wine for a brief while—full-sized, 750-milliliter bottles of Napa Valley wine. You can bet that surprised people. We knew it wouldn't last, and so did our customers, but they sure enjoyed it while we had it.

We got some great deals because companies changed the labels on their products and wanted to get rid of the old-looking stuff. The contents were as good as ever, no different in any respect from the stuff selling for five times as much, if not more. In search of closeouts and special deals, we tapped into a whole underworld of consumer goods. It was truly amazing what was out there.

The products we sold were almost infinitely variable, not only by item but by size. If we sold wrapping paper one Christmas that measured sixty square feet and the price subsequently went up beyond our means, perhaps we'd offer forty-five or fifty square feet the following Christmas. If chewing gum came five packs to the bag and the price crept upward, we could always sell four packs instead.

As long as we maintained our focus on offering great value, we'd be okay. We could maneuver our selection in any manner we had to, in order to keep the price.

We have never needed to change it.

It was, and is, for always.

. . .

Our commitment to the dollar changed the dollar itself, restored it as a viable unit of United States currency. That sounds like a wild, exaggerated boast, but think about it. Before we came along, the dollar had dwindled in significance. A buck no longer bought many candy bars, let alone a cup of coffee.

Fact was, no one in American retail gave a damn about the bottom end of the market, and no American shopper expected to find anything of quality for a single dollar. Nowadays, all the chains—Target, Walmart, Kmart, all the big-box discount department stores—have experimented with dollar sections. Those guys typically clear a section of their hundred-thousand-plus-square-foot sales floor up front near the doors and move all their dollar stuff into it. Their selection's not great, but they've recognized that the price point resonates with the public.

Same goes for your local supermarket and drugstore, where travel-sized health and beauty items have become a popular staple. We'll take credit for that.

And you can thank Dollar Tree for the dollar menu at your local fast-food joint, where the idea has found lasting traction. Dollar-menu items are mainstays now at McDonald's, Burger King, and Taco Bell. Meanwhile, our fixed price has won imitators around the world. Dollar Tree–style stores have sprung up in Japan (100 Yen Plaza), the United Kingdom (Poundland), Germany (EuroShop and TEDi), and South America.

The dollar-only concept enabled us to grow successfully among much larger chains without getting into a serious spat. We didn't hurt anybody's business. We just found a niche nobody had exploited on a large scale. Considering how well it's worked out, it's a little surprising that no new national players have come along to challenge us as dollar-only merchants. Of the three big American chains with *Dollar* in their names, we're the only one that actually sticks to that price. Dollar General, which originated in Tennessee decades before we came along, and Family Dollar, which appeared not long after, are mostly rural chains of small, low-end variety stores, with goods priced all over the park.

We have such stores of our own. In recent years, we've operated a chain of about two hundred stores called Deal$, mostly in the Midwest. These stores are roughly the same size as a Dollar Tree and sometimes occupy the site of a fixed-price store we've relocated; we've changed the name, changed the mix of merchandise, and reopened.

You might think that because the wares we sell there are a little more expensive, a Deal$ store achieves higher net sales than a Dollar Tree. But no. Now, the customer has to think before she buys, so she doesn't necessarily buy more. And the margins on what she does take to the counter are smaller.

So our experience demonstrates that the one-dollar price point is the better mousetrap. Shoppers are more cautious in a multi-price-point environment. They have to think before they buy. We sell great stuff for two or three dollars at Deal$, but it doesn't trump what customers can find for a buck at Dollar Tree.

■ ■ ■

But I'm getting ahead of myself. It's still early in the Dollar Tree adventure, with the company growing rapidly. By the end of 1988, we had 58 stores up and running. A year later, we'd almost doubled the number, to 102.

K&K was the bigger company, boasting more than 130 stores and a fatter gross income for each, but we could see that Dollar Tree had a much, much rosier future. Our only competition was regional; no one was operating dollar-only stores coast to coast. None of these regional players was poised to balloon into a category killer and thus create the claustrophobic competition we were enduring in toys.

We could make this work.

It was still too early to qualify as a sure bet, but by the beginning of 1990 the trend lines seemed to suggest that the little sister of our two companies could grow to dominate the pair. Modest sales, small stores, and therefore small rent. Don't try to do all the business, just try to make a profit on the business we did. That was our formula. And it was paying off.

The big question we faced was whether or not we could find enough merchandise to nourish our future growth. Our shelves and bins were dominated by the catch-as-catch-can stuff we found in closeouts. A little guy could make out quite well by trading only in the castoffs of other companies. He could buy in small lots. He could react quickly to opportunities. A little guy had some advantages over a big company. Now, however, we were outgrowing our supply chain. The lots were too small to supply us. Availability was unpredictable. The products we could find in sufficient bulk tended to be imports we bought from wholesalers, who bumped up the price.

Which was what drove me overseas, to see what I could find to buy there—just as, a century before, Frank Woolworth had been spurred to seek merchandise in Europe. I always aimed to find better goods at a better price, and because we could now buy at significant volumes, I thought we could nail down much better prices for foreign goods if we bought and imported them ourselves.

Price wasn't the only consideration. After years in the toy business, and after dealing with big toy companies that dictated what we bought, and how much, I wanted control. I wanted to be dependent on no one.

So we ventured back to Hong Kong, now with two companies to buy for. On our first trips over, in 1988 and 1989, I took two lieutenants with me—Alan Wood, who was buying for Dollar Tree, and Bryan Bagwell, who was now the head buyer for K&K. I can't imagine what that was like for those guys, who'd joined K&K straight out of high school and had never been out of the country. I'd been to Vietnam and had some feel for the Far East, but even so, Hong Kong was a sensory wonderland for me, bristling as it was with scores of skyscrapers clustered tightly below towering, tree-clad mountains and overlooking a harbor crowded with cruise ships, freighters, junks, ancient sailing ships. Double-deck ferries cutting back and forth between the island and Kowloon. Wildly decorated boats rafted six deep along the waterfront. Billboards for Double Happiness cigarettes. Laundry hanging everywhere, cars everywhere, neon lights, honking horns. The constant din of millions of people living right on top of each other. Weird, not always agreeable smells.

It was exciting to be there. The dollar business was new to the Chinese, but we won their ear because we'd earned credibility with our toy buying. They knew we'd pay our bills on time—which might seem a pretty low bar, but you'd be amazed at how many companies didn't. That reputation took us far. Our toy vendors introduced us to the people we needed to meet.

Even so, I didn't know many variety-goods vendors in Hong Kong, so I hired a guy, Glenn Collins, who used to work for Best Products, and he accompanied us there, serving as guide and go-between in exchange for 5 percent of the dollar value of any orders I wrote. Having been with what was then a much bigger company with a long history of working with the Chinese, he proved a valuable liaison, introducing me to vendors and product lines I didn't know. He made two or three trips with us.

By the time Glenn left us, my eyes were opened to what was available in Hong Kong, and it was a mind-blowing revelation. I'd go into these showrooms and they'd have a mountain of products for sale, so much that I couldn't take it all in. The showrooms were stuffed with merchandise from scores of vendors, all piled high. An eyewash of stuff, a tsunami of it—shelves completely packed and rising to the ceiling. Some of these showrooms must have had ten thousand items for sale, and a surprising number of them were within our means to sell for a dollar.

It was a world of merchandise I had no idea existed. If I had any doubts about the dollar business beforehand, my first few trips back to Hong Kong cured me of them. Look what was out there, waiting for us! Look what we could do if we got Dollar Tree up to top speed! I came home and talked to Doug and Ray about what I'd seen, convinced them we could have everything we wanted by dealing directly with the Chinese. We could control our product lines and slash what we paid for them. We'd have no further worries about supply. We could buy in any quantity we wanted, pay very little for it, mark it up to just a dollar, and still make a tidy profit. A few trips per year would keep us fat with merchandise.

At the time, any Chinese goods available through American wholesalers cost far more than those I saw in Hong Kong, because they'd gone through two, three, or four markups. Buying direct eliminated those built-in price hikes. We'd find an item in Hong Kong, buy it, put it on a shelf in America for a buck, and people went crazy. They were amazed to find the same things in our stores that they'd been spending three dollars for. Or more. We sold push brooms, straw brooms, and dustpans we'd bought there. Mops. Eighty-count packages of cosmetic wipes. Sunglasses. Sewing kits with fifty spools of thread, in fifty different colors.

People were even more amazed that we could be making money selling such stuff. Fact was, we were doubling our money on close to everything we sold. And still, we saw the opportunity to do even better—not only to spend less on the stuff we found in Hong Kong but to buy better, higher-quality merchandise that cost no more, if not less.

The key was that the Hong Kong showrooms themselves were applying a markup to the goods they showed us. They were run by trading companies, which was just another term for wholesalers. They were middlemen between Chinese factories and the United States market. Almost all were represented by Westerners or English-speaking Chinese nationals, which made buying from them easy, so few buyers for American stores looked beyond Hong Kong when they went to Asia to shop. It was a quick, painless, one-stop journey involving no foreign language.

But I'd heard of another marketplace that promised to make Hong Kong look like a ripoff. On one of our early trips to the Far East, I left the others to take care of business in Hong Kong and went off in search of the Canton Trade Fair.

. . .

The Canton Trade Fair, also known as the China Import and Export Fair, is a twice-yearly meeting for buyers and factories that's been held in its present form in Guangzhou, about a hundred miles northwest of Hong Kong, since 1957, and is said to date back in one style or another to the time of Marco Polo. Nowadays, it's a big deal that attracts hundreds of foreign buyers to a lavish campus of modern showrooms and a reception hall much like the Javits Center in New York. It's as fancy as the Taj Mahal.

In the late eighties, that wasn't the case. The fair was held in a cluster of World War II–era concrete buildings that looked like former barracks. Inside, those no-frills structures were home to huge rooms stuffed with booths set up by Chinese factories and their representatives. It was an extremely low-tech, bare-bulb setting.

But from my first hour there, I could see we'd be buying less from the trading companies in Hong Kong. Those guys were marking up stuff 25, 35, even 40 percent. On items we were in the hunt for, that amounted only to nickels and dimes, but percentage-wise the markup was immense. An item with a first cost of forty cents in Hong Kong might cost a quarter at the Canton Trade Fair. I was stunned.

Canton's buyers were Westerners and Middle Easterners. The factory reps tended to be Chinese women who spoke decent English. Many had Western names, or names they thought sounded Western. Stormy and Rain were popular. Fanny, too. One was named Tomato. I had a Chinese agent with me on my first visit and made it a habit afterward, because once we got into the nitty-gritty details of an order, both sides needed it. A lot of the buyers had their own interpreters.

To stand at the fair was to be awash in cultures and languages and visual stimuli—the buyers' foreign chatter layered over the stilted English of the factory reps and the insistent Chinese of the interpreters, while all around were sights too vast and complex to absorb. It was like a scene from *Blade Runner*, only busier.

And almost everything my eyes fell upon was a ridiculously good value. It was a real surprise, what we could buy. This was not the sort of stuff anyone back home would associate with a dollar store. This was merchandise of real quality and usefulness, priced so we could buy it, pay to ship it, cover the duty costs of landing it in the States, and still achieve a spectacular margin. It might be mind boggling to think we could buy anything of lasting value for thirty-eight or forty cents. But we could, since we were buying in large quantities—and of course, that was more the case in the years that followed, because as the company grew our orders became gigantic.

I traveled back to Hong Kong with samples of what I'd seen, some of which duplicated what we were already buying from trading companies at a higher price, and some of which was stuff we hadn't seen before—porcelain and hand-painted statuettes. We bought a little bit, and it sold fast. On subsequent trips, we spent a lot of time on porcelain and polyresin figurines. Polyresin was a plastic, of sorts, that had a heft to it. It felt expensive, and because it was molded it could be intricately detailed. These figurines came in every form imaginable. Just the Santa Clauses we had to choose from included tall ones, thin ones, fat ones, Santas in Victorian getup, Santas looking oddly rakish, others appearing to be of Middle Eastern extraction. Santas with children or bags of toys or stockings, Santas with wrapped presents, Christmas trees, or snowmen, Santas playing the violin.

If you wanted rabbit figurines, the Canton Trade Fair was your place. We bought hundreds of thousands of polyresin rabbits wearing summer dresses, or carrying baskets, or holding bundles of carrots, or counting eggs, or romancing their honeys. For those preferring mice, we served up cute polyresin rodents sailing on lettuce boats, sitting in piles of peanuts, posing with holey cheese or biscuits. Holding cherries. Eating grapes. We offered fridge magnets featuring the polyresin heads of every dog breed known to man. They all sold. We couldn't keep them in the stores.

And the margin on polyresin, which bordered on the obscene, was even more remarkable considering what went into these little knickknacks. Let me offer an example. It's from a few years into our trips to China, so you have to figure that, what with inflation, such buys were even better when we first started going.

We visited a factory where one of our polyresin figurines was being made. The factory was a long, low building with a corrugated metal roof. One wall

A Chinese factory worker paints a regiment of polyresin figurines. Finishing each finely detailed knickknack required many such artisans but cost pennies, making polyresin one of Dollar Tree's early successes.

Bryan Bagwell, standing at right, inspects the work at a Chinese factory cranking out figurines bound for Dollar Tree stores. That's Kay Waters just behind him and Benny Huen, our longtime trading agent, at far left.

PHOTOS COURTESY OF BRYAN BAGWELL

was brick, into which had been built a series of kilns. The figurines were cast in individual molds shaped a bit like acorns. After they cooked, a factory worker would pull them out of the oven, one mold at a time, crack them open, and extract the prizes inside—in this case, figures maybe five inches tall that we called "Bear on Books" in our records. It consisted of a little teddy bear sitting on one large book and using another as a backrest while intently studying another book that was open in his lap.

The cooled figurines were placed on a table, along which were seated eight men and women, each armed with a single color of paint and a variety of paintbrushes. The figurines, which came out of the molds a bright white, passed from one painter to the next, each applying a color—first an overall brown wash on the bear, then dark green on the books, then red trim on the books and on the bear's necktie, and so on.

It was fast, intricate work. In the half-hour of our visit, finished figurines—which were incredibly detailed in their construction and their paint jobs, with the look and feel of something found in a high-end gift shop—were placed a dozen to a tray at the table's end, and the stack of those trays rose to chest height.

At least nine people had touched each figurine, and that didn't count the folks making the molds or injecting them with polyresin. For all that labor, and for all that quality, the price the factory quoted us for each "Bear on Books" was thirty-three cents.

■ ■ ■

Now, some might read that and complain that we, an American company, were giving away work to the Chinese that Americans should have been doing. To which I reply: bunk. We are in the business of selling quality goods for a dollar apiece. American suppliers were unable to produce these types of goods at anywhere near the costs necessary to make that happen, let alone the prices we got from Asian companies. If we could have bought American, we certainly would have, but the math simply didn't work. U.S. labor costs were many, many times those of the Chinese. (That said, about half of the merchandise sold at Dollar Tree today—food, candy, paper products, and household chemicals—is American-made.)

Some others might read about "Bear on Books" and accuse us of exploiting the Chinese; they might say that, with our paying so little, those men and women on the assembly line couldn't have made more than pennies per hour.

I think it's probably true that they made very little money, but I believe it to be equally true that without our business they'd have had no work at all. That was certainly the case a few years into our importing, when Dollar Tree had grown to thousands of stores and our orders ran into the tens of millions of pieces. One line of figurines could keep an entire village employed for months.

We kept buying in Hong Kong, and we bought a lot in Guangzhou, but as time went on we ventured farther into the country, to rural areas where we met face to face with the people who made our products—the visit to the "Bear on Books" factory was on one such expedition—and came away with even better buys.

Sometimes, a group of factories in an area would stage a regional trade show for us. In China's Fujian Province, they'd set out all their wares in a hotel ballroom. We'd walk through it and select items we liked. We'd then leave the room, they'd remove everything we hadn't selected and replace it with different merchandise, and we'd come back for another pass. Then another and another, until eventually the room was filled with stuff we liked, and from that assortment we'd make our final picks.

The factories were eager for our business. They knew we wouldn't pay much per piece, but that we'd buy in such huge, almost incomprehensible quantities that they'd make out nicely. Ask the folks in Fujian if they felt exploited. I can tell you what their answer would be.

Our back-country explorations weren't limited to China. We went shopping around the world for merchandise without markups. The world had never seen anything quite like it. Buyers for Walmart and Kmart weren't getting in a car and driving for hours on dirt roads to find these rural factories. They weren't as hungry as we were, or as hell-bent on going to the source.

We were the Indiana Joneses of retail. We went to Italy to buy plastics, mostly kitchen and household items with modern designs and interesting colors. We went to India and bought hand-carved soapboxes and figurines made of soft stone. We found candy and cookies in Argentina. We bought handicrafts from Indonesia, which didn't have any manufacturing capability but had labor aplenty and could turn out merchandise in bulk. We got a letter from one Indonesian village that made decorative cornhusk scarecrows, thanking us for giving the entire population work for a season.

We went to Thailand in search of rawhide dog chews. Before then, you couldn't buy a dog chew in America for less than two or three dollars; the market was cornered and the price controlled by pet-supply companies such as Hartz and Sergeant's. We found this factory two hours from the nearest city, out in the middle of the rice paddies, a tin hut surrounded by racks of cowhide drying in the sun. It couldn't get much lower-tech. The workers would dry the hides, then soak them, cut them, tie them into shapes, and dry them again. When we asked about prices, the factory people offered us ten-inch rawhide dog chews for twenty-five cents. *Twenty-five cents,* for huge chews that would sell in a pet-supply store for four bucks. Even selling them for a dollar, we were looking at a 75 percent margin. We had to work hard to hide how excited we were. We bought the hell out of them, and back in the States, customers couldn't believe we had them in our stores. All it required was our wandering the wilds to find the factory.

Another example of how forsaking the beaten path paid off: Joan and I were browsing a museum gift shop in Virginia, and she found some Christmas tree ornaments she liked—nice-looking balls, hand decorated. They were ten dollars apiece. I examined one and saw that it was made in India. We were getting ready to head to India on a buying trip, so I told her to wait, that they were too expensive. She wasn't happy.

Over in India, we found the same balls—exactly the same ones—and they cost ten cents. *Ten cents.* Granted, that was before we paid to package and ship them, but still: ten cents.

It was a reminder that there is no relationship between the price on a piece of merchandise in a department store and what it cost to make it. A high-end, handmade import can carry a stiff price here at home, but ten thousand miles away, in the village where it originated, that ten- or twenty- or even thirty-dollar item might be worth just pennies.

10

Free of Distractions

K.R. was fond of sharing wisdom he'd picked up over his years in his varied businesses, and that he honed to short, memorable adages. One he shared with me early in my tenure at the variety store and with many managers afterward was, "Well displayed is half-sold." It's a foundational principle in retail, and if you live by it you see the results. Display, presentation, packaging—it's all important in attracting customers into a store, keeping them there, and sparking their interest in particular items.

In the early days of Dollar Tree, we violated the principle pretty flagrantly. We used inexpensive baskets, into which we dumped the merchandise. We did little to entice shoppers to individual items; our signage left much to be desired. And though our stores were clean and bright, they were disorganized, the merchandise situated with little regard for product categories and with little consistency from store to store.

The stores looked as cheap as they were, the reason being that we wanted to open them for the least possible money. We avoided anything that would run up costs.

But we grew out of that. As our shopping overseas brought more and more higher-quality merchandise into the stores, stuff that didn't deserve to be dumped into a basket, we shifted to traditional gondolas. And in keeping with K. R.'s philosophy, we organized the stores into firmer categories.

Gifts were a big driver in those days, occupying a cluster of shelves near the front of the store. Toys occupied a wall, on pegs, plus an aisle or two. Health, beauty, and cosmetic items—HBC, in industry parlance—took up another couple of aisles. Another stretch of shelf space was devoted to school supplies and stationery, and another to housewares.

From pretty early on, we recognized that party supplies and gift wrap were important. They were so overpriced in most stores, and so cheap to stock, that we knew we could offer some real bargains. The same went for seasonal merchandise. Nobody offered more quality seasonal decorations and doodads for less money than we did, and that's true to this day. We're the best merchants of seasonal goods there is.

Look around a store and you'd have seen that a huge portion of the shelf space, regardless of category, was devoted to items you'd give away to your friends, your coworkers, your students. Americans are very giving; our nature as a country is doing something for others. So we catered to teachers buying trinkets for the kids in their classes, to white-collar workers remembering friends at the office—mementos that cost only a buck but transcended their price in the giving. Dollar Tree became a supply house for the small but meaningful gesture.

For years, we've stocked plastic containers with lids, about the size of shoeboxes. There are "shoebox ministries" whose members buy these containers and fill them with toiletries, soaps, and such and send them to orphans or deployed soldiers or the down-on-their-luck. We sell mountains of them. If not for our price point, those containers might be too expensive for the charities to buy.

So if you visited a Dollar Tree as we entered the nineties, you'd have seen our stores evolving—the bins disappearing, the organization improving, the quality of goods getting better by the month. We were starting to use space with the same efficiency we controlled costs. At one point, we cut a deal with Wrigley's, which designed display racks for its gum that anchored to the backs of our cash registers. We hadn't even recognized that as selling space. The gum flew out of the stores. We did a calculation of how far all that gum would stretch, for some reason, and found it would circle the globe.

That got us thinking about other places in the stores where we might show off merchandise without disrupting existing displays. We started using clip strips—clear plastic strips with hooks—at the end of each gondola. We taped bags of ribbon and bows to the boxes of gift wrap. We did the same with tape and scissors, so everything customers needed to wrap presents used the same box for display. We bought white plastic chain-link, hung it from the ceiling, and dangled stuffed animals and other light products from it.

We were becoming a new generation of variety store, a variation of the old Woolworth idea—a place where people could drop in to buy favors for a birthday party, or Christmas decorations, or a slotted spoon they needed in the kitchen.

We didn't have the full selection a Woolworth did, because that grand old chain—on its last legs by this time—stocked merchandise at a wide range of prices. But our thinking was to build on the things people bought predictably, the merchandise that, so unlike the toy business, wasn't subject to fads or fashions. Easter, Halloween, and Christmas came along every year. There were events in every family—birthdays, graduations, anniversaries, recognitions of one sort or another—that required gifts, which required wrapping paper, ribbon, bows. Every fall, the kids went back to school and needed notebooks, pens, poster board.

One thing did not change as our stores grew up: we continued to emphasize the element of surprise, continued to bring in merchandise of such quality that our customers could not believe we were selling it for a dollar. Now, however, they didn't have to claw through bins to find it. We made it easier for them. Well displayed was half-sold.

That saw us blossom from 102 stores at the end of 1989 to 186 stores two years later. We had customers who knew what day the trucks unloaded; freight would land at the store, and they'd be there, waiting. They knew to buy items that day, too, because once they were gone we might not get more. We'd receive these import shipments, push everything to the stores, and bingo, it would be sold. You could look at our sales figures and pick out exactly when shipments had come in—there'd be a spike.

It was exciting for the people working in the stores, too. They were as amazed as the customers at what we were able to get. They never knew what was coming off that truck. Even with better-defined categories, we thus preserved Dollar Tree's treasure-hunt appeal. From week to week, people never knew what surprises might be waiting. Early on, we actually ran out of merchandise sometimes, especially at Christmas.

As he was leasing stores and trying to get them open, Doug used to fuss at me about not having enough merchandise for them in January and February.

I'd say, "Doug, we just don't have the goods. We can't *get* the goods." We were chasing our tail, trying to buy sufficiently early to land goods for the start of the next year, but we weren't sophisticated enough to keep that flow going.

Which of course was bad in one sense. Then again, turning our inventory that completely was the sign of a healthy company. We weren't maximizing our sales potential, but we were always getting something fresh. Turnover was constant. Which brought customers back, and kept them coming.

The takeaway for me was that we couldn't worry about what we didn't have. Just sell what we had. And we couldn't obsess over what we could have done. Just do well with what we had.

Still, we had some pretty Spartan-looking stores at times. Customers would walk in, look around at shelves wiped clean, and ask, "Are you going out of business?"

■ ■ ■

Our stores started to undergo another, more noticeable evolution in the early nineties as well. Up to now, our dollar stores had been located in shopping malls, and more often than not in malls where we also ran a K&K Toys. But for both businesses, the malls were no longer the lucrative locations they had once been.

Above all, they were expensive. Rent was steep, and it wasn't the same for everyone. There was no square-foot rate that applied to every business in a mall. Jewelers, for instance, operated small stores at a tremendous margin. They paid through the nose. Bigger, lower-margin stores paid a lower rate.

Maintenance fees for security, utilities, janitorial services, pretty plants in the central plaza—those were outrageous, and they weren't always shared evenly either. Oftentimes, a mall operator would make a deal with the big anchors—which he needed, more than anything, to make the place a success—that excused them from their fair share of those fees, and put a disproportionate chunk of the burden on the little guys.

Our dollar stores were small and had a big margin but modest income—after all, we charged a dollar for everything. And our toy stores were not the money machines they'd been twenty years before. As our ability to compete with Toys "R" Us and the other big-box retailers began to slip, and as we continued to be shut out of a healthy supply of merchandise by Nintendo, we turned to discount toys as our focus—the hot toys from a year before, plus the basics we bought direct in Asia. Our volume of business remained healthy, but our income from the toy business indicated trouble ahead.

The upshot was that mall rents and fees were a heavy load and growing heavier. We became dissatisfied with other aspects of indoor shopping centers as well. They were restrictive in design; it wasn't easy to expand or shrink a store, and the frontages tended to be small. Deliveries were a major pain in the neck, especially at the dollar stores, where we moved in a lot of small cartons.

We'd experimented with locating some toy stores in strip shopping centers and were pleased with the results. Now, a new kind of strip mall was springing up all over America: the power center, usually anchored by two or three big-box retailers such as Walmart, Target, and Office Depot, with an assortment of smaller retailers in between. These shopping centers were drawing traffic, and a lot of tenants we thought might be good neighbors for Dollar Trees. Their rents were far lower than those of the enclosed malls, maintenance fees were nonexistent, and they offered other advantages as well. Deliveries were easy— just pull a truck around back and unload directly through the store's rear door, rather than hassle with the twisty back corridors that linked a mall store with the loading docks. They were visible from the street, which brought in not only customers but job applicants, whom we needed.

Over the next ten years, we pulled Dollar Trees out of enclosed malls as our leases expired and moved into traditional strip malls and power centers. The trick was to get a storefront as close as possible to one of the anchors, preferably a variety anchor or a supermarket—a place where shoppers would be going as a matter of course. If those shoppers were already near our store when they left their cars, we figured they just might make a quick visit to Dollar Tree on the way in or out of our larger neighbor.

So that became our strategy: just as a remora attaches itself to a shark to take advantage of the bigger fish's supply of food, we shouldered up to big-box shopping magnets. And the strategy worked. Did it ever! In fact, it worked so well that some big retailers now write a ban against us into their lease agreements. It's annoying, but I can understand their position; they don't much enjoy selling merchandise for three bucks that we have next door for one. Once a customer sees that, she begins to wonder about all the other prices in that big-box store.

The lower overhead in the strip centers enabled us to experiment with larger stores. Throughout the nineties, we tried on a variety of sizes and configurations. Even within the dollar segment of the retail market, we faced some competition from small chains and mom-and-pop companies, and these stores (especially the ones in ethnic neighborhoods) tended to be larger. They might be small companies, but they impressed us with the sheer size of their outlets. So as we spread across the East and ventured west of the Appalachians, we found ourselves forced by competition to think larger. From our tiny, 2,000-square-foot mall footprints, we evolved first to 3,000 feet and then—as our Asian imports grew and we found more and better merchandise to stock— to 5,000 or 6,000. That was our standard size for years.

In search of the right size, we sometimes went too large. Our few failures typically came when we leased a former grocery store and tried to fill that 12,000- to 15,000-square-foot space with merchandise. Nowadays, we could do it. Back then, we couldn't pull it off; we'd have twenty facings of one item on the shelves just to create the illusion that we had tons of product. We didn't fool anyone.

■ ■ ■

The biggest changes at Dollar Tree, as we neared our fifth anniversary, weren't in the stores. In fact, they went unseen by our customers. But they ushered in dramatic shifts in the company's culture and focus.

The first came in 1990, when K. R. decided to retire at age seventy-three. He'd been working in Norfolk for more than a half-century at this point and had seen K&K grow from that little variety store at Wards Corner—which was still open for business, and where he still ate at the lunch counter most weekdays— to a toy-store chain that peaked at 136 outlets throughout the Southeast.

K. R. had never really managed the chain per se, but he'd always been our spiritual and emotional leader and was always a source of encouragement and wisdom to Doug, Ray, and me. He was a great motivator, the glue that held everyone together. We all owed everything to him. Had K. R. not convinced me to leave government service to work with Alice at the former Ben Franklin, I might well have retired as a naval intelligence agent, and you wouldn't be reading this book.

He didn't disappear by any means—K. R. kept his office and remained a beloved and respected presence—but he wanted to cash in his share of the company. The three of us bought him out. We went deep into hock to do it. Joan and I put up everything we owned as collateral to finance our share, and I know

Doug and his wife, Pat, had to scramble in similar fashion.

A few months later, another change occurred that at first glance might not seem nearly so earth shaking, but which forced me to change my role in the company. In the first four years of our Dollar Tree venture, Alan Wood had grown in importance to us. He reported to me, but for all intents he ran the show, since most of my attention centered on the toy business and the mounting pressures we faced from competitors and suppliers. Alan was Dollar Tree's chief buyer through its early, closeout-dependent days and our first few trips to the Far East. He was talented. I liked him, and the fact that I placed so much responsibility on his shoulders spoke to how much I trusted him.

In retrospect, his exposure to Asian culture might not have done him any favors. Here he was, a guy who'd risen through the company from the humblest of starts, as a stock boy at Military Circle; he'd spent his entire working life in southeastern Virginia and the Maryland suburbs around D.C. And now, suddenly, he was passing a lot of time in Hong Kong and Guangzhou, where vendors angled for his business by wining and dining him and smothering him with compliments. The bigger the pencil a buyer held, the more lavish their attention. I think that maybe Alan had his head turned by all the hype and came to believe he had grown too smart, too good for our dollar business.

That would explain why he quit out of the blue and went to work for one of our big vendors—and why, when he did so, he was confident we'd never survive without him. He made no secret of that; he told a lot of folks at Dollar Tree he was sure we'd fold.

He was mistaken. We thrived. But that's not to say it wasn't a blow to lose him, since we were as busy as could be and didn't yet have a corporate structure from which to promote a successor. Dollar Tree's entire office staff consisted of Alan, his assistant, Kay Waters, and the company's operations director, Tom Bowyer. And as capable and experienced as Tom was in operating stores, he had no buying experience, no track record in the one aspect of the dollar business that Alan had handled almost single-handedly: buying the stuff we sold.

Suddenly, the day-to-day oversight of the dollar business reverted to me, and I already had a full plate. I depended on Kay to help me understand what they'd been doing. With her backing me up, I quickly found that some common-sense reorganization could improve the dollar business's efficiency and its already impressive performance by 25 percent.

Trying to run the merchandise side of both K&K and Dollar Tree was too

Joan and I examine an abundance of baskets on a buying trip to the Far East. We visited some remote corners of the world together on such trips, to which we devoted several weeks per year.
COURTESY OF BROCK FAMILY

much for me or any one person. Fortunately, we'd hired a capable merchant named Steve Karp to help with the toy business. He was a toy veteran who'd worked in retail and been a buyer; this hard-charging New Yorker also understood K&K's health issues and had some ideas on how we might address them. It was Steve who was most responsible for bolstering our emphasis on discount toys, so we weren't competing item for item against the big-box operators. He brought a new and needed perspective to our toy buying.

Some in the company saw our bringing Steve aboard as a disruptive move, which I could understand. We'd always been a high-end retailer, and now we were importing new blood to embark on the aggressive pursuit of closeouts. It was a dispiriting shift to admit that, okay, we were probably not going to get the hot toys, so we'd offer great values.

But I needed his help. Steve was a stand-up guy and a good businessman, and he'd built relationships within the industry—the sort of bonds that would prompt a vendor to pick up the phone and call to say, "Hey, listen, I have some closeouts here of Masters of the Universe toys." He was also tireless, devoting every bit of his energy, his every waking minute, to the job. He spent every night at his desk, into the wee hours; he went home just to sleep, shower, and change clothes. I have worked beside many driven people, but few who worked as hard as Steve.

His presence enabled me to devote most of my attention to Dollar Tree. If I were to try to pinpoint when our efforts to reshape the stores into modern takes on Frank Woolworth's model kicked into gear—when we strengthened the categories of merchandise we carried so that the stores became better organized and understandable to our customers—it was right then, just after Alan left.

We committed ourselves to boosting our overseas buying and further reducing our dependence on serendipitous closeouts. We weaned ourselves of novelty merchandise, gimmicky stuff. We went hunting for great values for our customers.

It was up to me to do the buying. That first trip to Asia after Alan's departure, I took my wife with me. I figured Joan would enjoy herself, and I wanted her company. We both had such a good time that Joan became a fixture on my buying trips overseas. We've been to some out-of-the-way corners of the world together, places no vacation tour would think of going.

I remember a trip to Vietnam, years later, on which we visited a factory just outside Hanoi that made little clay incense vases. *Factory* was too grand a word for it; it turned out to be somebody's house, situated on a riverbank. All day long, the workers trooped outside, walked down to the river, and scooped clay from the bank. A worker would bring clay back into the house, dump it on a pottery wheel, and shape it into a little pot. Someone with a knife would get the pot next and cut little ventilation holes into the sides. A third person stuck legs on the bottoms, put the pots in trays, and slid them into a kiln in the corner.

That was the factory. Everything was done by hand. Our order was big, probably along the lines of fifty thousand vases. It kept that factory going for weeks.

A few months later, Joan and I were in a Dollar Tree in Virginia Beach, and there on the shelf were the incense vases. It was amazing to stand in that air-conditioned store in a well-to-do American suburb and recall our visit to a sweltering hut twelve thousand miles away—and to remember watching craftsmen fashion that fine-looking pottery from mud they had dug from their backyard.

...

Now came the biggest change yet. Over the previous year, we'd watched as the toy industry underwent a Darwinian die-off. In August 1990, for instance, the parent company of KB Toys bought one of our major competitors, Circus World—which, at 330 stores, was a pretty big fish. The *New York Times* reported the sale price to be about $95 million in cash.

That captured our attention. I remember that Doug and I looked at each other as if to say, *Holy cow*. It prompted a lot of contemplation about how unpleasant the toy business had become in recent years, and how much more unpleasant it stood to be in the future. Little guys like us were increasingly shut out by the big-box operators, and even the giants had been crippled by the recession of 1990–91; Children's Palace, a prominent operator in several of our markets, was hemorrhaging cash and was on the brink of shutting stores. It would declare bankruptcy a few months later.

In 1990, we had 8 percent of the toy business in southeastern Virginia— and the region was our stronghold, where we had history, strong customer relationships, and the greatest number of stores. Elsewhere, we weren't nearly so big. And as we looked ahead to the mid-nineties, when we'd have to renew many of our mall leases, we could see that rising rents likely would force us to close some stores.

So after a great deal of conversation and hand-wringing, Doug and Ray and I decided to approach KB's parent, the Melville Corporation, about taking K&K off our hands. We consulted with K. R. on this—it was his money and adventurous spirit that had built the business, after all—and he gave us his blessing. It was a sad decision. Our lives were braided tight with that company. I'd spent six days a week for twenty-three years building it. Doug had been a little kid when K. R. bought the variety store that started it all; its sounds and smells figured in his earliest childhood memories.

But this was business.

Melville was a big company with a lot of popular store brands. In addition to KB, which did more than $900 million in sales in 1990 (compared to K&K's $69 million), it owned CVS Pharmacy, Thom McAn, Marshalls, Chess King, This End Up furniture, and Linens 'n Things, among other brands. It also owned Peoples Drug, which had a giant outlet anchoring a section of Wards Corner just across the street from our original five-and-ten.

It agreed to an asset sale, meaning it wasn't buying K&K Toys per se, but its real estate, inventory, and most of its 941 employees. By this time, Dollar Tree, which would have 186 stores by year's end, had split off from K&K in the field; it had its own district managers, who oversaw a growing roster of store managers and sales associates with no link to the toy business.

The intricacies of the sale were not easy. To make a long story short, Melville was absolutely ruthless in its dealings with us, seeking any point of leverage to drive down our price. Every conversation seemed to be contentious. We each used different branches of the same accounting firm, and even those guys got to scuffling; at one point, Melville's people tried to accuse us of keeping two sets of books, which was just a pile of crap. They didn't actually find anything out of order, but it wasn't for lack of trying.

In the end, the purchase price wound up being less than the valuation we'd used to buy out K. R. We had to go to him, explain the situation, and request that if we had to take a haircut, he should, too. K. R., not surprisingly, agreed without hesitation. We adjusted things so we came out okay; the cash proceeds of the sale made us whole but didn't make us rich.

Melville did leave us with some assets, which we folded into Dollar Tree—the office and warehouse, our trucks, and, after KB was through with the transition, our pick of those K&K employees we thought could help us grow the dollar business. None of them knew the sale was in the works. No one did beyond a handful of our people—not even folks, such as Bryan Bagwell, whom I'd grown mighty close to. Steve Karp, one of the few who did know what was going on, pushed hard to get our sales numbers up to help the deal along, though he knew it would ultimately mean the end of his job. He was an entirely honorable man.

Our folks knew something was up, despite our secrecy. We couldn't hide the closed-door meetings or out-of-town trips. Bryan will tell you that on the September Friday he first heard a sale was in the works, he went home to his wife and two-week-old baby thinking his life was about to swan-dive. He got a call that night from our human resources director asking if he was available Saturday morning for a meeting with me. That probably didn't calm him any.

When he came in, I got right to the point. "Bryan, it's been a struggle, but we've made the decision to sell K&K Toys," I told him. "But we have a buying position available on the Dollar Tree side, and we'd like to offer that to you if you're interested. We need your help." I was relieved that he needed only about a tenth of a second to accept.

I'm relying on Bryan's recollection of what I said, by the way, because I had similar conversations with many people, and the details have blurred. Most of the folks I talked with agreed to come over to Dollar Tree. Some opted to stay in toys and went to work for KB. Some went that way for a while, then came back to us. I remember that many of the conversations brought tears.

But there was great relief, too. The timing was right. Toys were doomed. I have people say to me now, "Well, aren't you so smart?" My answer is that I guess it looks that way, that we were clairvoyant or something. But really, we knew only that we were getting pummeled and that a bigger operator might be able to preserve what we'd built. We knew we now had an opportunity to concentrate our efforts on a business that showed great promise.

A sad footnote: KB Toys went out of business in 2009.

11

Birth of the
Fire Chicken

W ith the toy business behind us, we got down to some serious over-seas buying for Dollar Tree. In March 1992, we visited Hong Kong, Taiwan, Thailand, and the Philippines, spending $13.5 million on merchandise we'd retail for more than $29 million—a markup of almost 54 percent. Seven months later, we traveled to Hong Kong, Guangzhou, Taiwan, Thailand, Indonesia, India, and South Korea, spending $13.92 million on merchandise we'd retail for more than $30 million—a markup, again, of almost 54 percent. We bought 386 products that were entirely new to our stores and reordered another 113.

Those margins might seem huge, and indeed they're pretty big, but they were actually typical, and maybe even a little low, for our purchases around the world. When we went overseas, we gunned for a bigger margin, not only because we were cutting out the middlemen who at home stood between us and the factories but because going overseas introduced all sorts of unanticipated expenses: language-barrier misunderstandings, late shipments, higher-than-expected duties. We also had to pay up front for our merchandise with letters of credit, and thus sometimes had to borrow to finance the buys.

Beyond that, our higher margins overseas enabled us to have more flexibility with what we bought at home. On domestic goods, we expected to earn less, sometimes quite a lot less. On occasion, we might mix in lower-margin goods as loss leaders, nearly unbelievable buys meant to deepen our customers' shock at what they found in the stores. Nowadays, we call them "Wow Items." So on our foreign ventures, I took a higher margin—in the 55 to 60 percent range—to balance things out. That way, the mix of domestic and foreign purchases fell within a certain markup range we established through careful planning.

When I went overseas, I had a rough "open-to-buy" target we'd aim for—so many millions of dollars available to spend for x type of items at such-and-such a margin. The margin might vary slightly from category to category. I might aim for a 50 percent margin on toys, for example, and 60 percent on housewares. I could overspend or underspend my budget depending on what I found; it was a general direction, rather than some holy, inviolable number. It wasn't like I had a boss looking over my shoulder, so our buying was flexible. We could take advantage of unexpected windfalls, great deals.

We always tried to buy the highest-quality stuff we could afford. If we were able to beat our margin target on one item, we'd sometimes use the extra cushion that gave us in the overall margin to buy another item of better quality than we'd initially considered. Water guns, for instance. We had a two-pack, which was an okay seller. If we wanted to really wow the customer, we'd make it a three-pack. It might go from a forty-cent first cost to fifty cents, but it still fit within our overall margin, so we'd do it.

If I beat my target, I could come home and be the hero. But more often than not, we decided not to try to beat the budget—we'd meet it instead, and shoot for better quality. Even with that kind of thinking, we were always able to exceed our planned margin through hard negotiation and volume. Every trip, we outdid our plans, because we were able to find good merchandise and buy it aggressively—by which I mean we walked into a negotiation knowing what margin we had to achieve, and that the size of our orders would give us leverage.

Within a few years, the figures from our 1992 buying trips seemed conservative—quaint, even. By the mid-nineties, we were spending twice as much. And not all of our trips were blind hunts; we brought shopping lists, too. Bryan Bagwell kept meticulous notes of his searches for items on those lists.

An example of one such item—a D cell flashlight with a magnet on its casing—might clarify just how much work and thinking went into each purchase.

Bryan approached a supplier in Chongqing, China, about such a flashlight and got a quote of forty-three cents each. From another in Jintan City, he got a quote of thirty-eight cents. That was a good price, but it only started the figuring he had to do to see if it made sense for us to buy it.

To the purchase price—the "first cost"—he added 10 percent (3.8 cents) to cover freight and 20 percent (7.6 cents) for duty when the shipment landed in the States. He added another 4.6 cents for our Chinese broker, who'd handle everything pertaining to the deal after we left, from ensuring the flashlights left the factory on time to seeing the containers were loaded properly onto a freighter. That yielded a total per-piece cost of 54 cents, giving us earnings on every flashlight of 46 cents.

Perhaps the most amazing thing about these trips is that we crunched all the numbers on every deal on-site. After an exhausting day of touring factories and negotiating prices, we'd hole up in our hotel rooms to figure the details of freight, duty, and such. We also figured out how many of an item would fit into a carton, the size of the carton, the number of cartons to a container, how many containers.

At times, what seemed a promising item would fail to pass muster in the number crunching. Oftentimes, the problem was freight. Goods that took up a lot of room—baskets, for instance—were expensive to ship, because we couldn't fit as many into a carton and could get only so many cartons into a shipping container. What seemed a wonderful deal in the showroom might collapse once we realized how much it would cost to get those baskets back to Virginia.

Likewise, containing costs prompted us to pay attention to how we packaged small merchandise. We were never elaborate in the packaging we ordered. We'd designate the thickness of the cardboard stock and work with the vendor to come up with sizes that maximized the number of goods per carton and cartons per container.

Assuming we cleared the freight hurdle, we'd work the numbers to decide how many of an item to order—"Okay, I want a carton per store, so I need 125 cartons, plus an additional 25, maybe, to back up reorders in the warehouse." It was seat-of-the-pants to a degree, because we were ball-parking our freight and duty costs, rather than dealing with actual charges, and sometimes those numbers differed by a wide margin. One thing we came to understand about overseas orders was that any number of complications could drive up our expenses.

With that in mind, we always built in an additional 5 percent cushion—an internal company charge we added to the cost to head off any surprises. In the case of that flashlight, it added another 1.9 cents, bringing our total estimated cost to 55.9 cents and leaving us with a margin of 44.1 percent. Not bad: for every 100 flashlights we sold, we'd make more than $44. If we sold 50,000 of them—not an unreasonable expectation—we'd clear $22,050. Even so, Bryan thought the deal could be better. He eventually talked the manufacturer down another 3 cents, to 35 cents a flashlight.

Since we were committed to selling items for a dollar, that three cents was a lot of money. And that's even more true today because, to a far greater degree than back in the nineties, modern Dollar Tree stores carry consumable goods—canned and packaged food, refrigerated food, even frozen—which is almost entirely domestic and yields a much lower margin. We balance those purchases with higher-yielding imports. The blend, the balance, makes the proposition work.

One final point about that flashlight: it was no cheap piece of junk. This was a big, heavy-duty sucker made of thick, durable plastic, available in two colors, with a sturdy magnet on its handle—the sort of flashlight a customer might hold onto for years. It was an almost unbelievable bargain at a dollar, a smart buy for us at thirty-five cents, and, as Bryan's careful notes testified, emblematic of so many surprising deals we found in Asia.

■ ■ ■

Back then, the "gift" category in our stores—knickknacks, picture frames, candles, and the like—was much bigger than it is today. People would walk into a Dollar Tree and find a whole section devoted to hundreds of polyresin figurines. They required a trained eye to buy, and Kay Waters developed that for us.

Kay made her first trip to the Far East in the fall of 1992. Through the nineties, she made three to four trips there a year, staying on the move for two to three weeks at a time. Though she bought a little of everything, her real touch was gifts. She became an expert at identifying the knickknacks that would resonate with American shoppers.

At first, she made her choices from samples placed before her in the various showrooms we visited. The manufacturers had more designs than can be imagined. Their in-house designers would dream up these figurines, they'd cast samples, and then they'd see if they could land an order. And we were the biggest importer of that stuff in the world. We went through millions of pieces.

But we also came to see that sometimes the Chinese didn't get things quite right. One vendor understood that Jesus was "olive skinned," for instance, and produced a bunch of Jesus figurines whose skin was painted olive green. Other miscues weren't quite so dramatic, but some aspect of the execution would often be a little off.

We all, but Kay in particular, took to tweaking the samples we were shown. We might like a Jesus figurine, for example, but would dictate the paint colors we wanted used for skin, hair, eyes. Sometimes, the colors of clothing on a figurine would be a little too bright for Western sensibilities, and we'd order the piece with more muted clothing instead. African-American skin tones were a challenge for the Chinese manufacturers. We did a lot of tweaking to get that right.

By the way, we took to tweaking many of the domestic products we carried, too. We'd go into the factory of a United States candy supplier and watch the workers put twelve bags of candy in a box, and four of those boxes in a carton. We'd tell them to throw all forty-eight bags loose in the carton, saving ourselves the expense of the four extra boxes.

But back to China. Our Chinese partners were always eager to make the changes. When we asked the Chinese for anything, the answer was always yes. Yes, they had it. Yes, they could get it. Yes, they could make it. It was a can-do culture. They made it work, even if at the time they promised something they had no idea how they'd pull it off. They figured it out.

Once we found a piece we liked and fine-tuned the color scheme, we'd photograph the sample from all angles, measure it carefully, and weigh it. If we didn't take those precautions, the manufacturer might try to sweeten its end of the deal by giving us a little less than we'd ordered—trimming the size of a figurine ever so slightly, perhaps, or hollowing it out to cut the weight, and thus pouring a little less polyresin for each piece.

We took samples back to Virginia, along with our measurements, and when the goods arrived at the dock we'd get an example from the delivery and check it against our sample and paperwork. We set up a whole process within purchasing to check every imported item upon arrival. If we ordered five colors and got only four, or if we ordered a three-inch figurine and it came in at two and a half, we had a beef to settle.

On the flip side, we sometimes shaved the cost of an item by suggesting minor changes in its detailing or construction. Polyresin is petroleum based, and as the price of oil climbed, Kay worked with the manufacturers to use a little less in order to keep the price steady. If she liked an item but it was too pricey for us, she might suggest the factory use six colors of paint instead of eight—and where, exactly, the colors should change. If she liked a picture frame but balked at the cost, she might specify how the frame might use just a little bit less wood, so the numbers fell into our range. It was still a damn nice picture frame, still a steal at a dollar, and often identical at first glance to the original.

It was a short hop from these sorts of tweaks to coming up with our own ideas for merchandise and ordering it from our vendors. We'd find an expensive figurine in Italy, take it to our Chinese suppliers, and say, "We'd really like to have this. See what you can do." On our next trip over, there it would be.

We started designing our own polyresin figures as well. Bryan and I were sitting together on an airplane flight, talking about what might excite American shoppers, and we hit on lighthouses. The idea struck us as perfect, seeing as how crazy people were for the lonesome romance of the seashore, and the beacons in particular. Bryan cut pictures of lighthouses out of magazines, lighthouses from all over the country, and we gave them to our trading partners. A little while later, we came out with our Lighthouse Collection, and it was a huge hit. For good reason, too: those little statuettes were beautiful, and authentic down to the last detail. Some of them even took batteries; when you flipped a switch on the base, the light at the top of the tower would shine.

On one trip, I got the notion that we should have some polyresin turkeys for Thanksgiving. While meeting with vendors in Guangzhou, I mentioned what I wanted. Turns out there are no turkeys in China. It's a Western bird. I tried to describe it—making "gobble-gobble" sounds—but it was clear from the stares of the vendors that they had no idea what I was trying to imitate. So I rounded up a picture of a turkey, and in short order they turned out a sample line of turkey figurines. That's not what they called them, by the way. They didn't have a word for the bird, so they made one up. The English translation was "fire chicken."

Kay, meanwhile, came out with a line of her own devising, called K's Collection—whimsical figurines of animals posing in clothes, as well as children, fairies, angels, ballerinas, singing nuns, castles, Victorian houses. I could take up a full page just listing the varieties. They've become quite collectible. Visit eBay and you'll find page after page of K's Collection stuff for sale—and you'll notice the pieces cost quite a bit more than a dollar.

As I write this, one seller is offering two of Kay's vases for forty-five dollars. If he pulls that off, he'll achieve a margin we never dreamed of.

. . .

We were good buyers, and we got better with time. Still, now and then, we misjudged how much of an item we should buy. Judging the quantity we needed was more or less a guess. We could sell a million pieces of something, but if we carried over two hundred thousand, we had ourselves a dog. We'd bought too many.

It didn't happen often—maybe with 2 percent of what we bought—but when it did we faced the challenge of getting it off the shelves, made all the more difficult because we didn't have sales, since our reputation depended on everything being one buck yesterday, today, tomorrow, and forever.

One of the things we came up with to clear merchandise was the grab bag. We printed up little paper sacks—half in pink for girls, half in blue for boys— and into them we put an assortment of merchandise, always several items, and together worth well over a dollar, so there was no doubt in the customer's mind that she was getting a deal. Among the stuff inside would be two or three items that hadn't sold well, along with candy or some other small thing. We'd put up an endcap where we displayed the bags for sale.

People never knew what was lurking inside. They loved the mystery surrounding the bags, the surprise of ripping them open. We cleared a lot of low-selling merchandise that way and sometimes put pretty great stuff in there; it wasn't just junk. Customers came back for them week after week.

It was such simple, common-sense merchandising and great buying that helped propel our sales and income through the roof in our first year of doing business solely as dollar-store operators. In 1992, our net sales jumped by more than 70 percent, from $71.1 million to $120.5 million. Our net income—profit—stood at $10.5 million. And by year's end, we had 256 stores and plans to open more than 70 in 1993.

. . .

The biggest key to this rapid expansion, far bigger than any other factor, was our people. The early nineties saw us move some new executives into positions from which they helped aim the company high.

I mentioned Tom Bowyer awhile back, so I'll start with him. Tom joined K&K in 1987, when Dollar Tree had only its original five stores. He'd been working for Circus World in Newport News, a few miles northwest of Norfolk, when Doug walked into the store and sweet-talked him into jumping ship; he was an attractive hire, because before Circus World he'd worked in Detroit and Louisiana for KB Toys and knew the business well.

Doug had Tom meet him at the five-and-dime, where a scene unfolded that illustrates just how humble and unpretentious the whole organization still was. "We're walking through the store, and this young black kid is buffing the floor," Tom recalls. "Doug says, 'Let me show you how to do that.' And he does—he's swinging the buffer back and forth. The kid says, 'Who are you?' Doug says, 'I work for the company.'"

At that point, it had been about eighteen years since Doug's stint as a stock boy in that very store. The company's top management was never far from its origins.

Tom was born in Kalamazoo, Michigan, so we moved him back to Detroit as a district manager overseeing K&K and, before long, a Dollar Tree store—the thirty-second location we opened was in his district. Michigan soon became one of the company's big states in terms of store count. He entered the dollar business reluctantly. When he learned he'd be overseeing a Dollar Tree in Michigan, his reaction was, "You don't really want me to run that junk store, do you?"

That was not an uncommon reaction among our longtime toy people to this upstart company, but they came around. Tom did so with a vengeance. He'd just opened our sixtieth store when we moved him back to Norfolk in 1989 to join the Dollar Tree team as our director of operations.

Big job. He hired store managers, promoted them to district managers, managed the whole company in the field. He worked with Doug to figure out where we should look to build new stores. Later, when we acquired other chains as Dollar Tree spread across the country, he played an important role in integrating the newcomers into our systems and our style of doing business.

Tom really paid attention to the needs of his people. Until we grew to hundreds of stores, he knew the name of every one of our store managers and something about their backgrounds—where they came from, what they'd done. He'd experienced that kind of personal touch himself when he first came aboard. When we moved him to Detroit, he found he couldn't make ends meet on what we were paying him, so he called Ray for help. Ray asked what he needed, then saw that he got it. As Tom will tell you, "That *never* happens in retail."

Over the next ten years, Tom became a Dollar Tree vice president, then a senior VP. His duties didn't change much—it was just that we got so big that he needed people working for him. So as the organizational chart deepened beneath him, his title got ever more grand. Even then, he says, "we didn't just run lean. We ran anorexic."

Another important addition was Eric Coble, who joined the company in 1989 as controller, becoming the first formally educated financial officer we'd ever had. Eric had an accounting degree from the University of Virginia, worked for a "Big Eight" accounting firm his first four years after graduation, then moved to Royster, the same Norfolk fertilizer company where we'd found Ray Compton. He was working there when he heard our controller was leaving. He wound up having lunch with Ray and touring the office just before Halloween—and finding the entire staff in costume. He was hooked.

Eric turned out to be far more than a number cruncher for us. Among the first things he did on the job was to read through the minutes of our board meetings, which were pretty informal and candid, not at all like the carefully sanitized minutes of public companies. The minutes amounted to a history of the company and a portal into its culture. In the years that followed, Eric became de facto historian for the rise of Dollar Tree. He also became the company's chief financial officer.

Another important executive was Len Intrieri, our human resources chief. I'd met Len at my church, where we were both on a committee charged with buying an organ for the sanctuary, and he impressed me so much that when Ray mentioned we needed an HR boss, I suggested they meet. Len was retired from the navy and one of the warmest people I could hope to meet—not a detail-oriented guy by any means, but so irresistibly likable, and so interested in and empathetic toward his colleagues, that he became a sort of glue binding the work force. Everyone at K&K and Dollar Tree loved the man.

Len's kindly presence helped us through the goodbyes that accompanied the sale of the toy business. He kept us laughing, too. I recall that on one occasion, a federal workplace safety official showed up to inspect the print shop in our Norfolk warehouse and told Ray he'd need to see our OSHA log of accidents and such. Ray passed the request on to Len. Later in the day, Ray returned from lunch to find a big chunk of firewood on his desk with a Post-It attached, reading, "OSHA log." That still cracks Ray up twenty years later. Mind you, Len had the real OSHA log at the ready. It wouldn't have been much of a prank if he hadn't.

Other key players you've already met—Bryan Bagwell, Kay Waters, Darcy

Stephan—became even more important to the organization as it expanded. We were a company of diehard loyalists, many of whom had started as teenagers stocking shelves or loading trucks and now ran the show. Take Lewis Mitchell, the sailor K. R. had picked from the bank line to work at the five-and-dime. After managing stores, a district, and several regions around the South, he became our store display manager and Doug's right hand in getting dollar stores designed, built out, and opened all over the United States.

Perhaps the most important people on the payroll were the hundreds of store managers and thousands of workers we now had at Dollar Tree, meeting our customers every day. Lewis Mitchell will tell you that working for Dollar Tree is among the hardest jobs in American retail, second only to managing a Dollar Tree. Just the physical aspects of the job are demanding. Anywhere from twenty-two hundred to three thousand cartons of merchandise show up at a store per week and have to be carried to the right aisle, unpacked, and displayed.

The pace is relentless. The press of customers is constant. And our store associates—even those we hire part-time or just for the Christmas season—manage to accomplish their tasks with a smile. We've found that when we give them the room to do what they're capable of doing, they almost always pleasantly surprise us. You can't *make* people do anything; they have to want to do it. So if you communicate with them openly, and share information, and encourage them, coach them, and train them, they'll perform.

To a large extent, those people in the field are the real story behind Dollar Tree's success. We try to treat them respectfully and honestly. We try to pay them decently and to provide them with good benefits so they'll choose to grow with the company. We try to catch people doing something right, and to praise it.

We try to encourage ideas from our associates on just about any topic. When we improve some aspect of our stores, the idea almost always comes from someone with an up-close view of our day-to-day habits. We try to promote independent thought and initiative in our people, to impress upon them that whatever their decision is—and of course they have to make decisions, everybody does—if they do it for the right reasons, with honesty and integrity, they'll generally come out okay.

They have proved themselves worthy of trust in all but the rarest of cases and have repaid anything we've given them with a dedication to hard work and customer service that is the envy of the industry. So as I continue with this story and the flurry of developments that saw Dollar Tree become a retail giant, bear in mind that throughout, the real story of the company's success was playing out every day in our stores, one on one with the customers who walked through the doors looking to be delighted—and always were.

12

Fifty-fifty or Nothing

===========

Considering how well Dollar Tree was performing and how lucrative that was for Doug, Ray, and me, it might seem counterintuitive that in the middle of 1992, not yet six years into running the company, we were actively looking for someone to buy a piece of it from us.

We had many reasons. First and most importantly, we wanted the best for the business. We'd started it on a shoestring with little direct investment and had seen it grow beyond our dreams. It had been a fun, exciting, and deeply gratifying experience. But now, with Dollar Tree having eclipsed K&K's size in a handful of years, we had reached a point at which the company's continued growth was beyond our experience and required a more seasoned hand. We knew nothing about big—really big—business. I was a marine. Doug had no more professional training than I did. Ray was a fantastic financial planner and disciplinarian but was almost as far out of his element as we were. And with few exceptions, our senior management team was likewise inexperienced. Some of our most important people had topped out, education-wise, in high school. They'd grown up with us. They had chutzpah but no real experience or expertise beyond Dollar Tree.

In sum, we needed help.

The second reason, and it was a distant second, was that Doug, Ray, and I had all of our personal assets tied to Dollar Tree. We'd collateralized everything we owned to get bank loans to finance our expansion. And while it's nice to be comfortable on paper, it's a lot more so to be comfortable in liquid form. When your house and future are mortgaged to your business, it's like that old Tennessee Ernie Ford song—you owe your soul to the company store.

So, no bones about it, we wanted to take some chips off the table. We wanted to have money in our personal bank accounts. We wanted to find someone to share the benefits, and also the risks, of growing Dollar Tree to its fullest potential. We were willing to surrender a stake in the company in exchange for that.

This wasn't a thought that just occurred to us in 1992. In fact, we'd first sought a partner back in 1987, less than a year after starting the dollar business. We'd forged an understanding with the Jordan Company, a New York investment firm. We were in New York that October, ready to close the deal, when the markets collapsed on the infamous Black Monday, the Dow Jones Industrial Average suffering its worst one-day decline in history. Our financing evaporated on the spot. We closed the books on the deal and flew home to Norfolk.

We went looking again in 1991, just after K. R. cashed out. This time, our potential partner was a New Orleans investment company, Jefferson Capital Partners. We were on the phone with one of its people, going over deal points, when he suddenly hollered, "Oh, my God, we've just bombed Iraq! I have to get off the phone." That ended that.

So we'd come close to acquiring a partner twice before and had seen global events derail our plans. Now, we started sniffing around again. We thought the most straightforward approach might be to find a bigger retail operator to play the role of synergistic partner, but we couldn't find any we were comfortable with or that were willing to take us on. So we looked for a private equity firm to recapitalize us.

A recapitalization partners an investment firm with an entrepreneurial company that isn't reaching its full potential. The firm buys into the company, offering cash in exchange for a piece of the action; typically, it acquires a majority stake in the business so it can call the shots, though the company's management remains in place. The investment, along with the firm's expertise and guidance, enables the company to expand without its bosses being personally liable if the business tanks. In exchange, the firm sees the value of its investment grow (assuming the business succeeds) and returns the earnings from that investment to its own backers.

These arrangements are not meant to be permanent. The investment firm typically sticks around for a few years, helps grow the company, then exits the partnership by taking the company public and selling its shares or by simply selling out to a hungry buyer, either option yielding more money than the investors have at stake, and thus giving them "a second bite of the apple." Of course, none of this is as simple as it sounds. To successfully go public, a company has to show strong, consistent performance, to convince the stock market it's a good bet. It must grow in value at a rate that makes potential buyers of stock sit up and notice. But these daunting expectations for growth and performance were part of what attracted us to a recap. Ultimately, it would force us to be better.

When we sold K&K, we'd been impressed by a fellow working on behalf of Melville named Josh Goldberg. He was with an investment bank, Financo, that worked only with retailers, and he had a retail background himself—his family had founded the Stop & Shop supermarket chain in Massachusetts. We hired Josh to serve as our broker with investors. With his help, we produced a prospectus and sent it out. Four investment firms were interested, two very much so. We interviewed them in early 1993.

One was a D.C.-area concern with a strong record of investing in real estate, shopping centers, and the like. It was a bit of a rough-and-tumble group, sharp elbowed, aggressive, its leadership consisting of members of a single family. We met with the son, rather than the old man at the top.

The other was a New York firm called Saunders Karp. It was fairly new, having just one big transaction under its belt. Josh called a young partner in the firm, John F. Megrue Jr., and told him not to laugh, but that he was representing a dollar business.

Megrue had never stepped into a dollar store, but he was a smart guy—a Cornell graduate with an MBA from the Wharton School and six years in the finance business, during which he'd handled a number of buyouts and recaps—and he heard Josh out. He was intrigued enough to do some digging into our operation, assisted by an associate at Saunders Karp named Barron Fletcher. What they discovered got them excited. They liked that our stores consistently paid for themselves in their first year of operation. They were encouraged that we were opening seventy new stores that year. They admired the way Doug, Ray, and I complemented each other.

We were impressed with them, too. Their senior partner, Thomas A. Saunders III, was a local boy—born in Suffolk, twenty-odd miles southwest of Norfolk. He'd attended Virginia Military Institute, spent eight years in the army, and obtained an MBA from the University of Virginia before going to work for Morgan Stanley in 1967. By the time he left the company to start his own firm, he was a managing director there.

Both Megrue and Saunders struck us as off-the-charts smart, as straight shooters, as men of integrity. I felt a connection with both of them straightaway. But though Megrue had some experience in retail, the firm as a whole did not, and being a new venture, its track record was a blank. We had no yardstick by which to measure how we'd do with Saunders Karp.

We went with the other guys.

■ ■ ■

One thing I should point out is that the bottom line was the same with both potential partners. We figured Dollar Tree's enterprise value at roughly $73 million, a figure that included all of its assets, its debt, and the cash on hand that we founders planned to pull out of the business once the deal was inked. We planned to pocket about $25 million among us, which left about $48 million in equity to split with a suitor looking for a 50 percent stake.

That wasn't subject to much negotiation. We were confident the company was worth every penny we said it was. In fact, years later, people would ask why we wanted to sell the company for so low a figure—suggesting, in that question, that we'd fleeced ourselves. We didn't. The question applied knowledge of what came later to a deal with more uncertainties than guarantees, and to a time when we remained a pretty modest undertaking. At the end of 1992, we operated 256 stores. Our annual profit stood at $10.5 million. We were nowhere near the Dollar Tree everyone knows today.

The whole reason for doing the deal was to try to become a bigger, savvier company. The $24 million price seemed a good deal for both sides.

Except that before we signed on with our new partners, they underwent some serious internal turmoil—ugly, intergenerational family stuff that looked to sink the whole firm. We wondered if they were the right match for us. Heck, we wondered if they'd survive long enough to be partners with anyone.

John Megrue had impressed me by staying in touch after we'd gone with this other outfit. Every month, he called to ask how things were coming together. When he called in June 1993, I had to admit that our deal with the other guys was falling apart.

John immediately resumed his pursuit of Dollar Tree. And we were happy to be pursued; Doug, Ray, and I viewed Saunders Karp as the lead candidate after the first deal did in fact unravel. What the firm lacked in experience, it addressed with intense study of our business. It understood our concept and loved it. And it brought a broader world view; as individuals, the partners had worked with many companies, were old hands at dealing with banks, understood Wall Street. They had much to teach us.

I think we fascinated them. We seemed to be defying gravity. As Tom Saunders put it, "It's hard to understand how you can improve your quality and your margin and never change your price, year in and year out, no matter what's going on in the world. The whole thing is counterintuitive. You say to yourself, 'It's just not possible. How could this thing work?' "

It took them awhile to trust what they were seeing, "to get comfortable that people were as good as they were at Dollar Tree," Tom said. "We could see that this was very, very profitable. High margins—some of the highest margins in retail. We knew they were on to something."

Still, they were cautious. The age-old question—whether or not we should stick to the one-dollar price point—loomed large in their worries. The seven years since Dollar Tree's founding had seen annual inflation average an uncharacteristically low 3.7 percent, which hadn't been much of a threat to us. But looking at all of the previous twenty years, the average rate was 7.6 percent, and in 1980 it had topped 13 percent. What would happen to the price point if inflation headed back in that direction?

They fretted, too, that most of the stuff we sold was made in Asia, where many countries screwed with the value of their currencies in order to boost their trade with the United States. What would happen if they stopped doing so and the dollar fell versus the yuan, baht, dong, kip, or whatever? Could we still buy so cheaply as to hold steady on the dollar price?

They wrung their hands over our buying. China, our biggest supplier, had seen its relationship with the United States go to hell after the Tiananmen Square massacre of 1989. Congress had been battling over possibly pulling China's most-favored nation status ever since. What would become of Dollar Tree if that happened?

It was part of the firm's modus operandi that it created financial models to help assess a potential partner's future performance, so John Megrue and Barron Fletcher built three models corresponding to three sets of circumstances. The first was ours: Dollar Tree management assumed we'd continue opening seventy stores a year, and that those stores would do about the same—which was to say, very well—as those we'd opened to date. Scenario two assumed circumstances that saw our opening stores at a slower pace, and those stores performing at a lower level than existing outlets. Scenario three saw us opening stores for a few years, then hitting a wall on new openings—and at the same time, the new stores failing to perform as well as earlier ones.

Not surprisingly, the models painted different futures. If we hit our in-house projections, Saunders Karp would make tons of money for its institutional investors. Everyone would be happy. Under the other two scenarios, however, the firm would not get the return it needed.

So whether or not this was a good deal for Saunders Karp came down to a gut call. It recognized that we were disciplined operators. It was impressed by our past performance. It believed us to be honorable. But other discount stores had gone bust, and none of us could predict how public tastes, international relations, or global economics might change in the years to come.

■ ■ ■

Actually, Saunders Karp had another concern, and it was the biggest, a potential deal breaker.

I wanted any alliance, whether it was with Saunders Karp or someone else, to be a true partnership—fifty-fifty, us and them. Equals. No majority partner. No minority partner. No one controlling anyone else. No one giving the orders, and no one taking them. The way I saw it, if we were going to be partners, then damn it, let's be partners.

I knew this wasn't the way most recapitalizations worked. Typically, an investment firm took at least 51 percent of the control. Often, it took a lot more than that. It might leave the company's management in place, but the real shots were called by the majority owners.

That typical structure didn't interest me. I'd rather have done without a partner than give up control; I wanted to share the business, not surrender it. And I didn't want to have our side serve as majority owner, either. I wanted both sides truly to be in this thing together. Saunders Karp did business under the motto, "Partners with management." I took that at face value.

Tom Saunders did not share that view. He wanted someone to have a majority, because he feared that a fifty-fifty split might lead to stalemates. He came to me and said, "We can own 51 percent-plus, or you can own 51 percent-plus, and the other party will have minority rights." In other words, whoever was the majority owner couldn't sell the company without the minority's agreement. I kept going back to him, saying, "No, we want to do fifty-fifty." And he kept saying, "This doesn't make sense. Somebody has to be in control." Over and over.

We were able to calm the firm's other fears about the deal. We explained that we could offset inflation by buying in large volumes and tightening down on inefficiencies and unnecessary expenses. We showed it that failed discount retailers hadn't tanked because their business model was bad but because their execution was flawed. But on the question of equal ownership, we were at an impasse.

In a way, I suppose, Tom's fear had come to pass. He worried that if the board deadlocked on a decision, we could put the company in jeopardy. He feared, for instance, that if we failed to meet our performance targets, Saunders Karp would have to earn the full board's assent before it could adjust the company's strategies. If we didn't sign off on the firm's plans, we'd be dead in the water.

Which brought up a related point: Doug, Ray, and I were adamant that we not be told how to run the business. We knew how to do that better than anyone. As we went back and forth over ownership, I became ever more unyielding on this. In fact, the longer the negotiations dragged on and the wearier I grew of the whole process, the more I wondered if we needed a partner at all. I began to question our need for outside money. I grew unconvinced that we should share our profits, when our return on investment was so quick. It seemed to me that we might be able to finance our own expansion and relieve ourselves of any worry over ownership and control. Mostly, though, I was sick to death of too much talk and too little action.

We were still hung up when, as part of his due diligence, John Megrue asked for a tour of a representative Dollar Tree store outside of southeastern Virginia, so that he and Barron Fletcher could gauge how much "white space" we required; that's an industry term for how close to each other our stores could operate without stealing customers from each other. Did a store require a two- or three-mile radius, or did it have to be twenty? I decided we'd visit stores in the Detroit area.

John, Barron Fletcher, and I explored several stores there over a couple of days in early September 1993. They were clearly excited by what they saw. The stores were busy with shoppers, who were doing what Dollar Tree shoppers did—reacting with shock and delight to what waited on the shelves. Coming in for one item and leaving with several. Buying far more than they'd planned. I have to be honest: even I was impressed.

Afterward, in a lounge at Detroit Metro Airport, John and I waited for our flights home. He was obviously eager to get back to New York, to share with his partners what he'd seen. I had come to like John a great deal over the course of our conversations, had come to feel we had a real chemistry, and was pleased that he was blown away by what we were doing every day.

But despite his excitement, he seemed resistant to commitment. He didn't want to be rushed. And I was through waiting. I'd had enough. I had a trip to Asia coming up at the end of the month, and I was so fed up that if we didn't have something pinned down by the time I left, I was willing to walk away. So I turned to John and said, "Either we finish in the next three weeks or the deal is off."

This announcement surprised John, to say the least. "I knew him reasonably well," he says of me and the episode now. "He's a pretty mellow and balanced person. Some people you don't see as having that style, genetically, in them, but he'd obviously thought a lot about it."

I later learned that on his flight back to New York, he wondered if the deal, so long in the works, might collapse, wondered if his partners would balk at joining forces with a guy who resorted to ultimatums. Eventually, his takeaway was practical; he had a deadline to meet. "In our business, there are times you need for various reasons to do things that might not be in one's ideal zone or time frame or price," he says. "But you have to make sure you keep the major items separate from the minor items."

In contrast, on my flight back to Norfolk, I couldn't have felt more relaxed. It was clear to me that without a firm deadline, the talks would drag on. And as I ate the little bag of pretzels the flight attendant passed me, I realized that Doug, Ray, and I, along with Dollar Tree, would be fine however it all turned out. It was up to Saunders Karp to meet our demands.

In the meantime, we had a business to run.

■ ■ ■

As it happened, John's partners saw more benefit than danger in the deal, despite our insistence that ownership be evenly split. "We reluctantly agreed," Tom Saunders says now. "In my better judgment, it didn't make sense. But we decided to do it."

I'll let him explain the reasoning. "In most of these things," Tom says, "it all comes down to relationships. Big numbers are thrown around all the time, but better deals and partnerships and better experiences together are because of relationships.

"It is all about character and integrity, someone you can depend on to do what he says and never attempt to one-up you or take advantage of a situation. You can take what they say to the bank. And it was our view that the character of these founders, all of them, was great. We knew that we could take them at their word, that they'd always be straight up with us and lay it on the line, and we would try to respond with the same behavior. And I think that bond, the recognition of that, is what provoked us to take what we perceived as a risk.

"If we got into this and it wasn't working out, it would be very difficult. All the textbooks tell you not to do this. You have the risk of doing damage to the institution if the arrangement is dysfunctional. The only way we got over that concern was because of who they were, and we felt comfortable in a relationship that was not structurally sound in terms of control, but was very strong in terms of character.

"Even if you get into a tough situation, if you're working with good, honest people, the probability of solving it is much, much higher."

We felt exactly the same way about Saunders Karp. The deal turned out to be the right way to go for everyone involved. If either side had walked away, we would have missed out on one of the greatest deals in equity investment history—and an incredibly powerful partnership.

Not to mention a lucrative one. Saunders Karp paid Doug, Ray, and me a total of $23.6 million to buy half of the company. Each side wound up with exactly the same amount of stock—8.274 million shares. We stripped the operation of its built-up cash and reentered business as a new corporation that borrowed to fund our operations.

The much-feared deadlock never happened. All of us were united in purpose from the first day we together oversaw the company. Saunders Karp taught us the ways of the world of finance and big business and left us to run our stores as we saw fit, with one difference: because it had to provide substantial returns to its investors, the new Dollar Tree grew at a much faster pace than we'd ever imagined.

We might have continued to prosper without Saunders Karp. But if there's a pivotal point to this story, the merger's magical fusion of talent and vision was it. Without Saunders Karp (which in short order became Saunders Karp

Megrue), we were just a bunch of local guys who'd capitalized on a good idea. We were hardworking and smart but lacked the strategic know-how to become the company we are today. Tom calls the union "the best relationship we ever had with anyone," and I can't imagine its having gone better.

Years later, Tom and I participated in a case study of the deal at the University of Virginia's Darden School of Business. We headed to Charlottesville and went into the classroom, and the professor split all the students into two camps, some on the Dollar Tree side, some SKM. Each of the sides split again into several teams, and each was assigned to analyze the situation that faced us as we negotiated the deal, and to answer the pivotal question: what would you do?

Then we all went into a large auditorium, where Tom and I explained what we had done, and why. Many of the students were surprised. Quite a few would not have done the deal—the fifty-fifty split was a snagging point, as was our selling price, which some thought too low. But it was impossible to argue that everything hadn't turned out well.

And by the way, throughout all the negotiations and deal cutting, Dollar Tree kept growing. By the end of 1993, we had 328 stores and sales of $167.8 million—more than double the sales of a year before. The average customer spent $6.50 per visit.

With the help of our new partners, we almost doubled the number of stores again, to 737, over the next three years, and our sales almost tripled, to $493 million. This at a time when several of our competitors—including Jamesway, 50-Off Stores, and the venerable Ben Franklin chain—stopped trading publicly.

13

Lifting
Our Kimonos

The Dollar Tree that took shape with the arrival of our new partners was a different company from the rather seat-of-the-pants operation we'd been until then. It was, first, a more formal and professional business. We convened monthly board meetings that Tom Saunders, John Megrue, and Alan Karp attended regularly. We began to revamp our hiring practices with an eye to bringing educated pros aboard as we grew—technically trained people, unlike most of us old originals, but with the humble manner our culture had always bred and valued.

We examined our systems for measuring performance and giving feedback. We refined our systems for developing financial targets. We were poised to grow, and to grow quickly, and doing it successfully depended on keeping track of everything at once. That meant leaving our mom-and-pop style behind in favor of having systems. So we built them.

Nowhere in the company was this more apparent than in logistics. It became clear by the time we joined forces with Saunders Karp that our warehouse was no longer capable of servicing all of our stores, which by the end of 1993 numbered 328 and were spread over eighteen states. The distances involved in trucking merchandise to the farthest-flung locations—in western Kentucky and Tennessee, Indiana and Michigan, as well as others we were planning to

Dollar Tree's board of directors shortly after the company went public in 1995. Standing in front is John Megrue. In the second row are Doug, Ray, Alan Wurtzel (CEO of Circuit City stores), and Frank Doczi (who ran the Home Quarters Warehouse chain). At the rear are me, Tom Saunders, and SKM partner Alan Karp.

open in Louisiana and Arkansas—had grown so vast that we were in danger of outrunning our supply lines.

Servicing those western stores kept our trucks committed for so long that we couldn't efficiently service the stores closer to Norfolk without boosting the number of trucks we had on the road to a level that didn't make economic sense. Plus, the mileages involved were high, and it cost so many cents a mile to move a truck. The smarter solution was to open a second distribution center to service our continuing expansion, especially as we pushed farther west.

There was a time early in our history when I'd resisted the notion of a second warehouse. I was leery of growing too fast and spreading too wide, lest we run into the same troubles that had doomed Everything's A Dollar. But it was clear that we'd now reached the point where we'd be doomed if we didn't take this step. We were stretched way too thin.

We recognized this new warehouse would have to meet several requirements: it would have to be accessible to interstate highways and easily reached from major ports; it would have to be far enough west of our Virginia headquarters to enable us to rationally divide up our territory, so we wouldn't spend too long on the road to reach any group of stores; and it had to facilitate our opening stores in new parts of the country, not only to ease our current logistical load but to enable us to grow.

We concluded that the logical location was the Memphis area, which was close to both east-west and north-south highways, just a few miles from the Mississippi and in striking range of the new opportunities west of the river, and home to a ready work force. After hunting around, we found and leased an existing 244,000-square-foot warehouse on the southern edge of town, just above the Mississippi state line. We started operations there in January 1994.

Following that move, Dollar Tree became an infinitely more complex company to operate. We have eleven gargantuan distribution centers today, sprinkled from coast to coast, but the most difficult transition wasn't going from two warehouses to those eleven; it was going from one to two. We had to develop new systems for shipping merchandise to the United States from around the world, so an appropriate share of the stuff we bought would be delivered directly to each warehouse.

Think about that for a moment. Our trading agents in China now had to split our shipments among containers headed to different destinations—shipments that were coming to the docks from dozens of suppliers. The job suddenly became way, way more complicated. And here at home, we had to develop new trucking routes that made the optimal use of time and fuel. Where we previously had warehousing and delivery systems, we had to develop systems of systems.

Since Kenny's death, Ray had overseen our distribution functions. Now, however, he begged off the duty, arguing that the company's growing sophistication demanded an expert in logistics. He was right, of course. Our ability to maintain the dollar price point depended to a large degree on maximizing the efficiency with which we moved merchandise from the factory to the shelf— depended on controlling costs, combining tasks, and boosting speed and service. We needed systems we could put in place right away but would be expandable as we opened additional warehouses in the years to come.

So it was that Stephen White joined Dollar Tree in June 1994 as our director of transportation and distribution, a function he fulfilled for the rest of his career—though he became a vice president in 1995, a senior vice president in 1999, and was chief logistics officer for thirteen years, beginning in 2003. He came aboard while we were still in the process of integrating the new Memphis center into our operations, and he made a difference from the day he arrived. In an organization as populous as a medium-sized city, there are few to whom I can point and declare, without hesitation, that we wouldn't be where we are today without that person. Steve is one of them.

Steve grew up in Greenwich, Connecticut, earned degrees in business and finance from Northeastern University in Boston, then embarked on a career in transportation and distribution that educated him in every aspect of the work he'd do for us. He oversaw a trucking fleet and a distribution center for a New England industrial supply company, ran all the internal transportation logistics on two continents for Eastern Airlines, and built a distribution network for a pharmaceuticals firm in Florida.

Before we landed him, he spent eight years with Ames, a fast-growing regional department-store chain in New England and the Mid-Atlantic, running its transportation systems. In 1988, the company swallowed up a bigger chain of discount stores, Zayre. Ames wound up with a nasty case of indigestion in the form of a bankruptcy, but the experience proved useful to Steve. "It made me very objective as far as how to run a business," he says, "and I learned an awful lot about what not to do in an acquisition and merging two companies together."

As it happened, Ames used the same overseas agent to consolidate its container shipments as we did, and it was through that outfit that Steve heard we were looking for someone to ride herd on our supply chain. He'd never heard of Dollar Tree—we had no stores in New England, where Ames was based—and had never been in a dollar store. Still, he came down to Norfolk to talk with us, and found that the job we described would combine everything he'd learned so far.

It was perfect timing. We got the guy we needed at exactly the point he had become that guy. Under his leadership, our logistics improved markedly, but in steady, controlled fashion. We honed our systems little by little. We shaved time from our functions and introduced metrics to analyze our warehouse efficiency. Every day, we tweaked the machine.

As we contemplated new distribution centers, Steve and his team designed networks to take advantage of them. We hired no consultants. All of our modeling was done in-house, based on current store locations and our real-estate plans for the coming three years. We thus managed our growth, never building more warehouses than we required but always having enough to meet our needs.

Steve hadn't been with us long when he started talking about introducing some changes that went far beyond the incremental. Our warehouses were still an entirely manual operation. We unloaded by hand shipping containers filled with new merchandise, then "picked" that merchandise off the shelves and loaded it onto our trucks the same way. That couldn't last. And wouldn't.

∎ ∎ ∎

Of the changes Saunders Karp introduced, one had an especially profound and lasting effect on me.

If you had asked most of the people working for Dollar Tree in late 1993 who the company's bosses were, they'd have had no trouble rattling off the names of the Three Musketeers, as they referred to Doug, Ray, and me. If you asked them for our official titles, on the other hand, I think you'd have stumped a lot of them. For the record, Doug was our chairman and chief executive officer. I was president and chief operating officer. Ray was executive vice president and chief financial officer.

Those titles had never meant much. The three of us led the company as a team, each of us complementing the skills and interests of the others. Doug and I, in particular, operated as equals; we owned equal shares of private stock, reached decisions via consensus, and always relied on one another to take care of our respective pieces of the business. Neither of us was in a position to tell the other what to do, and wouldn't have been inclined to do so anyhow.

Our new partners weren't looking to change the dynamic we enjoyed any more than necessary. For example, they weren't interested in acquiring titles themselves. They merely took places on our board. And I think they admired the way we three led the company as a unit, a melding of personalities. But about one thing they were firm and consistent: Dollar Tree needed to have one leader, one public face. That leader should hold the rank of CEO. And that CEO should be me.

To Tom Saunders, the issue seemed pretty straightforward. He and his partners at Saunders Karp weren't in the business of running retail chains. They were using other people's money to buy into our operation, with the expectation that they'd be able to help us boost our income, thereby providing their investors with a good return. Eventually, they'd "deleverage," or remove themselves from Dollar Tree's ownership, either by helping us sell the company or by taking it public.

All of this depended on their spurring us to grow at a much greater pace than we'd managed so far. That commitment to growth, and the prospect of our eventually courting Wall Street in an initial public offering, or IPO, required that we have clear and unambiguous leadership.

Their belief that I was the logical choice for CEO came down to two things: I was the company's merchandising boss, and I felt at ease performing in public. The merchandising was probably the lesser of the two factors, but it figured in our partners' thinking. Dollar Tree could not have prospered without Doug's expertise in getting us good locations for our stores. Many a good concept has failed because it opened for business in the wrong place. Real estate has always been a vital component of our success. But what most excited our new partners was what we chose to sell in the stores and our ability to stick with our price point regardless of what was happening in the world. In their view, that's what made us truly remarkable and set us apart from any other retailer in the country. "What should you put on the shelf? That's the key," Tom said. "If you don't get that right, it doesn't matter what else you're doing. The merchant is the most important person in a retail company. You cannot survive without a really great merchant. What he buys is key."

Because I was the lead player in that end of the business, I had a leg up as the choice for CEO. But a more important factor, I think, was that I was comfortable in public—in front of a crowd, in front of the cameras, talking on my feet. I'd always enjoyed being the center of attention, going all the way back to my cut-up days in junior high. It came naturally to me.

It didn't come as easily to Doug. He was as gregarious and outgoing as a person could be. To get on an elevator with Doug was to find yourself in a conversation, no matter who you were, how you looked, or even whether or not you spoke the same language. He could make friends with anyone. But he wasn't nearly as comfortable at a lectern, speaking to an ocean of listeners.

If Saunders Karp took us through the process of becoming a public company, we'd have to sell ourselves in an entirely new way to the American public. The style and confidence with which we made that pitch would be essential. "We needed a spokesman. Your CEO has to play that role, and he has to be believable," Tom said. "It's like picking the quarterback of your team. Who can throw the tightest spiral and still stay in control in the toughest conditions and get the job done?" He felt that I "had the best chance of being the quarterback successfully, and doing what we needed done."

When I reflect on the thirty years since we started the company, that decree from our new partners ushered in my greatest period of discomfort. I understood why they insisted on it. I came to understand why they thought I was the guy for the job. But because our partners were mandating that one of Doug's titles be transferred to me, titles suddenly became very important indeed.

The issue was that Doug and I were family. I'd been married to his sister for thirty years. He and I had worked side by side for his dad for more than twenty years, had founded Dollar Tree together as a stepchild of the Perry family business. Our roles had been entirely interdependent. The business would not have flourished without him or without me. So the idea that just one of us was now going to be the boss did not go down easy for any of us. If we could have kept on going as we were, I would have voted that we should. It was comfortable. It worked.

But only for us. For our new partners, comfort wasn't much of a priority. They wanted results. They wanted the company's sales to grow at 20 percent a year. They wanted us to roll out new stores at a greatly accelerated pace. To that end, what motivated them was "not a family harmony obligation, it was a responsibility to our investors," John Megrue said.

All of which made sense. But the situation created a tension between Doug and me that we'd never felt before, and that I still lament to this day. Doug retained the title of chairman, and as such, an undiminished voice in Dollar Tree's leadership. He was as important to the company as ever. But I think his perception of his place at the table was altered by the title switch, and it probably didn't help that John Megrue and I became close friends over the next two or three years. John was a regular guest at a beach house that Joan and I had on the Outer Banks, and we went on motorcycle tours together to the Blue Ridge Mountains, the Rockies, down the West Coast.

That was hard on Doug. We were undergoing a shift in the balance of our longtime partnership, which had produced everything good that we'd enjoyed to that point. Those early days had been fun. They were exciting. We'd all been trying something new, making it up as we went along, entirely the masters of our destiny. Now, Dollar Tree's chemistry was changing. Our heady, adventurous days as hungry entrepreneurs were giving way to the duties of running a big business.

■ ■ ■

Then again, it was hard to complain about the benefits the shift brought. They made themselves apparent quickly. In 1994, our first full year with our new partners, our sales jumped from $167.8 million to $231 million, and by year's end we'd opened 81 new Dollar Trees. We now operated 409 stores, including 5 each in Louisiana and Arkansas, our first ventures west of the Mississippi. We had become America's undisputed leader in $1 retail.

By year's end, it was clear, too, that the national economy had regained a robustness it hadn't seen since before the Gulf War, and that the company was sufficiently strong to weather the scrutiny of Wall Street. With a push from John Megrue, we applied to the Securities and Exchange Commission to take the company public. We figured we'd sell 15 percent, the public shares evenly split between us founders and Saunders Karp. That was a pattern we followed through several successive public offerings, by the way; we sold exactly the same number of shares as our equity investors, so we maintained the fifty-fifty ownership I'd been so hell-bent on achieving.

In the weeks before the IPO, Doug, Ray, and I spent a lot of time making public presentations, speaking for the company. It was a punishing schedule of meeting after meeting with representatives from big investment funds, institutional investors, and banks that had investment divisions, made all the more challenging by our audiences' initial skepticism. They knew that other dollar-store companies had run into trouble, à la Everything's A Dollar. And most of our listeners were men, who didn't shop nearly as much as women, who therefore didn't have as firm a grasp on how much consumer goods cost, and who thus had to be educated on just how outrageous our success really was.

Doug would explain our real-estate strategies, which were smart, and Ray would go over the company's finances, which were compelling. I'd carry a suitcase into the room. It was filled with merchandise from Dollar Tree and similar but much more expensive stuff from other retailers. I'd pull out a hammer costing four or five bucks up the street, then pull out a Dollar Tree hammer. I'd pull out a squirt gun that went for three dollars elsewhere, then a comparable Dollar Tree squirt gun. You could see amazement in the Street guys' faces. They were accustomed to companies telling them what they were about. We showed them.

We had another hurdle to clear in those meetings that required a little more finesse. Most of the time a company seeks public buy-in, it's to raise money to enable it to grow. Investors are comfortable with that. They like the idea that with their money, a company will be able to ratchet up its activities and its earnings and turn into something big.

But our IPO was not to raise money for the company. Rather, we were going public to take our own chips *off* the table and pocket the money we raised. Dollar Tree was a company making piles of cash, one with no apparent need for outside help. How could we convince investors to buy in when we were doing the opposite?

The answer proved to be pretty simple. We flipped the usual pitch to the Street. We didn't need their money, we told investors. But if they'd like to share in our success, we'd welcome them aboard.

Investors scrambled to buy stock. And who could blame them? Our face-to-face presentations were backed up by our prospectus, which Eric Coble pulled an all-nighter to strip of the legalese doublespeak the lawyers and bankers had pumped into it, and which made an irresistible case: "The company's net sales increased from $52.2 million in fiscal 1990 to $231.6 million in calendar 1994, a compound annual growth rate of 45.1 percent," the prospectus read. "In addition, operating income increased from $3.4 million in fiscal 1990 to $26.9 million in calendar 1994, a compound annual growth rate of 67.2 percent."

Holy cow! When you looked at our performance over five years, you saw a company that was exploding in value. I'd have pulled out my wallet to buy stock, had I not been busy trying to sell it.

"In calendar 1994, the average investment per new store, including capital expenditures, initial inventory and pre-opening costs, was approximately $138,000," the document continued, "while the average new store (i.e., a store for which 1994 was its first full year of operation) had net sales of approximately $602,000.

"The company's stores have historically been profitable within the first full year of operations, with an average store level operating income of approximately $139,000 (approximately 23 percent of net sales) for stores whose first

The Dollar Tree brain trust meets in an informal session. Clockwise from bottom are Darcy Stephan, Bryan Bagwell, Bob Gurnee, Len Intrieri, Steve White, Joan, Tom Bowyer, Eric Coble, and Ray Compton.

full year of operation was 1994. The operating performance of the company's stores has been very consistent, with over 85 percent of its stores having store level operating income margins in excess of 15 percent in 1994."

No hard sell was necessary. Our initial public offering came on March 6, 1995. We offered 2.5 million shares of common stock at $15 apiece, which—after subtracting commissions and such—brought us just shy of $35 million. By the time the market closed for the day, the stock price was climbing fast. A few months later, we sold another batch of stock at nearly twice the IPO price, and at year's end the stock was trading for more than $30 a share.

Did becoming a public company change us? In one respect, it certainly did. Everything we did was now subject to public scrutiny—how much we made in salaries and bonuses, every little detail of our earnings, every major decision we made about our strategy or merchandise mix. We had to lift our kimonos and give the world a long, close look. That took some getting used to. Being private and family controlled, we'd always kept the curtains drawn and the company's financial information to ourselves.

But I'd guess that, compared to some other companies, we didn't have nearly as tough an adjustment. Doug, Ray, and I had always managed for the corporation. We'd never cheated, never charged things to the company for our personal benefit—cars, weekend homes, club memberships, any of that nonsense. We'd paid ourselves salaries and bonuses that we figured were appropriate, and from there paid our own way. We treated ourselves as employees of the company.

The same went for the high officers who'd worked with us for years. None of us took goods without paying for them—not so much as a polyresin Santa figurine. That did not go unnoticed. The officers lower in the company's hierarchy had adopted that style as their own, and their charges had followed them. The whole culture was straight-up.

That's one aspect of the Dollar Tree adventure that makes me especially proud. We always wanted to be successful, but to do it the right way—with honesty, with integrity. Those are big words, and so high minded they almost sound naïve, but they really do capture the philosophy by which we managed the company, and K&K before it. From K. R. Perry, to Joan and Doug, to Ray and me, we'd always placed high value on playing by a few simple rules: being honest, being straight, paying our bills, and treating people well.

That was equally true whether the company was private or public. We had nothing to hide; actually, we had a lot to show off. The fishbowl took a little getting used to, but my attitude was, again, that sunlight is the best disinfectant. Whatever discomfort it caused, public scrutiny was good for the company.

■ ■ ■

The next couple of years bore that out. At the close of 1995, we had 500 stores in twenty-three states, and more than $300 million in sales. A year later, we had almost half again as many stores—737—and our sales had risen by 64 percent, to $493 million. In ten years, we'd gone from 5 tiny stores of closeout wares tossed in bins to a half-billion-dollar company.

Our store count jumped in 1996 because we swallowed up another dollar retailer—Dollar Bill's, a Chicago-based chain of 136 stores in sixteen states. They were bigger stores, mostly in urban areas. Dollar Bill's had little or no direct imports; it bought from domestic vendors and devoted a lot of its shelf space to consumables.

We'd absorbed a small, Louisville-based toy outfit back in the K&K days, but this was the first time we made such a move in the dollar business. We relied on a lawyer named Will Old to handle many of the details. He was with a Virginia firm we'd worked with since our K&K days and would eventually become our in-house legal counsel. In the Dollar Bill's deal, he was my eyes and ears and a key player in the negotiations, and he'd occupy that role in every major acquisition we undertook from that point on, right up to the present day.

It took some time to integrate Dollar Bill's into the Dollar Tree family, because it did business differently. And we saw that we could learn from some of the things it did. As with most of the acquisitions we'd make in the years to come, we got more than just real estate and market share when we bought a company—we got smart people and their ideas, if we were willing to listen.

We listened. With that buyout, we recognized that adding consumables to the mix in our Dollar Tree stores made sense. Everyday needs such as snacks, sodas, candy, kitchen cleaners, toothpaste, and shampoo brought people through the doors at greater frequency. We didn't attempt to launch a bona fide grocery department, but we reasoned that we could make ourselves a convenient alternative to Walmart or a two-acre supermarket if we just carried a few must-haves. At the same time, we boosted the proportion of our traditional Dollar Tree wares in the Dollar Bill's stores, so that our mix became more or less uniform. We eventually rebannered all of its stores as Dollar Trees.

The Dollar Bill's deal cost us $52.6 million in cash plus $2 million in inventory. Looking back, that was a bargain. In addition to the stores, we got its modern, 250,000-square-foot warehouse and distribution center in Chicago.

That was bigger than our Norfolk warehouse, which was fast becoming a serious issue. Our old systems were breaking down under the stress of receiving, sorting, and shipping merchandise for so many stores. The shelves were overstuffed; storage was straining capacity.

Our attached corporate headquarters, built for a company with a hundred stores, now bulged with the administrative staff necessary to service seven times that many. In our accounting office, sixteen people were squeezed into a space the size of a suburban living room. And we had no way to expand; when we chose the site, we hadn't anticipated growing out of it and hadn't bought any spare land.

So in the summer of 1996, Steve White and Ray worked on plans for a new distribution center that would last us awhile, a much larger, fully automated warehouse next to a 76,000-square-foot office building. After nosing around town, we chose a site in the Norfolk suburb of Chesapeake, just off Interstate 64. We bought fifty acres of land, which gave us plenty to spare, just in case.

We broke ground in February 1997. Virginia's governor, George Allen, came to turn a shovel and say a few words. He loved Dollar Tree, he told the crowd that had gathered in a field in Chesapeake's Greenbrier area. "It is the one place where I can take my kids shopping," he said, "and I can make them spend their own money."

14

The Power
of No

Let me take you on another tour, so you can best understand just how revolutionary our new approach to warehousing and distribution was. We'll drive north from Fort Worth on Interstate 35, up over the board-flat North Texas plains and across the Red River into Oklahoma. Fourteen miles north of the state line, a gray shape takes form on the highway's left side—an enormous rectangular box.

And when I say enormous, I mean the box stands five stories tall, measures a third of a mile long, and has a roof spanning twenty-three acres. This is Dollar Tree's Marietta Distribution Center, from which the company services 670 stores in five states. Search "Marietta, Oklahoma" on Google Earth and you'll spot the building immediately; it's the bright white rectangle that's bigger than all of downtown Marietta. Seriously. The entire business district and several blocks more would fit inside.

At a little over a million square feet, Marietta is not the biggest of our DCs—that distinction belongs to our 1.45-million-square-foot center in Joliet, Illinois—but it's typical of the last several we've built. Opened in 2003, expanded ten years later, it sits on eighty-five acres just off the interstate's Exit 15. Swift Transportation trucks roll in and out six days a week, bringing containers in from our vendors and hauling merchandise out to our stores.

Our imports bound for Marietta land on American soil aboard ships calling at Houston or one of several ports in California. The containers on those ships are loaded onto rail cars and pulled to a hub facility in the Dallas–Fort Worth area, where they're transferred to trucks and pointed toward the appropriate DC.

Once they check in at the entrance to the Marietta lot, truckers are directed to their proper places among the 121 receiving docks built into the DC's short southern and long western sides. At any given time, several trailers are being unloaded, their contents stacked by hand on pallets. Meanwhile, each trucker hands over his load's paperwork to a "checker," who verifies that what's coming out of the trailer is what the manifest says it should be: he or she opens one carton, checks that it contains the proper number of items, then—when a full pallet of a particular product is amassed—tags the pile with a barcode that identifies what it is and where it's to be stored.

In short order, a battery-powered forklift whizzes up to the pallet, and its driver scans the barcode with a hand-held reader. A video screen in the forklift's cockpit tells him where to take it—for example, to Zone 61, Aisle 34, Slot 7-Alpha—which is assigned by computer on a space-available basis; the warehouse's shelves are not arranged by product type, in other words, but by when merchandise arrives.

All of this happens at a brisk pace, because the DC lives or dies by the speed at which we can get stuff off the trucks, onto shelves, and back out again to the stores. Checkers process thirty to sixty pallets per hour. Forklift drivers are expected to move twenty-two pallets in the same time. The men and women unloading the trucks tackle several trailers a day, and those loading the outbound rigs are expected to handle a minimum of 400 cases an hour—and most manage 450 to 700.

For every 10 percent over the minimum they achieve, they earn an extra twenty-five cents an hour. It's not unusual for a DC worker to take home six hundred dollars in bonuses per month.

Now comes a point in the process when the DC begins to resemble something out of science fiction. As orders come in from the stores, some of them automatically generated and some by store managers, a computer spits out pick tickets for those items—stickers with barcodes identifying the products, their locations in the warehouse, how many cartons are needed, and their destinations. It goes beyond that, actually. The computer knows where the products

"The merge" at Dollar Tree's Windsor, Connecticut, distribution center, where feeder lines from the stacks of stored merchandise feed into a main chute and onto the company's trucks. Such automation was key to getting goods from ship to store at a breakneck pace.
USED BY PERMISSION OF DOLLAR TREE

are and prints each sticker in the order in which the items are arranged on an aisle, so that a "picker" pulling products off the shelves for outbound shipping need only walk down an aisle, never reversing direction, from one slot to the next.

These stickers are produced in stacks of several hundred, which fit into a holster on a picker's belt. On all four levels of the "mods," or stacked shelves, are conveyor belts running the length of each aisle. A picker pulls a ticket from his or her holster, finds the bin it identifies, pulls a carton, slaps on the sticker, and puts the carton on the belt—and keeps doing it until he or she gets to a sticker for another bin.

Sixteen pickers usually work on a shift. Each is expected to select four hundred cases an hour, but that's well below the output of most. Consider Daniela, whom we'll follow for a grand total of three minutes as she works an aisle. She pulls two cartons from one bin, thirteen from the next, and so on, until she's picked forty-seven in 180 seconds—on pace to more than double the minimum.

The belts in each aisle dump into one of eight bigger conveyor belts, or feeder lines, which run parallel down the east side of the warehouse. From above, this huge array of belts looks like a rail yard, and the cartons moving down the lines at a jogger's pace resemble train cars. On average, 190 to 220 cartons of merchandise move out of the mods and into this rail yard every minute. Considering that the feeder lines are hundreds of feet long (the biggest measures 580 feet), thousands of boxes are typically on the move at any moment.

Near the building's southeast corner, the cartons on all the feeder lines dump into a single big conveyor belt at a point called "the merge," their flow regulated by photoelectric eyes that open and close gates into the main line. Moving faster, the cartons on this main belt climb a ramp, negotiate a horseshoe bend, and race past an electronic scanner. In an instant, the machine reads the sticker on each carton, identifying its contents, the store to which it's bound, and the loading dock where a truck waits to carry it to that store.

Because the conveyor moves at a constant speed, the scanner can also measure the exact distance between the carton and its nearest neighbors. The belt, now high above the floor, takes a left turn down the building's south side. Branching off its left edge are chutes aimed downhill at each of the building's twenty-eight loading docks. As a carton reaches the appropriate chute for its destination, the system (having used the scanner's input to calculate the box's exact place on the line) deploys a "shoe," resembling a shuffleboard tang, which slides from the right side of the belt and shoves the merchandise on its way.

A carton at Marietta is touched by human hands just three times: once as it's unloaded from an inbound truck, once by the picker, and lastly when it's loaded on a truck headed out.

Some products are so popular and stay so briefly in the warehouse that they don't even enter this "roller derby," as I nicknamed it when we were developing our first automated DC, in Chesapeake. Bottled water, paper towels, toilet paper, bleach—essential household goods that just fly out of our stores—never make it to the mods. Instead, seven of our docks at Marietta can be configured to move merchandise directly from an inbound truck to an outbound. These "cross docks" are fitted with retractable conveyors that can be extended deep into a trailer to off-load cartons, which then travel by belt to a neighboring dock and into another rig waiting to head out.

It all seems like magic. I'm utterly mesmerized when I stand on the catwalks overlooking the merge and the scanner, watching the shoes push cartons down the chutes, listening to the roar of the belts, the hiss of the compressed air that drives the whole system. An hour there passes quickly. I'm astounded that it works.

But it does, and without much fuss. The system drives the process; it pretty much just happens. At peak capacity, Marietta moves two hundred thousand cartons of merchandise a day.

■ ■ ■

The new Chesapeake DC differed from Marietta only in scale; its automation was even more mind blowing a generation ago, when we brought that first center on line. I delegated the entire task to Steve White. As I did with anyone working with me, I trusted him to get the job done. He was the expert, not me, and besides, I never saw much sense in attempting to do other people's jobs for them.

Still, I was nervous as the time approached in January 1998 for the roller derby to kick into gear. I asked Steve more than once, "Are you sure this thing is going to work?" And I told him more than once, "Steve, this thing had better work."

They were wasted worries. When we flipped the switch on our first automated DC, it worked just as advertised. In the old warehouse, it would have taken three shifts to move twenty thousand cartons. In the first week at the new DC, we moved that many in a single shift on four separate occasions. Right from the start at Chesapeake and all of our DCs since, we've filled store orders correctly and on time 98 to 99 percent of the time. Not a bad average.

What we learned at Chesapeake informed our designs and systems at all of our later DCs. Today, the scale of our logistical operation is almost unfathomable. In 2015, we imported forty thousand shipping containers of merchandise. *Forty thousand.* Just juggling the containers is a huge task. At each DC, we want the twenty-odd containers that arrive today emptied today, so we can have the empties ready for pickup tomorrow; an incoming truck will drop off a full container and haul away an empty. We have a negotiated deal with a single trucking company for each of our DCs, and we're usually among that company's biggest clients.

Right now, we have more than 9 million square feet of warehouse under roofs, with our eleventh DC having just gone on line. In 2015, we shipped 365 million cartons of merchandise. We shipped 75 million just out of the gargantuan DC in Joliet.

The Chesapeake DC is now our smallest. It services 330 stores, less than half the load carried by Marietta. But the warehouse operation was only half the story when we opened it, because the DC shared the site with our corporate headquarters, which opened at the same time.

Our new offices required almost as much thought as the automated logistics, because we needed a home that would enable us to run a big company and give us room to get bigger, but one that would still reflect our traits since the K&K days, which Doug, Ray, and I viewed as real strengths. We wanted a home that fostered communication among different pieces of the operation. We wanted a certain level of informality, an atmosphere that encouraged everyone to mingle. We wanted it to feel like a small, family-run business—intimate and friendly—but to work efficiently.

And the 76,000-square-foot headquarters gave us all we sought. At its center was a soaring atrium topped by high windows and flooded with sunlight, which served as a sort of town square for the company; it was a natural gathering spot and meeting place. Just off the atrium was a soda fountain with refrigerators for brown-baggers and a mock-up of a Dollar Tree store—we felt it important to have a constant reminder on hand of who we were. We had a 150-seat cafeteria. Scattered all around were "enclave" conference rooms, specially designed to be easy to duck into for impromptu meetings.

A grand staircase switchbacked to the second floor. Light was plentiful throughout. We made one decision I thought was particularly important: most of the building's windows would be shared by all. Only top management had private offices, and only five of us had offices with windows. In fact, the whole building had just one corner office.

Otherwise, the setup was egalitarian and communication-friendly, with plenty of space for two hundred in cubicles. It was a long, long way from our first cramped office in the Perry Building and the tiny space we grew K&K from in Virginia Beach.

No sooner had we opened the new campus in Chesapeake than we upgraded our operation in Memphis. We bought forty acres of land in Olive Branch, Mississippi, twelve miles south of our old warehouse, and built a fully automated, 420,000-square-foot distribution center that today services 407 stores. Its thirty-six receiving docks and thirty-one loading docks move freight a heck of a lot faster than the old place, which had a grand total of eighteen docks for everything.

Right behind that job, we started revamping the Chicago warehouse we'd acquired with the Dollar Bill's purchase.

And as we made all these improvements to our logistics, to the behind-the-scenes machinery that made the company run, what we did on Main Street put us before a soaring number of consumers. At the close of 1997, when we were finishing the Chesapeake DC, we operated 887 stores that served more than 112 million customers and generated more than $635 million in sales. Our new stores were larger, thanks to improvements in the shopping experience we'd seen at Dollar Bill's; they now averaged forty-one hundred square feet. To keep up with our need for well-trained managers, we took a page from McDonald's and ran almost three hundred trainees through an education program we called Dollar Tree University.

Woolworth closed the last of its United States stores that year. Stuck with once-prime locations in withering downtowns, the company had lost one of its greatest assets—convenience—and had fallen out of favor. Our strategy of locating Dollar Tree stores near the anchors of strip shopping centers made us the heir to Woolworth's role as America's variety-store destination.

That became even more apparent in 1998, when the new Chesapeake DC went on line, Olive Branch was under construction, and we broke the 1,000-store barrier. By year's end, we had 1,156 locations, including our first stores in New England and Oklahoma and—thanks to our acquisition of another competitor—California and Nevada.

That purchase came in December. We bought the 98 Cents Clearance Center chain from Step Ahead Investments Inc., owned by Gary Cino. It consisted of sixty-six stores and a warehouse in Sacramento, California. We'd been eyeing it since just after the Dollar Bill's purchase but initially shied away because when we toured its stores, we found they were messy and filled with low-quality goods. We didn't care for that.

We met with the chain's top executives and told them we were interested, but that their current style was so different from ours that integrating their stores into Dollar Tree would tax us. Step Ahead took everything we said to heart and transformed the company over the course of a busy year. When we went back in 1998, we found the executives had turned everything around. Unfortunately for us, they'd boosted the value of their company, and thus the asking price, in the process. But the integration was a smooth one.

Compared to Dollar Tree outlets, the former 98 Cents Clearance stores were bigger—ten thousand to fourteen thousand square feet—with wider aisles, lower-profile displays, and a larger selection of consumable goods and party supplies. You could stand at the doors and see pretty much the whole store, too, which was something you couldn't do at our traditional Dollar Trees, where merchandise was piled high.

We liked that open feel to the stores, the higher impact that more shelf space brought to the products without the need for a whole lot more inventory. Once again, we learned from a competitor we brought into the fold. We started experimenting elsewhere with bigger stores of about ninety-two hundred square feet. Wider aisles enabled us to put shopping carts in our stores for the first time—and shopping carts encouraged our customers to buy more. And they did.

California would become our biggest state over time, and home to some of our hottest stores. This is how eager Californians were to embrace us. We had a particularly profitable store in San Jose, in a neighborhood where everybody had money. Even the poor people there were well off by national standards. We opened a new, bigger store down the street. People at headquarters figured we'd have to close the old store—it was too close to the new one, and sure to chew into its business. A lot of debate ensued; eventually, we decided we'd close the original store if either seemed to be ailing, but that for the moment we'd keep both open.

Hell, we never looked back. They both performed off the charts. They were almost within sight of each other but were both among the hottest stores in the whole chain.

In 1999, just thirteen years after opening the first tiny Only $1.00 in Dalton, Georgia, we broke the threshold of $1 billion in sales—hit close to $1.2 billion, actually, up 26.9 percent from the year before. The new distribution center in Olive Branch opened that January. We started building a new, 317,000-square-foot DC in Stockton, California, to replace the Sacramento warehouse.

We also acquired a chain of 24 New York stores trading as Only $One—which, added to the 180 other stores we opened by year's end, gave us 1,383 stores in thirty-three states, employing more than eighteen thousand people.

. . .

While all this was happening, I was still making several buying trips a year to Asia, along with Joan, Bryan, and Kay. We were all seasoned hands by this time, but that didn't mean we didn't experience some hiccups. Sometimes, the language barrier caused headaches. On one trip, we stayed in a Sheraton hotel in Kowloon. Kay and I had an appointment across the harbor in Hong Kong, and the folks we were meeting arranged for a driver to collect us in the hotel lobby. So we came down from our rooms and found this driver. We told him our names, he nodded, we climbed into his limo, and off we went. He snaked through the streets and over a bridge to Hong Kong proper, and we got to a high-rise. The driver escorted us to the fourteenth floor, where we met a group of Chinese businessmen. They glanced at us and shook their heads at the driver—we weren't the people they were expecting. We'd taken the wrong limo to the wrong meeting.

Our hosts sent the driver back to the hotel to pick up the correct passengers and pretty much threw us out. The mix-up had been their driver's mistake, but they didn't care; we were abandoned to find our own way to our appointment. I was hopping mad. Outside, I tried without success to hail a cab until Kay stepped in and told me that no one would pick us up as long as I was wearing such a scowl. She managed to flag a taxi, but we never made the meeting.

That was a rare event, thankfully, mostly because we had good trading partners who looked out for us. I rarely went on a buying trip on which I didn't have one of our Chinese traders at my elbow, introducing me to people I needed to meet, steering me away from people I didn't, and helping me bridge the language and cultural chasms separating us from the manufacturers.

Unfortunately, even a trading partner didn't protect us all the time—especially when the problem was that trading partner. Through most of the nineties, the most important of our partners was Rayman Trading. This was the company I had chosen years before to accompany me to Guangzhou to trade directly with the factories. Since then, it had worked with us on all of our trips to China, serving as our translator and navigator; when we flew back home at the end of each buying trip, it was Rayman Trading that served as our eyes and ears on the ground there, because we had no infrastructure in China. It inspected merchandise, scheduled shipments, supervised the loading of containers, did everything we needed.

Rayman was owned by a fellow named Vincent Au. He and his wife, Millie, were Chinese nationals who'd spent years in the United States; both had been educated here and seemed nearly as American as I was. Joan and I socialized often with the Aus and grew fond of them. We considered them friends. We looked forward to seeing them. And we were good to them. Dollar Tree was doing big business, buying in vast quantities, and Vincent was making a lot of money. We were paying him a 5 percent commission, which was a good chunk of change. And on top of that, he was making untold piles on the side.

This was how: We'd agree to pay forty cents, say, for an item made by supplier A. Once we flew back home, Vincent might hunt down a supplier B, who'd agree to make the same item for thirty-five cents, and he would switch to this new supplier and pocket the nickel. Back in Virginia, we wouldn't know the difference, assuming the product came to us exactly as we'd ordered it.

It wasn't like we could have put a stop to it even if we'd been fully aware of what was going on. That was the Chinese style of business. My philosophy was that we needed the merchandise. If we got it and it sold and we made our margin on it, I couldn't worry about what lower price I might have been able to get. I had to run the company. The point was that Vincent was making quite a bit of money off the books. I didn't know how much, and as long as he was true to his agreement with us, it wasn't worth caring about.

Except that after years of working with us, Vincent went bad. I don't know what happened, or why. But I do know that before the British handed Hong Kong over to the Chinese in 1999, many people there got nervous. They didn't know whether Hong Kong would be allowed to continue doing business and they'd be able to carry on with their capitalistic enterprises, or whether the People's Republic would put the brakes on trade and send everyone off to re-education camps.

Maybe Vincent panicked. Whatever the case, we had a huge shipment slated to leave Hong Kong—close to $2 million in Halloween and Christmas merchandise—and had a sharp-eyed woman handling our end of the logistics in Virginia, LuAnne Cox McCarty, who'd come to work for us at the Wards Corner five-and-dime when she was fifteen, in the early K&K days. Since then, LuAnne had held several jobs in the company and in the mid- to late nineties was our lead person on seeing to it that shipments left Asia when they were supposed to, that they were filled with the stuff we needed, and that our paperwork with United States Customs was in order.

She spoke to Vincent often by telephone, because Rayman was notorious for shipping late. If it had a window of July 1 to 15, for instance, it always shipped on the fifteenth, if not later. LuAnne's first clue that something was amiss was that on this occasion, Rayman shipped early. Her second clue was an email from a Chinese manufacturer informing us that it had our merchandise ready for pickup. *Wait a minute*, she thought. That stuff should have been at mid-ocean by then, part of that early shipment of twenty-one containers bound for Virginia.

Suspicious, LuAnne examined the invoices for the shipment and found that everything was screwy. They said the containers were packed with far more merchandise than would fit, and that the weights were out of kilter with the supposed cargo.

We were paying by letter of credit. When Rayman had goods ready to ship, Vincent would present documents to his bank, which would then receive payment from our stateside bank. The letters were as good as cash, and irrevocable; once approved, they could be stopped only by court order. In this case, Rayman had been paid something like nine hundred thousand dollars for this early shipment. A second payment of roughly the same size was pending.

LuAnne went to Ray and told him something was wrong, and that we should stop payment. We managed to cut off the second letter of credit and to get Vincent on the phone. He pled ignorance. As far as he knew, the shipments were fine, he said. He'd get to the bottom of it.

Ah, but two or three weeks later, when the containers arrived at the docks in Norfolk, we had the first one trucked over to our warehouse, and I went out to open it. And inside was nothing but air and a little trash. We'd been ripped off. The entire shipment was a sham. Our merchandise was still sitting in factories scattered all over China.

I dispatched LuAnne to Hong Kong to try to sort things out. Vincent showed up at one of these meetings; LuAnne said he kept his head down and didn't have much to offer. After that, he vanished. We haven't seen or heard from him since, and as far as I know he's never been spotted. It's like he dropped off the face of the earth, and his family with him.

We haven't seen the money he took either, and the damage didn't stop there. When this went down, we were in the midst of planning a secondary stock offering. We were at the lawyers' offices discussing an upcoming road show to sell shares, and the lawyers, as part of their due diligence, asked, as they always did, if there was anything they didn't know.

I raised my hand and said we had a situation, and that I didn't know where it was going. And I told them of the fraud that was unfolding as we sat there. The offering evaporated at that moment.

Far worse, we lost the shipment we needed for Halloween and Christmas. We had a company to run, and we couldn't do it without merchandise.

I flew to Hong Kong. A competitor suggested we speak with another trader there, Benny Huen, so I met Benny in a restaurant, and we hit it off. I told him what had happened, and he went to work finding the merchandise we'd ordered, which had been manufactured but had never made its way into the containers. He found most of it, and we got it in time for the holidays.

I was indebted to Benny, and he became our favored contact in Hong Kong. We still work with him today. The disaster thus had a happy byproduct. But there weren't many others: A friend betrayed me. We wound up paying twice for the merchandise. And needless to say, our margins were a little off that year.

■ ■ ■

As we grew into a retailing giant, we necessarily became more sophisticated in how we safeguarded ourselves against fraud and other dangers. We couldn't eliminate the risks that came with buying from people on the far side of the globe, but we could install systems that minimized them. Take, for instance, the lessons we learned when we inadvertently infringed on the copyrights of some manufacturers, and what we've done to ensure we don't repeat those mistakes.

Dollar Tree devotes far less shelf space these days to the polyresin figurines that commanded so much of our attention and spending back in the nineties. But at the height of their popularity in our stores, we had to be wary of buying merchandise that was already owned by others. We recognized some of the popular lines of figurines, such as "Precious Moments," on sight, and knew to avoid buying them, since we'd surely be sued. We knew to stay away from classic Disney characters, Winnie the Pooh, and National Football League figures, all of which were officially licensed.

But we didn't know every copyrighted product out there and thus didn't realize that a line known as "Snowbabies" was already owned by a company called Department 56. We had never seen them before. We'd never heard of them. A vendor showed them to us, and we liked what we saw: little babies in snowsuits in dozens of poses—frolicking in the snow and cavorting with puppies and hugging geese, whatever. Bryan and Kay bought them by the truckload.

They were a hit until we got a letter from a lawyer informing us that we had infringed on an existing brand. We had to pull the figurines off the shelves, destroy every last one, and stroke a big check to Department 56.

That sort of thing happened often. We'd walk into a showroom in China, see something we liked, and ask the Chinese to build it for us, based on that sample, and they'd do it. Lo and behold, maybe the style of the piece, its color scheme, or some telling detail was copyrighted. Our good vendors would tell us, "Wait a minute—that's somebody else's." But not all spoke up; some vendors would do anything to get our order. In China especially, knockoffs were a stock in trade. If we didn't know better, and the vendors didn't tell us, we might have the item churned out by the thousands, ship it back home, and not long after find a letter in the mail. And our headaches were not confined to polyresin figurines; we were nailed for all manner of goods.

I won't claim we were always the guileless victim. We were in the business of "parallel marketing" anything that was popular, and by that I mean we intentionally sold items that were pretty darn close to stuff available in other stores for a lot more money. We pushed the limits. Twenty years ago, our attitude was that it was better to seek forgiveness than ask permission. When we were caught, we were quick to make amends. Those other companies had to protect their brands and their prices. We understood that and gave them their due.

But as you can imagine, all the legal wrangling grew to be a real pain in the neck, not to mention a major expense. Over time, we decided we'd be better off buying far less merchandise from samples and instead going to China with our own product designs. These days, we no longer rely on copying what we see in the showroom. If an item in our stores has a design on it—whether it's a plate, a gift bag, or the packaging on a store brand—odds are we created it in-house. We have our own art department staffed by our own designers. We create our own patterns.

It's tweaking, taken to a new level. We can fashion a more attractive pattern than the Chinese designers—or at least one that sits better with American consumers—and we avoid any infringement issues. It also enables us to match bags with bows and gift wrap. And ours have the same popular look as stuff at department stores. It doesn't have to be ugly because it's only a dollar. Buy one of our gift bags and you have the best you can get.

Eventually, we grew so big that we found ourselves getting sued whether or not we'd done something wrong. The bigger you are, the fatter a target you make for lawyers. There's a whole industry of lawyers in this country who do nothing but sue companies for their fees. Do we settle when we'd like to fight it out in court? Well, yes, sometimes. We protect ourselves any way we can.

I'll give an example. I came up with a gift-bag line. We wanted a brand name on the bottom of these bags, so I suggested a period in history: Renaissance. We stamped that on the bottom of every gift bag and sold millions. Well, two or three years later, we faced a lawsuit. A gift-card company with Renaissance in its name sued us for infringement. We weren't selling cards, remember—these were gift bags—but the company sued us just the same. I wanted to fight it. I thought we could win. But we settled, agreeing not to use the name anymore. Now, our bags are branded "Voila!"—which is a pretty good name, too. Better, actually, now that I think on it.

Such hassles notwithstanding, Joan and I still loved going overseas with the team; we continued to have great adventures on every trip. And as the new century approached, the dynamic of negotiation shifted to favor us even more. I could approach a vendor about a plastic cup, for instance, and say, "I'd like to buy two million of these cups." The vendor might say, "Very well, that cup costs sixty-five cents." To which I could say, "No, I need to make a 47 percent margin on this cup, so I can pay fifty-three cents. Thank you for your time." And walk away.

I could do that because I knew we now had "the power of no." We were buying in such quantities that before I flew home I would without a doubt find a vendor to make me that exact cup for fifty-three cents. And I also knew that any vendor who wanted to stay in business (let alone trade with us in the future) would have to do some serious soul-searching before turning down an order for two million of anything, even if it meant agreeing to a few pennies less per piece.

More often than not, I didn't walk far before the vendor came running after me.

15

Going Coast
to Coast

I n March 1998, Dollar Tree was spreading faster than the flu across the United States, its value headed for the heavens. The stock had split several times and was now worth six times more than it had been three years earlier, when we'd gone public.

So Doug, Ray, and I decided to take a few more chips off the table. We sold a bunch of stock, as did Saunders Karp Megrue. Doug and I had been comfortable before then, to be sure, but with this sale we reached a point where the biggest worries we had about money were which worthy causes we'd give it to.

We also began to wonder, each in his own way, how much longer we could play the roles we occupied, and if it was time to have someone else come in to keep the goose laying golden eggs. Doug felt he'd done well enough as a working man—an understatement if ever there was one—and that it might be time to take it easy, see the world, have some fun. Ray had worked hard for decades—he was at the office seven days most weeks—and now faced great pressures related to our public status, especially dealing with a board of directors that asked what seemed silly questions. On top of those frustrations, he had some health issues that wouldn't abate unless he slowed down.

The guys at SKM started to deleverage, as they'd intended all along. Their first responsibility was to the institutional investors who'd bankrolled their partnership with us, and now they had an opportunity to return big piles of cash to those lucky backers. In that March 1998 stock offering, SKM trimmed its stake in Dollar Tree by a third.

As for me, I worried that our improbable venture might soon outgrow us. We'd achieved success so far by instinct as much as anything, going with gut decisions on everything from personnel to store locations, relying on adventurous entrepreneurship in our overseas buying and product mix. But the innate skills that had brought us to this point weren't going to take us much farther.

John Megrue had been telling me for years that I'd face some difficult decisions about our corporate leadership, because we were outrunning the abilities of the team members who'd been with us from the early days, and who had risen through the ranks as we'd grown. We would need experts in big corporate systems, he said, experts in new technologies. We'd need leaders who were humble enough to mesh with the Dollar Tree culture but whose business training gave them the wherewithal to wrangle a company grown so big that it was difficult to comprehend, let alone direct.

I had resisted John's advice. I didn't want to hear it. I was close and grateful and beholden to the people who had helped create Dollar Tree; it was impossible to separate who we were from their efforts. I couldn't bring myself to cut and run on them. But over time, I realized John was probably right, that we'd need more experienced senior management.

I came to this realization because I saw that everything he said applied to me, too. I was an instinctive leader. Along with Doug and Ray, I had created a vision of what we might be, and had pursued it successfully. But I had no formal management training. I had no formal business training of any kind. My notions of good leadership and effective decision making were products of the marines' Basic School. My experience had come on the job, beginning with my apprenticeship under Alice Parlett. She and K. R. had been my only real mentors.

I needed help—people with not only brains and hustle, which we had aplenty, but with a grounding in complex business systems that were by then used by almost all large retailers. We could try to set up the systems, but they'd be worthless if we didn't know how to run them.

We'd reached a thousand stores by keeping everything as simple as possible—no credit cards (why complicate a small, straightforward transaction?), no checkout scanners (why bother, when every item cost the same thing?), no inventory control (unnecessary, since until now we'd simply sold merchandise until it was gone). But I had only to study our store operations and merchandise distribution to see that further growth would require a much more sophisticated approach.

We were now carrying more consumable goods, which turned over quickly and had to be replenished if our customers were to come to rely on us for such merchandise. How would we know when to replenish, and with how much? The answer seemed to lie in installing point-of-sale scanning at our checkout counters, in automating store inventory in the same way Steve White had automated our distribution centers, so we could better keep track of what each store had, what it needed more of, and what it needed less of.

Darcy Stephan, who'd computerized us out of the Stone Age and managed the company's ever-growing information systems since, was at the forefront of our first experimental forays into installing point-of-sale automation. The system identified each item we sold by a "stock keeping unit" number, or SKU, which was encrypted in a barcode on its packaging or on the product itself. The customer might find three bottles of a detergent on the shelf and buy one of them. At the checkout, the scanner would read the detergent's SKU and send a message to the distribution center: "Hey, store 123 just sold a bottle of detergent, reducing its stock to two, and our automatic replenishment protocols require that we keep three bottles on hand; send more detergent." The computers logged the order, and the next time a truck rolled out that way, it brought a resupply.

Automation would help us determine how much of a product to buy on our shopping trips overseas, too. Our distribution network moved cartons efficiently from the docks to the distribution centers to our stores, but even so, we had no system in place to manage how many cartons to send to each—and thus, how to buy at the proper levels. We might find an item in Hong Kong we liked, a good item we knew would sell. But how many should we buy? We used to work out those numbers on the back of an envelope in our hotel rooms: we had so many stores and figured we could sell so many items per store, so we should buy x number of items. Then we had to decide where to send it—how many to warehouse A, to warehouse B, and so on. Who would get it and who wouldn't? We used to buy merchandise and simply push it out to the stores. But that could land us in trouble, because when we were flying blind and pushing merchandise to the stores simply because we had it coming into the country, we could jam some stores with too much inventory and leave some with too little. Stores had unique temperatures, different ethnicities, varying demographics. Some products had regional popularity and didn't move the needle elsewhere.

Pushing inventory could throw our distribution centers out of whack, too. Some would get swamped with merchandise while others were hungry for more, to the point that we'd have to shift stores from one DC to another. If Chesapeake was supplying some stores because it was physically close but Olive Branch was heavy on merchandise, we'd take some of Chesapeake's stores and have Olive Branch supply them, even though it was farther away, until the inventory was back in balance. It was much cheaper to run trucks to stores beyond a DC's normal frontier than it was to move merchandise from one DC to another. Financially, it penciled. But it was a pain in the neck, especially because we knew it was avoidable, if we had the right tools.

We needed systems that spoke to each other, that integrated everything we did, that showed us how much merchandise to buy, where to send it, when to replenish a store's supply, when to buy more. We needed to be able to track hot-selling products versus those that lingered on the shelves. We needed more than mere data; we needed the data analyzed, to give us information we could use to make intelligent choices. Computers could take this seemingly too-vast bundle of tasks and simplify it, because they broke down complicated problems into a bunch of small decisions.

I was sure automation was key to our future growth and health, but I was equally sure I didn't have the knowledge and skills and experience to figure out how to build such systems. I knew that to maintain our momentum, we had to change. It wasn't an emergency—we weren't in trouble and could keep going as we were for a while. But as the company continued to grow, its needs would grow, too. It made sense to address them now.

Besides, I was fifty-six in 1998. Even without the challenges facing us, even if we hadn't needed a new type of leadership, it was time to start thinking about succession.

■ ■ ■

This was occupying my thoughts when Doug came to me with the news that he had decided to retire.

Dollar Tree's history has been marked by a few turning points: our seeking an equity partner and joining forces with Saunders Karp; the decision to go public; and now, in 1999, the departure of a founder—in fact, the man whose 1986 visit to Tower Mall had sparked the creation of the company.

Doug's announcement took me by surprise, though I should have seen it coming. He had never voiced an intention to work into his old age. He'd always been one to smell the roses whenever possible. Of the many, many, many things I admire about Doug, that ranks high. He always viewed work as a means to doing what he really wanted to do.

I reckon he figured the time was right. Five years had gone by since my ascension to CEO. Still Dollar Tree's chairman, he wielded a strong hand in the company's direction, but with all the attention Wall Street and the press paid to a CEO, I'm sure he felt a little left out. Plus, I'm sure he recognized, as I did, that meeting the challenges we faced would change the company. If he was going to do something else with his life, the time seemed right. Doug was still a young fifty-one.

Doug's understudy in the real-estate sphere, Bob Gurnee, had learned the trade at his boss's elbow and was well equipped to take over locating stores and getting them opened. We'd no longer have Doug's instinct and judgment in choosing real estate, but we could get by. The greater impact of Doug's leaving was psychological, cultural. He was a huge piece of the company's identity.

The folks who ran the company's quarterly newsletter, *Dollar Tree Ink*, captured his place in the culture nicely. "Doug Perry respects and cares for each and every one of his fellow Dollar Tree associates," the newsletter noted shortly after he announced his intentions at a "town square meeting" in the new headquarters. "He is one of the most selfless individuals you would ever meet; in fact, he would probably ask that we didn't write this article."

It continued, "It is the little things that build a person's character and Mr. Perry's character is evident throughout the entire organization. On any given day, those of us in the [headquarters] may see him walking around the office, introducing himself to new associates along the way. In doing this, he identifies himself as 'Doug,' not as a founder or as the chairman."

All true. He was one of the faces of Dollar Tree, his presence an assurance that no matter how big we got, we'd always be a company with a personal touch. It was tough on everyone to lose him.

Especially me. Doug and I had been partners for thirty years. We knew each other as well as we knew ourselves. We relied on one another completely. We'd been a terrific team; any success we'd enjoyed had at its heart the synergy between us. Neither of us could have done it in the same way alone.

The pain of losing Doug was compounded some months later when Ray—who in addition to his health worries was probably the most heavily burdened of us after we went public—came to me to say he was going to retire, too. He'd wrestled with it, had been reluctant to go through with the decision, he said; he didn't want to leave me high and dry. But he felt he needed to go. Eric Coble, his understudy, was on deck. Ray had trained him to take over as chief financial officer, and Eric was smart and capable. He was up to the job.

Still, Ray understood that losing a second founder should be a gradual process, for the company's sake as well as mine. He set up how he'd exit, how he'd manage his step-by-step handover of our financial affairs as carefully as he'd managed our spending and growth. I was grateful for that. It bought me time. I was used to having two partners, and soon I'd have none. The company was public, and things were happening faster and bigger and harder than ever, and I'd be on my own. It felt, as the old saying goes, lonely at the top.

Doug's and Ray's impending departures jump-started our quest for a new style of leadership. At that time, I was on a board at First Union Bank—a local board, not the national—which was buying Signet Bank. A friend from that board was the odd man out in the bank merger and found himself looking for work. He'd gone to Randolph-Macon, and I knew and liked him. So I hired Zeb Holt to help me think about and manage things, especially in the area of acquiring fresh talent, and to help me hold it together in general. He didn't know retail, but he was a smart guy who understood people. He helped me sort things out.

Once he was on board, I started looking for the next generation of company leaders. First, I interviewed search firms. I went to New York, had meetings with three or four of them, and chose Herbert Mines Associates. It assigned one of its headhunters to my case—a hard-charging, no-nonsense woman I admired—and she came to Chesapeake to interview me. She found out who we were, who I was, and what I wanted: a chief operating officer—not a CEO just yet, but somebody who could rise to it. And I wanted a merchant, someone who had experience in retail.

She set off on the search and came back with the names of prospective candidates. We sorted through the stack and wound up with a short roster of people to meet. I interviewed four men. A couple were working for Office Max, and one was at Kmart. The last was a fellow named Bob Sasser, employed by

Roses, a chain of discount department stores.

In the meantime, Zeb Holt introduced me to a hiring process he'd been exposed to at the bank—a battery of interviews and tests administered by an industrial psychologist named Keith Jacoby and designed to analyze a job candidate's skills, aptitudes, and fit in an organization.

I figured that before we put any candidates through the regimen, we ought to submit to it ourselves, to find out who we were—or rather, to find out if we were who we thought we were. I asked all of our top men and women to take part in the analysis. Not all of them were thrilled by the idea, but I promised that nothing we gleaned from the tests would count against them, and that their results would be kept completely private. I also promised I'd take the tests, too.

Keith interviewed all of our people. That process determined what the existing management team was like, all of our traits—how we communicated, our verbal skills, our management style, our critical thinking, cognitive strength, IQ. It pointed out our assets and weaknesses.

One thing that came through, of course, was that for all our strengths, none of us had classic business educations or the kind of technical know-how the future demanded. I tried to soothe the ruffled feathers over the interviews by pointing out that our success was exactly the sort of thing business schools studied. Still, our people pushed for formal business education, so I signed some of them up for executive training at the University of Virginia's Darden School. They ate it up.

Now that we knew ourselves a little better, I turned my attention to analyzing the candidates for the COO job. I asked each to participate in the same testing, then consulted with Keith on the results. He offered insights on who they were and how they operated. He was completely unbiased in helping me assess them, so I could select the leader who'd fit best with our style but also take us higher.

They were all strong, but Bob Sasser emerged as the top contender. He seemed the kind of person I wanted to help me run things. He was user-friendly, an easy guy to get along with, and smart in ways I wasn't, skilled in ways I needed; Bob had a propensity for numbers that exceeded mine by a large measure, as well as the professional training I lacked. I asked Doug and Ray to meet with him. He passed their smell test. With that, I made him Dollar Tree's number-two guy.

. . .

Bob Sasser joined the company as chief operating officer after a long career in variety retail—and brought with him brains and an understanding of the changes we'd have to make to harness our runaway growth.

USED BY PERMISSION
OF DOLLAR TREE

Bob Sasser was forty-seven when he joined us, and his past suggested he'd understand what we were about. Born in Columbus, Georgia, where his dad was a civil servant at Fort Benning, he moved with his family to Panama City, Florida, when he was a kid. While majoring in marketing at Florida State, he worked part-time at Sears and W. T. Grant, the latter a big discount variety chain for most of the twentieth century, a competitor of Woolworth and Kresge.

On graduating in 1973, Bob ran several stores in the Southeast for Grant before the company started to tank, which it finished doing in 1976. Before the end came, he jumped ship to Roses, based in Henderson, North Carolina. He worked for Roses first as an assistant manager, then as the manager of stores in Georgia, South Carolina, and Kentucky, moving seven times in five years until he was transferred to headquarters as the chain's sales and promotions manager in 1983.

A little more than ten years later, having risen to vice president, Bob left

Roses to follow a former boss to Michaels, which at the time was a chain of about a hundred arts-and-crafts stores. He spent three years and change with the company in the Dallas area, during which Michaels more than quadrupled in size.

By then, his two kids were out of high school, and Bob missed the East Coast. So he left Michaels to return to Roses, this time as senior vice president for merchandise. The company was in flux; Roses had filed for and emerged from Chapter 11 and had been sold to a private company in Raleigh. He set about rebuilding the organization.

Which was what he was doing around Christmas 1998, when he got a call from our headhunter. Without identifying us, she asked if he was interested in a job as chief operations officer. Well, no, Bob said, not really—he hadn't been back long in North Carolina and felt obligated to stick with the new owners. Besides, it was Christmas. He was busy.

But he pressed the headhunter for the name of the company she represented, and at home he asked his wife if she'd ever heard of Dollar Tree. Oh, yes, she answered—why, she'd been shopping with us just that day. She showed off what she'd bought. He was intrigued. Over the next few days, he strolled through a couple of stores, taking in the product mix. He read over the paperwork the headhunter sent him. Then, early in the new year, he came to Chesapeake to meet with me.

I liked him right away. We shared interests in the arts and history, as well as business, and I appreciated his experience. Here was a guy who'd done just about every job in retail, from cleaning bathrooms to helping customers to running a chain—and not just in retail, but variety retail. At Florida State, he'd pursued engineering before veering into business, which was a great combination for a guy who'd be leading our charge into new technologies. He also tested as really smart. Bob had a lot of gray matter, a lot of bandwidth. He was from the South, too, which didn't hurt. We sealed the deal at a diner in South Hill, Virginia, a little town on I-85 roughly halfway between Norfolk and Raleigh. I made an offer. He accepted. He joined us on March 1, 1999.

Over the next two years, he planned and tested, with Darcy's help, the new technologies that would help us keep better track of our inventory. In 2001, we tried point-of-sale scanning in ten stores near our headquarters. Each sale was logged into a computer system that we eventually married to our automated warehousing and distribution, so replenishment was all but automatic.

It eliminated waste and guesswork. Stores no longer got product simply because we had it, but because they needed it. Our supply chain thus acquired the same hands-off efficiency, top to bottom, that our warehouse operations had. And though a store manager could tweak the system to request more or less of an item, he or she wasn't required to order anything. We could have all gone on vacation at once and the computers would have kept the stores stocked with merchandise. It was a little scary.

From the start of the ten-store experiment, we gained a clear picture of product movement from container to customer. It was like having an MRI picture of the company's guts, compared to having to guess what was going on in there. This took me back to my days in the Marine Corps in some ways. At Basic School, much discussion had focused on battlefield awareness—on how a key to success in combat was knowing where your opponent was, and where you were in relation to him and your reinforcements, and how to keep him in the dark as to what you were up to. That's what the emerging Dollar Tree systems gave us: battlefield awareness.

Bob devoted a lot of energy to strategic planning as well, because he recognized that if we were to grow as we wanted to—doubling in size every five years or so—we would have to think three to five years ahead. Our infrastructure would have to be in place ahead of our stores.

We started systemizing the company using his leadership, even as I gave Bob more and more responsibility. I exposed him to Wall Street, which he'd never dealt with; he'd never had a public role in his past jobs. He was a quick study. By 2001, he was ready to take on bigger responsibilities, and I was ready to relinquish them. I promoted Bob to president. I remained the CEO, handling Wall Street and our place in the larger world, while Bob ran everything else. At the same time, Doug, who'd remained chairman of the board after his retirement, became emeritus chair, and I moved into the chairman's slot.

It may not have been obvious to observers outside the company, or even to people within it, but I'd started the process of handing over the reins.

■ ■ ■

Meanwhile, in April 2000, Dollar Tree acquired Dollar Express, a chain of 106 stores based in Philadelphia, for $306.8 million in stock. Founded in 1941, Dollar Express was a strong presence in that part of the country; it did $155.5 million worth of business in 1999, and its bosses had announced their plans to take the company public. We got to them first. Not only did the deal eliminate a competitor that would have been difficult to dislodge, it gave us great store locations in Philadelphia, where it was hard to find decent real estate.

We finished 2000 with 1,729 stores in thirty-six states. We opened the new distribution center in Stockton, California, that year, and bought land for a new DC in Savannah, Georgia. The first three quarters of the year were record breakers. We entered the holidays with Dollar Tree looking better than ever. At least on paper.

Out in the stores, however, something was off. The fall and early winter brought fewer customers than we expected. Consumer confidence was down all across America, which translated into less spending. Miserable weather in December kept shoppers indoors. Our new Dollar Express stores—which we didn't immediately rebanner with our own name—were particularly sluggish.

Our fourth-quarter sales weren't awful by any means, and our figures for the year were stellar; just the same, we were printing money just a little less quickly than the Wall Street forecasters thought we would. When we crunched the numbers in mid-December, we saw that our fourth-quarter earnings would likely come in at fifty-nine to sixty-two cents a share—well below the market's guess of seventy or seventy-one cents.

Now, these were Wall Street's projections, not ours, and anyone owning Dollar Tree stock still stood to make a tidy sum. We were a company on fire. Just the same, when I gathered at the office with Bob Sasser, Eric Coble, and the vice presidents, we knew we had to give the world a heads-up that reality wasn't quite going to measure up to the market's forecast. We were a public company, and as such we were servants of the public trust. We felt obligated to report it.

We knew what it meant to issue such a warning. We were committing hara-kiri. There'd be immediate bloodshed. Wall Street didn't give a damn then about long-term performance, and it doesn't now. It doesn't give a damn about the past or the future either. It focuses only on what's shiny and right under its nose. The market has a notoriously short attention span.

So never mind that we'd beaten the Street's forecasts every quarter since we'd gone public, or that we'd been investors' darlings who could do no wrong. Never mind that Walmart and other discount retailers were also downgrading their expectations. We'd stuttered. And we would pay for it. I woke at six on Tuesday, December 19, 2000, as I did every workday. I made my usual three-mile run. I ate some breakfast. Then I began what by any standard was a really crappy day at the office.

Pandemonium erupted. In what financial analysts called a massive overreaction, almost a third of the company's stock, more than 32 million shares, traded hands in six and a half hours. The stock price, which had opened at $36.38 per share, nosedived 44 percent to $20.44, and at one point dipped as low as $18.69.

Here's a holy-crap statistic: at the market's close, the value of our outstanding stock had free-fallen from $3.93 billion to $2.2 billion. It was a blue Christmas in Chesapeake, let me tell you. I felt like shouting to the market, *Are you people blind? Do you understand just how much money this company makes, and how much more it'll make in the years to come?*

We did our best to shake it off and get back to business, and over the next three months the stock slowly rose back to $24.19 a share. That's where it stood on March 16, 2001, when we had to issue another warning. Our first-quarter earnings, sucker-punched by weeks of fierce winter weather that closed our stores repeatedly and stole seven thousand store-days from our business calendar, had once more fallen short of the Street's best guess.

We took it in the shorts again. The stock price dropped 25 percent this time, all the way to $18.19. Dollar Tree's market value was half of what it had been three months before. That was mighty frustrating.

The hell of it was, we had amazing runs in 2000 and 2001. Our sales in 2000 were $1.69 billion, up 24.9 percent from the year before, which was a heck of a growth rate for any year. Our operating margin was 13.7 percent, which was incredibly high. I noted in our annual report, "Our total sales are up, our earnings continue to rise, and we are focused on profitable growth. Our average transaction per customer in 2000 was above the prior year's level, and the quality of our merchandise remains high."

The following year, sales hit $1.99 billion—so, so close to another amazing threshold—and we opened 246 new stores, along with the new DC in Savannah and another in Briar Creek, Pennsylvania. The soft American economy produced a slew of brand-name closeouts and fantastic deals, which we scooped up and offered to surprised shoppers. In my state of the company address at our annual stockholders' meeting, I pointed out that we'd attracted a quarter-billion customers in the past year.

A few statistics underlined the scale at which we were operating. In 2001, we went through 300 million shopping bags—enough to fill 150 shipping containers, so many that our decision to print the Dollar Tree logo on just one side saved $184,000. That year, our utility bills ran upwards of $17 million. We spent $1 million just on tissue paper to wrap polyresin figurines.

We enjoyed some vindication shortly after the stock pounding, when we made the Forbes Platinum list of America's best big companies. We'd made the list the year before, too, but it was particularly sweet now. And our debt-to-equity ratio was 3 percent, in an industry where the average was 34 percent.

That was just a prelude, because the following years made it obvious there was no ceiling on just how big and profitable this once-humble dollar business might get. By the end of 2002, we operated 2,263 stores in forty states, and they were steadily expanding; the average new Dollar Tree now ranged from seven thousand to ten thousand square feet. Company-wide, our square footage jumped by 31.6 percent in 2002.

Not least, we posted $2.33 billion in sales—over $2 billion for the first time, an achievement that would seem puny when we topped $3 billion just two years later. We were growing at an almost exponential rate—over the past five years, we'd grown an average of 30.5 percent per year—yet were able to manage it. We broke ground on the DC in Marietta and pursued the automation of our in-store inventory controls. Scanning equipment at our checkout stands, test-run in that handful of stores in 2001, was installed in more than a thousand stores by the end of 2002.

Halfway through the year, our stock had fully recovered. And from there, it only grew. And grew. And grew.

In May 2003, we bought out another competitor—Greenbacks Inc., a chain of ninety-six stores scattered through the Rockies and based in Salt Lake City, Utah. The $100 million purchase price was steep—we could have built our own stores for less—but the deal gave us an already established network of really good locations and a speedy way to move Dollar Tree into Arizona, Colorado, Montana, New Mexico, Utah, and Wyoming. We got a distribution center out of the deal, too.

We were now in forty-seven of the contiguous forty-eight states, with 2,513 stores. The only blank spot on the map was North Dakota.

We opened a store there the following year.

16

Twenty-one
Little Words

I t might be easy for an outsider, reviewing the crazy growth of Dollar Tree through the end of 2003, to dismiss it all as the product of underselling the competition, to say we achieved success simply because our products were so inexpensive. But that's not the way I look at Dollar Tree. I never have. Our success has always seemed to me the result of trying to do the right thing for the right reason.

Those aren't just words. I reckon we could have bought cheaper, less worthy stuff at a higher margin on our buying trips and offered it for a dollar, and our customers would have been none the wiser. But we didn't do that. We strove to treat our customers as we'd want to be treated—and that meant getting the best quality we could afford.

We could have looked after our own people poorly, could have paid our sales associates and warehouse teams the minimum, without benefits, and not bothered with performance bonuses and investment options. But we didn't do that. We can't pay them as much as they're worth to us—because if we did, we'd have gone bankrupt long ago, considering how high a regard we have for them—but we pay them decently and always try to treat them fairly. We train our managers to "catch people doing something right"—to praise them, encourage them, show them how important they are to the company's success.

Because without question, they're the most important assets we have.

We reward initiative and smarts with advancement into the management tiers. And at the rate we've grown, those opportunities have come along frequently.

We've always tried to give our people a way to share in our success. Early on, when we were running K&K and still a private company, we made it possible for our rank-and-file folks to obtain stock. Some of them made out very well when we sold the toy company. We tried to deal them into the dollar company when we were private, too. And when we went public, we had forklift drivers who pocketed a lot of money—and by that I mean anybody's idea of a *lot* of money.

At some point amid this expansion, we held a big retreat in Williamsburg, Virginia, for our top managers, and one of our activities was writing a company mission statement. You can go on Dollar Tree's website today and find that statement pretty much as we wrote it then: "Dollar Tree, Inc. is a customer-oriented, value-driven variety store operating at a one dollar price point. We will operate profitably, empower our associates to share in its opportunities, rewards and successes, and deal with others in an honest and considerate way. The company's mission will be consistent with measured and profitable growth."

That "measured and profitable growth" line came straight from Ray, by the way. The wording did a nice job of summarizing the discipline and care he brought to the company's finances.

Around the same time, I had cards printed up for every Dollar Tree employee, emblazoned with the company's core values. They were the size of business cards, so they'd fit easily into a wallet. On the front of each were three words: *Attitude, Judgement,* and *Commitment.* Under *Attitude* were the words *Responsibility, Integrity, Courtesy.* Under *Judgement* was this: "Do The Right Thing For The Right Reason." Under *Commitment* was "Honor And Respect For Self And Company." Those few words—twenty-one, all told—crystalized what we held dear. They were the traits we wanted our people to keep uppermost in mind when they were on the job, because they were what we tried to demand of ourselves.

If you go to the Dollar Tree website now, you'll find those values on display just as they appeared on the cards—except that *Judgment* is spelled correctly, which wasn't the case when I was the guy holding the pen.

My point is that we took this seriously, and we still do. We were not simply in the business of making money. We were still striving to be straight-up and by-the-book, just as we had tried to be on our first toy-buying trips to New York. We still hewed to the idea that to be good operators we first had to be good. As we grew big, I reinforced the values in pretty much every edition of the company's quarterly newsletter. Now that we're huge, Bob Sasser uses distance-learning technology to keep the work force up to speed on core standards and Dollar Tree culture.

You're probably reading this and thinking, *Wait a minute. This guy's talking like these people are on some holy mission, when what they're doing is running a bunch of dollar stores.* Fair enough. But those stores fill an important niche. They provide a service.

Let me offer a story that illustrates what I'm saying. Darcy Stephan brought us into the computer age at K&K, built our computer network at Dollar Tree, consulted with Steve White on the development of our logistical systems, and started the process of automating our stores. But she didn't spend a whole lot of time in those stores. She was always saturated with tasks at our headquarters.

Sometimes, at Christmas, when the stores were overwhelmed with customers, we all had to pitch in on the front lines. Darcy had helped at K&K stores early in her tenure, and one holiday season in the early nineties she found herself working the floor in a Dollar Tree.

Until that night, Darcy hadn't much understood the appeal of our merchandise. Now, she was approached by an older gentleman, who asked for her help in picking out a Christmas gift for his wife. The country was in the grip of a recession. He had five dollars to spend.

It was a moment both wonderful and devastating for her. Suddenly, she had a sense of what the company was all about, of how much its customers had come to depend on it. She helped the man select a pair of earrings and a vase or some similar knickknack. He left happy. She ended her shift a true believer.

So, sure, it's a dollar store. But the mission and values mean something to me. And the fact that they remain virtually unchanged since we wrote them might not mean much if we weren't a very different company in a great many respects from the Dollar Tree I led at the close of 2003.

None of the change was revolutionary—it came, as Ray might have phrased it, in steady, measured fashion—but a veteran from a dozen years ago would hardly recognize today's operation. If things go as I hope they will, it'll be a much different company again in another dozen years.

Why? Because in retail, if you're not changing, you're dying. We have to strive to stay fresh, to keep surprising our customers. We can't make that happen by embracing the status quo, even for a minute. Yet I like to think that our mission statement and values will still be in place in a dozen years and beyond, and remain guideposts by which Dollar Tree finds its way.

. . .

It can be a tough thing to admit to yourself that this wondrous entity you had such a hand in creating has left you behind, but by 2003 that's exactly what many members of the company's old guard found ourselves confronting. Dollar Tree had to change, to morph into a different style of company, if it were to grow—or even if it didn't grow much more, just to last. And we barnstormers weren't the people to take it on that journey.

So while Bob Sasser was president, he and I began the process of hiring managers trained and educated in using the new systems with which he proposed to take the company to new heights. Inevitably, these new talents took over pieces of the business that had been overseen by pioneers. He had his own candidate in mind for chief operations officer. Tom Bowyer, who'd handled the job from the K&K days, was offered another post at Dollar Tree, opted not to take it, and left us. Bob hired a new chief of information systems, Ray Hamilton. Darcy took her leave a few months later. Eric Coble vacated the chief financial officer position to become corporate secretary before he, too, departed.

Kay Waters (now Kay Waters Bousman) kept buying through the first few years of the new millennium—and was stranded in China on 9/11—but eventually came to feel it was time to try something new. Bryan Bagwell, who'd risen from warehouse stock boy to senior vice president for merchandising, and who proved himself a smart, savvy, detail-oriented, and incredibly energetic executive, left the company after twenty-seven years of service.

Those were bittersweet times. The shifts hurt. But we needed the strongest, most capable people we could find for this new systems-driven style of business we were transitioning into. We couldn't afford to find ourselves saying, "I hope this person works out."

I was well aware that what went for the other pioneers went for me, too. What the company needed was no longer my personal style of leadership, but a CEO with the sort of organizational skills to manage a corporate giant. I knew I didn't have those abilities. So I began my own exit.

Succession from a company's founder to someone new is, I'm told, one of the most difficult transitions that can take place in business. Few transfers of power happen smoothly. The work force has a hard time accepting new leadership in place of a boss who had a hand in building the enterprise, and the founder has a heck of a time letting go. Who, after all, knows the business better? In the course of a company's history, that founder has done everything from buying paper clips and mopping the floors to devising long-term strategy. And perhaps more importantly, he embodies the vision everyone in the work force has shared, the goals toward which everyone has labored.

In theory, it shouldn't be such a big deal. If you build a company with the right structure and with the best possible people in each slot, you should be able to swap out individual executives like components of an engine; personalities shouldn't count for nearly as much as competence. But companies aren't machines. They're living, breathing entities, susceptible to organic stresses and ailments as surely as you or me. You can put two companies of equal size to the same task, and it won't take long to see that their success or failure turns on elements that are few in number, hard to measure, and entirely human: their commitment to the mission, their overall morale, their collective determination. A committed, pumped-up work force will always outperform a competent but uninspired bunch. Personality counts.

And no one's personality is as visible, as influential, as that of the man or woman at the top. That person is ideally both a symbolic and a real leader in the company's culture; he's a cross between a car's hood ornament and its driver. He gives the business a face. He's shorthand for the brand. And he has a tremendous role in charting its course.

So I knew, on deciding to hand over the CEO's title and duties to Bob, that the company depended on me to handle the transfer correctly, and that meant succeeding at what might be my greatest challenge as a Dollar Tree executive: Doing nothing. Keeping my mouth shut and staying out of the way.

I was fortunate because in all my years of working with Doug and Ray, we'd managed to hold one thought highest in our minds: the company was more important than we were. Doing the right thing for the right reason almost always meant putting Dollar Tree first and subsuming our egos to whatever the business needed. And now, what was best for Dollar Tree was clear to me. Caring about the company, putting it first, meant handing it over to a new generation of leader who could do better than I could. It meant surrendering my role as leader and taking up that of statesman.

It helped that I had examples to follow. On deciding to retire, Doug and

Ray had remained on the board and were enthusiastic participants in its activities, but both trusted the officers who followed them to safeguard and nurture the baby they'd created. Their examples helped me accomplish the best thing I've ever done as a businessman, other than help found the company.

. . .

Here's how it happened.

Working with Bob and seeing that he had the confidence and chops to run the company and lead it through its necessary metamorphosis prompted me to start grooming him for the CEO post. In large measure, that mentorship consisted of taking him with me on my presentations to Wall Street. I wanted not only for Bob to gain the experience of dealing with New York financiers but for them to get a good look at him—and to see we were leading the company together.

Whenever I went on a road show, Bob came with me, and we both spoke. After I made the decision to retire as CEO, we chose to announce it in the fall of 2003 but to have it take effect a few months later—again, giving the Street time to digest the news and to watch Bob in action. I wanted our transition to seem orderly and inevitable, so it would be greeted with "*Of course* Sasser is taking over," rather than "Oh, my God, the last founder is leaving. What's going to happen?"

I would not be leaving completely. I'd take the title of executive chairman of the board, which would give me a management function. Bob would run the company, but I'd be there to work with him and the board to further ease the transition. So much of this plan seemed common sense to me that I was a bit surprised people made such a big deal of it. It was considered remarkable in that we went from a family company to a public company, then turned the company over to a new regime and still achieved great success. As a matter of fact, the University of Virginia's Darden School did another case study on that succession.

I guess I looked at succession as a last opportunity to do something right. We'd founded the company, instituted great ideas, and earned a reputation for being good retailers and running a great company; the next thing to do was to figure out how to keep it going.

So on January 1, 2004, Bob Sasser became Dollar Tree's CEO. I came into the office most days and had plenty to do in my new role, but by and large I

Bob Sasser, left, and I hobnob at a company get-together, shortly after he took Dollar Tree's reins and spurred growth that eventually saw it reach $8.6 billion in sales—even before the purchase of the larger Family Dollar chain.

Used by permission of Dollar Tree

stayed out of the kitchen; he was the chef, and I left the cooking to him. I wanted him to succeed, wanted it desperately, and I figured the best way I could encourage that was to stay out of his way unless he needed my help.

He didn't need it much. Bob proved himself the ideal new leader for a company that kept growing and becoming ever more sophisticated in its corporate systems and logistics. At the end of his first year at the helm, we had 2,735 stores, and point-of-sale scanning gear had been installed in 2,600 of them—an astounding achievement just three years after we first toyed with the technology. We opened two new distribution centers in 2004, in Joliet and in Ridgefield, Washington. Oh, and we busted the $3 billion threshold in sales.

The following year, we bought a 138-store chain of discount variety stores based in the Midwest and Southeast and kept the stores' name unchanged. Deal$ was our first foray into running stores that did not hew to the dollar price point. We figured we could use it as muscle in some markets against low-end competitors with similar product mixes—namely, Family Dollar and Dollar General. The purchase, from SuperValu Inc., cost $30.5 million in cash and $22.2 million of inventory, which was a bargain.

Was this a signal that we intended to dump the price point someday? Not at all. We opened hundreds of new Dollar Trees at the same time, and they operated at much higher margins than our new Deal$ stores. The dollar price point remained, and remains, magical for us. It's who we are. But the Deal$ purchase did give us a feel for running bigger, broader stores with product mixes we hadn't experienced since the early days at Wards Corner—which would come in handy a few years down the road when we made a bid for the much, much bigger Family Dollar chain. I'll get to that.

Meanwhile, we busted the 3,000-store threshold in 2006—broke it by a wide margin, in fact, ending the year with 3,219 stores—and further enlarged the average size of each. Our acquisitions had shown us that having more space offered advantages in enabling the use of shopping carts, displaying merchandise effectively, and creating a pleasant environment for lingering. But the steadily growing size of our outlets was a minor change next to the shifting mix of merchandise we filled them with.

. . .

In our early years, we concentrated almost exclusively on nonconsumable stuff—imported dry goods from around the world, along with interesting things we were able to get domestically. We offered a few consumables, and they always sold well, but the margins were so much lower that I allowed only so much of them in our product mix.

That shifted dramatically early in Bob's tenure. He saw value in boosting the share of every store devoted to food, snacks, toiletries, and household essentials that customers needed on a frequent basis. Gift wrap and greeting cards might bring shoppers in a few times a year, but toothpaste, paper towels, toilet paper, and soft drinks might bring them in several times a week. "Needs-based items," he called them, to make a distinction between this new concentration and the sort of serendipitous, treasure-hunt merchandise we'd started with.

So the stores shed most of their gift items, such as the polyresin figurines that had figured so prominently in our rise. We still sold a few, along with vases and picture frames, but far less space was given over to knickknacks and far more to household cleaners, laundry detergent, shampoo. We carried name brands as well as private-label merchandise, which amazed our customers. It was one thing to find a completely unknown brand of toothpaste for a dollar and quite another to find the same brands sold next door at the supermarket.

That we were able to offer these name brands was sometimes a function of what's called the gray market. A toothpaste's brand managers can't allow their wares to be undercut by a dollar price point. They're selling to Walmart and Winn-Dixie and Kroger, after all, and they want to protect that business; they're not about to offer their stuff so cheaply that Dollar Tree can sell it and kill business to the retailers charging three or four bucks for the same thing.

So we buy bounce-back goods from other markets—Mexico, Europe, South America. It's made for those foreign markets but for whatever reason ships back into this country, and we can get it on the bounce. We sell Colgate Total toothpaste in a 1.9-ounce tube. It's made in the United States. Right beside it are Colgate Deep Clean and Colgate Max Fresh toothpastes in much bigger tubes—2.8 ounces. Examine the packaging and you'll see that they're made in Mexico. The Aquafresh fluoride toothpaste a short ways down the shelf comes in an even bigger 3-ounce tube. It's made in Taiwan. The stuff inside the tubes is the same as next door in the supermarket. We're not selling fake versions of the name brands. Our procurement is different, and that's all.

As for the private-label foods we sell, it's all decent, quality merchandise, and our customers get a lot of it for the money. Is it as good as the name-brand stuff? Probably not quite. I'd be lying if I said it was. Our cookies and crackers aren't Nabisco. But they're good enough. The name brands cost four times as much, and our cookies are simply not four times worse. They're almost as good. They'll do.

We don't make much money on each consumable item we sell—not compared to the margin on our imported dry goods, at least. The thing is, though, that our volume is so high that even at a dollar such items generate a pretty fat income. Vendors say we buy so much of an item that it defies belief. Another chain might buy twenty-four tubes of toothpaste for a store; we'll buy a dozen times that number, and we'll sell it all faster. Dollar Tree might clear only a nickel or a dime on each item, but the number of sales makes it work.

Our growing selection of foodstuffs invited an ever wider cross-section of the population into our stores. While we'd always scored big with savvy middle-class and upper-middle shoppers on the hunt for great bargains, we began attracting lower-income customers who'd lacked sufficient disposable income to shop for nonessentials (the old polyresin figurines, for example) but now found products on our shelves that they needed at prices they could afford.

So it was that we ended 2005 with freezers and coolers installed in 632

Dollar Trees. And behind the glass, our customers discovered the same sort of surprises they had always found elsewhere in our aisles. A half-dozen eggs for a dollar? Milk? TV dinners? Seriously?

Yes. Seriously.

Our unbeatable prices on consumables have made us a threat to other retailers. Nowadays, right many supermarket chains exclude us in their lease agreements, or at least try to. They'll locate in a strip shopping center on the condition that we're not their neighbor, or that if we are, we don't carry food.

And if they believe we're selling too many of the same items, they sue. We were sued by Winn-Dixie not too long ago and had to defend ourselves—hire lawyers, spend millions of dollars. It was all a huge waste of time, effort, and money. Winn-Dixie didn't want the competition from us, though I'd argue that our presence in its shopping centers meant more traffic for everybody.

We posted $4 billion in sales for the first time in 2007. Topped $5 billion just two years later. Made the Fortune 500 list of America's biggest public companies for the first time in 2009. Jumped 102 spots in our second year on the list. Started accepting debit cards, then credit cards, then phased in food stamps. Opened our four thousandth store in 2010.

As we steadily increased our presence throughout the lower forty-eight, we also crossed the Canadian border to become international in 2010. That October, Dollar Tree bought the eighty-six Dollar Giant stores, based in Vancouver and scattered across four provinces—British Columbia, Alberta, Saskatchewan, and Ontario. We stick to a fixed price point north of the border just as we do in the States, only there—where the dollar packs less punch than the United States note—we sell everything for $1.25 Canadian.

The new territory was hungry for the sort of surprises we'd been offering our American customers, and we hurried to satisfy it. Within a few months, we had ninety-nine Canadian stores and had spread into Manitoba. We've since more than doubled that presence.

I could go into greater detail, but the litany of firsts and records and achievements is so long and varied that it almost gets boring. Suffice it to say that the company almost doubled in size in the first five years of Bob Sasser's leadership as CEO. And the percentage rate of growth stayed pretty steady as the company acquired this monolithic scale, which meant that the bigger it got, the faster it got even bigger. Our 2010 annual report listed our sales at $5.9 billion. The report of two years later put the figure at $7.4 billion.

It had taken us fourteen years to achieve our first $1.5 billion year. Now, we were growing by that much in two.

. . .

I spent about five years as executive chairman of the Dollar Tree board. Over that time, I found myself with much to do outside the office, so eventually I moved out of the executive chair and took the far less demanding role of chairman. I'd spent forty years in retail. I figured I had earned a little more free time.

How did I spend it? Well, as it happened, Joan and I were as busy in our retirements as we had been in our working lives. I was asked to join the board of trustees at Randolph-Macon College, and served as its chairman for ten years. While I held that post, Joan served as chairman of the trustees at Virginia Wesleyan College, a coed liberal arts school in Virginia Beach. It was interesting, both of us leading schools of similar size at the same time. It made for some pretty unusual pillow talk.

We gave more than our time to education. Through Dollar Tree's growth after Bob took over as CEO—an expansion that saw the company reach $7.8 billion in sales and 4,992 stores in 2013 and $8.6 billion in sales and an incredible 5,367 stores a year later—we remained among its biggest individual stockholders. We realized that our longtime mantra—doing the right thing for the right reason—applied to us now more than ever. It was incumbent upon us, we felt, to share the benefits of our good fortune. To try to do good.

So we gave a lot of money to the schools that had helped make us who we were. Our first big gift, back in the mid-1990s, had helped build the Brock Center, a state-of-the-art sports and recreation facility at Randolph-Macon. Ours was the lead gift toward meeting the center's $9 million cost.

That whetted our appetite to do more. We gave money to renovate two Randolph-Macon classroom buildings, Fox and Haley Halls, and redid the college's boardroom and president's office. At Longwood University, Joan's alma mater, we helped finance the construction of Brock Commons, a central plaza of greens, fountains, and sculpture garden that replaced a busy, traffic-choked street; it united the whole campus and really transformed the character of the place.

Later, we donated money toward the construction of another Brock Commons, at Randolph-Macon, this a lavish, 26,000-square-foot student center with meeting and dining facilities. More recently, we've made a commitment to remodel the Copley Science Center and to build a new science building along-side it.

There's more than sentimentality to all this. My feeling is that colleges such as Randolph-Macon and Longwood are real contributors to the life of the state and its people, and that they should be preserved. I can hold myself up as an example of the transformative power of a liberal arts education at a small college. Randolph-Macon is where I became a productive member of society.

No surprise, then, that education has been one of the primary focuses of our philanthropy. Joan pursued a master's degree in humanities at Old Dominion University in Norfolk, so we directed some of our money there, too; it has enabled the school to build a mighty attractive outdoor amphitheater and a wetlands pathway linking the performance space to the campus's northern edge. At Virginia Wesleyan, we endowed the director's post in the Center for the Study of Religious Freedom and kicked in help on scholarships and campus renovations. We built a primary school in Sierra Leone and continue to support it. We've endowed a number of faculty chairs and made other gifts at colleges throughout Virginia.

In 2009, Randolph-Macon thanked us by conferring honorary doctor of laws degrees on both Joan and me. I doubt our teachers back at Granby High would have been the least bit surprised to see Joan get such an honor, but I'll bet a few of them didn't see it coming to *me*.

Most recently, we donated money to the Eastern Virginia Medical School to help create the M. Foscue Brock Institute for Community and Global Health—named for my dad, who died in 2002 at age ninety-eight, and dedicated to the sort of community-minded work on public-health issues that he embodied throughout his twenty years at the tuberculosis sanatorium. I think he would have been shocked to see a medical-school institute named for him, but I think he might have been pretty tickled by it, too.

Our other big giving targets have been the arts, the environment, and the disadvantaged. We've long been supporters of the Chrysler Museum of Art in Norfolk, which has a heck of a collection. Joan was a docent there for years, and both of us have chaired the museum board; Joan was the first woman to do so, in 2006. We helped lead a major capital campaign that expanded and remodeled the whole place in 2012. Now, the museum's main building is named for us. Doug and his wife, Pat, have been big Chrysler Museum supporters, too. Their names are on the museum's glass studio, where visitors can watch some of the world's greatest glass artists at work.

At Pleasure House Point in Virginia Beach, we built the Brock Environmental Center, a striking complex perched on the edge of the Lynnhaven River that has earned accolades as one of the greenest buildings around. The Chesapeake Bay Foundation operates the center as a resource for students and teachers in their study of challenges to the ecosystem. That's a double hit in both education and the environment.

And Joan devotes herself to another twofer: we've made large contributions to the ACCESS College Foundation, a scholarship program that guarantees a higher education for worthy but less advantaged kids in southeastern Virginia. Joan, who's led the foundation, has really overseen its growth. She's also an avid supporter of the United Way Women's Leadership Council, which raises money for the charity's work with women and children.

Neither Joan nor I would have enjoyed our success without a lot of help. Giving back is important to us, and we've found it easy to do. And the one thing that all of this largesse has in common is the source of the money. Should you find yourself gazing at a beautiful painting at the Chrysler Museum, or attending a seminar on saving the bay at the environmental center, or chatting with friends on the lovely promenade at Longwood University, bear in mind that the gifts we've made to those worthy causes have all been outgrowths of Dollar Tree. Those stores produced the earnings, one dollar at a time, that made our giving possible. And the principles to which the company and its thousands of dedicated workers stay true have made such giving a no-brainer. We're just trying to do the right thing for the right reason.

Not bad for an idea many folks thought was crazy, one that couldn't possibly work.

17

Parachuting from Twenty-five Thousand Feet

========================

For my fiftieth birthday, in 1992, Joan surprised me with a Harley-Davidson Sportster motorcycle. I started taking the bike on weekend trips with friends, Joan sometimes riding on the seat behind me, and I fell in love with it—the wind in my face and the feeling of total freedom, of release, cruising smooth blacktop at a mile a minute on a big, powerful machine. On the Harley, I could escape completely from the pressures of the workday. I was one with my surroundings. So many details of flora and fauna, of landscape, that I'd missed driving a car were obvious when I was on just two wheels.

Before long, I traded up to bigger and bigger Harleys, and as we embarked on more ambitious trips out west I switched to a BMW and eventually a Honda Gold Wing. When our youngest child, Macon, graduated from college, we met in Denver and celebrated by riding through the Rockies. John Megrue also took up the hobby, and we made many trips together. We rode the crest of the Blue Ridge Mountains, and up the Pacific coast, and toured the deserts, canyons, and mesas of Arizona and New Mexico. We drank in the wind-swept, austere beauty of the Great Plains.

Those long, glorious days in the saddle answered a calling I'd always felt to see America. I'd spent weeks every year for the past two decades overseas, buying for Dollar Tree in Asia, Europe, and South America, but I'd never had the time to experience the United States on the ground, up close. Once I started handing over the company's leadership to Bob Sasser, I had the time, and I chased the opportunity whenever I could.

It wasn't always easy—bad weather is a million times worse on a motor-cycle—but I found it glorious to be out in the open air, experiencing some new corner of the lower forty-eight. The first couple days of a long trip, I probably looked what I was: a corporate suit dropping out of everyday life. But with hundreds of miles behind me, my beard grown out and my face roughened and tanned, I was indistinguishable from tens of thousands of other bikers. That was something else I loved about riding: it was a great equalizer. When you're stopped at a light and another biker pulls up beside you, it doesn't matter that you're a buttoned-down desk jockey and he's a rowdy diesel mechanic. You share a fraternity.

Wherever I rode, I was never far from a Dollar Tree, and though I was out there to escape the pressures of work, I found it difficult to ride past. That's still the case today, on the bike or behind the wheel of a car. If I see a Dollar Tree on the side of the highway, I'll often stop in to have a look around and say hello.

I probably don't see the place the way most people do. I know the story behind how we get most of the merchandise on the shelves, for one thing. I know the high-margin goods from those on which we earn just a few pennies. I recognize the hot sellers and the old reliables.

For me, our stores are filled with codes. On the side of a carton of Puffs tissues waiting to be unpacked, I can find the sticker applied by a picker back at the distribution center and tell you where in the warehouse that carton was stashed. I know the brand names that identify an item as a Dollar Tree (and only Dollar Tree) import, such as Royal Norfolk and Greenbrier Farms, our house peanut butter brand, named for the Chesapeake neighborhood where our headquarters is located. Ditto for Greenbrier Kennel Club, the label on our dog chews. Some house brands aren't such immediate giveaways. Breckenridge Farms is the name on our lineup of jarred pickles: kosher dills, spears, and sand-wich slices, sweet pickles, bread and butter chips—all products of India. Search the back of the label, however, and you'll see that those pickles are distributed by Greenbrier International, Dollar Tree's importing arm.

We sell batteries that are branded "Sunbeam" in the same script you'll find on that company's electric appliances. Here's some news: Sunbeam doesn't make batteries. We pay it a licensing fee to use its brand on perfectly good bat-teries that otherwise would bear an unfamiliar label and that many customers might not buy for that reason, and only that reason. The name sells the product.

In sum, a trip to a Dollar Tree holds little mystery for me. I understand how we're able to score such terrific deals and pass them on to our customers. Yet despite that—and notwithstanding all my years in the business and my experience as a buyer and my insider knowledge—I can't help being excited and a little amazed on my visits.

Take, for example, a stop at our store number 137, in the Chippenham Forest Square shopping center in Richmond, Virginia, about a hundred miles west of our headquarters. In August 2015, it was welcoming back-to-school shoppers. The first thing I saw as I passed through the doors was an island of school supplies and simply peerless deals. A dollar bought four glue sticks, or four yellow highlighters, or eight retractable ballpoint pens, or a dozen number 2 pencils. It bought crayons in packs of thirty-six or sixty-four colors, spiral notebooks divided into three or five sections, or two-hundred-sheet packets of notebook paper. We might have offered some such stuff back in the day, but not nearly this broad or deep a range. Dollar Tree's expanded size and buying power means customers can find almost everything they need for school right here, down to the goodies they include in their children's lunches.

All through the store were items that even I could not have expected to find for a dollar. Back in the refrigerated section waited packs of fresh turkey bacon, plenty big enough for a typical family's breakfast. Ribeye steaks—precooked, three and a half ounces each, vacuum-packed, and a hell of an alternative to burgers. And most amazing to me: four-ounce salmon fillets. Wild-caught salmon fillets. I was well aware of what went into making these items available for a dollar. Still, it floored me to see just how far we could make pennies stretch. It made me proud, too. And it reassured me that Dollar Tree is going to stick around for a long, long time. Nobody else does what we're doing.

Occasionally, a visit exposes mistakes in organization or attitude, but I don't see many. Most stores are clean, bright, and well stocked whenever I walk in. Our people are almost unfailingly helpful and polite. Consider again store 137, where a van drove through the front windows in March 2015 and a car did the same thing just a month later. Fortunately, no one was seriously hurt either time—and the staff kept the store open and serving customers.

During my August visit, a customer approached one of the store's associates with several items in hand. "Are these a dollar?" she asked. The associate answered, "Everything's a dollar, darlin'," in such a warm and friendly tone that I'd never have guessed she was asked that question, as she later said, "about a thousand times a day."

Every once in a great while, I do encounter a problem. Some time back, I was way down south in the Mississippi Delta, on a trip with friends tracing the history of the blues, when we decided to take a break and pulled into one of our stores. I walked in for a look around. The place was a complete and utter wreck. It was filthy, for starters—a big breach of our standards, because the first thing that should surprise and delight customers on entering a Dollar Tree is the clean, bright, and well-organized look of the store. Shelves were empty. Unpacked boxes of merchandise were stacked in the aisles, blocking the way to shopping carts. Nobody seemed in a hurry to restore order to the mess.

I was flabbergasted. Everything about the place was a refutation of the company's respect for customers. I pulled out my cell phone, called Chesapeake, and got the vice president of operations on the line. Turned out the store's manager had been out sick, which suggests just how important those folks are. Still, that wasn't much of an excuse, and you can bet the store straightened up in a hurry. The whole district got a close eye for a while thereafter.

I say this to make the point that I'm only *semi*-retired. I still consider myself a Dollar Tree associate, even when I'm out exploring back roads on a motorcycle, and I reckon I will for as long as I live. I'm immensely proud of the company, its people, and the quality and value we've been able to bring to our customers, and I'm so, so grateful to have been part of it.

I take its triumphs and missteps personally. Your local Dollar Tree didn't materialize out of nowhere. It's the product of a long evolution that began among the popcorn, toys, and fishtanks of that Wards Corner five-and-ten. It embodies what we learned, often the hard way, during our long apprenticeship in the toy business. It testifies to decades of sweat, moxie, and discipline from a dedicated group of people with a shared sense of mission, people who truly believed that if we did the right thing for the right reason, we'd succeed—and who proved that belief true.

I've introduced a few of those people in these pages. I wish I had the space to recognize the contributions of many, many others. The company they helped create has grown beyond any of our wildest imaginings. It's a much bigger, systems-driven organization today, and most of us old-timers would find it probably a little less fun and exciting than the seat-of-the-pants Dollar Tree of old. But it continues to grow and continues to hew to the guiding principles that we established and lived by.

I think that most of the founding staffers share my parental love for Dollar Tree. I'll bet most of them are customers, as I am, and that on many of their

Bob Sasser straightens a display at a Dollar Tree in Virginia Beach, demonstrating that the company's executives are not far removed from workers in the field, though the venture today is unimaginably bigger and more complex than the humble chain we started in 1986.
PHOTO BY MACON BROCK

shopping trips they catch someone doing something right. I'll bet they'd have been as steamed as I was by that rogue store I encountered in the Deep South.

I reckon the next time I'm in that town, that store will be the cleanest, best-stocked, brightest, and friendliest Dollar Tree in the country.

No telling when I might get down that way.

Could be next week.

Could be tomorrow.

Look sharp, people.

• • •

The *semi* part of my semi-retirement is mostly taken up by my duties on the Dollar Tree board, which I share with Doug, Ray, and our old equity partner,

Tom Saunders, among others. As directors, we've all helped guide the company on a part-time basis, and at some distance from day-to-day operations. Bob Sasser, whom we consider "Founder 2.0," has been CEO longer than I was. He doesn't need much help from us, and when he does, it's almost always on strategic, big-picture questions.

It's been fun, and deeply satisfying, to watch him take what we started and turn it into something several times bigger and richer; today, Dollar Tree's more than six thousand stores blanket forty-eight states and five Canadian provinces. We've watched, intrigued, as he's overseen the expansion of our stores to an average of about nine thousand square feet and transformed the product mix to equal parts customer wants and customer needs. More than four thousand Dollar Tree stores now have freezers and coolers offering a wide assortment of foods. The typical customer now spends more than eight dollars a visit.

We've seen the advent of Dollar Tree Direct, our online shopping system, which now offers twenty-six hundred items for sale and gives customers the option of having their purchases delivered to their doors or to their nearest Dollar Tree, which saves them the cost of shipping. About 80 percent of the orders are picked up at the stores, which is fine by us, because it earns those stores additional visits and other opportunities to delight and surprise customers—and to sell them something.

In short, Bob has been a stellar CEO. It's been exciting to have a continuing hand in a company grown so big and complex that we couldn't hope to operate it ourselves. That we did so good a job early on that we made ourselves obsolete has turned out to be a good thing. That we had the sense to make room for a new generation of leader is just plain great.

■ ■ ■

The most exciting days for Dollar Tree are still ahead. In July 2015, we on the board of directors made an audacious turn in the company's course, one that promises to reshape it in just about every respect. We closed on a deal to buy Family Dollar, a North Carolina–based chain of eighty-one hundred discount variety stores.

It was a bigger company than Dollar Tree, and a different style of retailer. Founded in Charlotte in 1959, Family Dollar was never a single price-point operation, despite its name. Its merchandise mix early in 2015 was far more skewed to consumable goods, which accounted for a whopping 73 percent of its products, versus 49 percent of ours. Its typical shopper had a lower income than a Dollar Tree customer, despite our lower prices, and while most of our stores were in America's suburbs, the bulk of Family Dollar's were in small towns and urban neighborhoods.

It had more in common with Walmart than with us. If you took a Walmart Supercenter, shrunk it by 95 percent, and ditched most of the surviving electronics and clothes, you'd wind up with something like a Family Dollar store. Yet Family Dollar did resemble us in two respects. One, it was convenient. It had survived big-box competition by giving customers a place close to home to dash in for a few needed items, in place of a time-sucking jumbo store several miles away. And two, its discount retail niche, like ours, wasn't much affected by the ups and downs of the economy.

While I was CEO, I paid the chain little mind. It didn't take much of our business, and vice versa. It was just a little country store that catered to the underserved in mostly Southern markets with little or no competition. But in May 2014, an activist investor, Carl Icahn, gained control of 9.4 percent of Family Dollar's stock and thus became the most powerful shareholder. Almost immediately, he pushed for the company to put itself up for sale. The stores underperformed, he argued, and only new blood would set things right. He figured there "would be significant interest from strategic and financial buyers who could recognize massive synergies from an acquisition of the company."

He was right. Family Dollar didn't have anywhere near the margins we did, or fare as well in other metrics of retail performance. It made money, but not nearly as much as it should have. And it so happened that we *were* interested.

To simplify a long and complicated story, we talked with Family Dollar and in late July 2014 sealed a deal to buy it for $8.5 billion cash and a pile of Dollar Tree stock. We also agreed to assume $1 billion of its debt, which effectively jacked up the price to $9.5 billion.

That prompted Dollar General, a Tennessee-based chain of 11,500 discount variety stores, to make its own bid for the company. Dollar General and Family Dollar were direct competitors that occupied similar markets, carried similar ranges of merchandise, and asked similar prices for their wares. In August 2014, Dollar General offered four dollars more per share for Family Dollar stock than we had.

Family Dollar rejected the bid, saying a merger would almost surely invite an antitrust action and kill the deal. A big dustup ensued before the company's stockholders ultimately agreed to and approved our purchase in January 2015. We closed on the deal six months later.

Now, we're wrapping up the process of integrating these two very different companies, which together have more than fourteen thousand stores, operate twenty-one huge distribution centers, and post sales of almost $19 billion. We're melding two different cultures and synchronizing different ways of doing things. We're already seeing ways to improve ourselves in Family Dollar's operations. We're on the lookout for those, as always. When our eyes and ears are open and our attitude is humble, we never fail to learn a lot.

We're going to the vendors we share, comparing the deals they've made with each of us, and demanding the better price for the combined company. And they're agreeing to that, because any purchasing power we enjoyed before the merger is dwarfed by "the power of no" we'll wield from here on out. Over time, we'll be able to nail down lower costs for goods all over the world.

We've rebannered some of the Family Dollars into Dollar Trees and even rebannered a few Dollar Trees into Family Dollars. We're figuring that out market by market, store by store. We're picking up some of Family Dollar's store brands—those we can sell for a dollar, that is—and it's taking some of ours.

In most places, we are operating the chains side by side, trading on the strengths of both. We're improving efficiency, productivity, and product mix at Family Dollar to boost its performance. Dollar Tree is tapping Family Dollar's expertise in selling consumables. We're revamping both logistical systems to use all of our warehouses to our best advantage. And we'll keep adding stores to both chains. We'll continue to grow.

It won't be easy. This is a complicated marriage. Bob Sasser is fond of saying that finding Dollar Tree products overseas and getting them delivered to an individual store "is like parachuting from ten thousand feet into a teacup." Now, it's going to be like doing it from twenty-five thousand feet. The company has more than doubled in size in one fell swoop. Anything can happen.

But I have great confidence that Bob Sasser, our staff, and their new colleagues from Family Dollar will find synergy in the merger. It should mean lower prices at Family Dollar stores and even higher-quality goods at Dollar Trees. It should mean higher income and profits and a better return for our stockholders. It should turn out better for everyone.

■ ■ ■

It's a tenet of memoirs that every life is a study in patterns, that each of us has certain built-in default modes to which we return time and again, for good or ill, and in those tendencies are the keys to success or failure. In the process of telling this story, I've been searching my own memory, and tapping Joan's and those of close friends, for patterns of thought and behavior I can identify in myself.

I've had no trouble finding a few that have directly affected my career and my place in the story of Dollar Tree. The eighth-grade cutup who loved attention became the corporate boss who found it easy and invigorating to stand before a crowd to tell his company's story. The one-time underachiever who strove to prove himself to his parents and teachers never lost that yen to show the world he was worthy, and thus never lacked for incentive to bust his hump to reach a goal. The young marine captain who trusted his more seasoned sergeants to do their duty was rewarded for that trust, and so repeatedly gave it to his coworkers throughout his career, almost always with positive results—which encouraged him to offer that trust more freely.

It's pretty easy to see such patterns in those close to me on this adventure, too. In K. R., I see a life informed by an independent streak, quiet and disciplined planning, and educated risk taking. Doug Perry's tendency toward modesty was as obvious when he was Dollar Tree's chairman as when he was buffing the floor at the dime store, and his friendliness and empathy for people endeared him to thousands within the company—and made him a disarmingly effective negotiator to boot. Ray Compton's attention to detail and careful methodology not only contributed to his success as an accountant and financial planner, it made him the calm, rock-steady center of Dollar Tree's sometimes cyclonic corporate atmosphere.

The people who worked with us, who grew up with the company, all brought with them innate traits on which we came to rely as a business and a culture, traits that weren't the product of classrooms but were hard-wired into their personalities. And our spouses and families demonstrated behaviors that abetted our efforts in the office, on the sales floor, and in the remote back blocks of Asia. Joan's inexhaustible energy, bright mind, and desire to give, to contribute to the greater good, were evident in middle school, flowered in high school and college, and kept us afloat as a family while I was off in Vietnam and enduring the misery of West Virginia—and made her an indispensable ingredient not only to Dollar Tree's success but to my own happiness.

Fact was, the miracle of Dollar Tree was due to a synergy of all these wide-ranging personalities, all these ingrained tendencies. We needed all of them to become the company we built. If lessons are to be gleaned from this tale, I think it's these: First, nobody achieves anything worthwhile on his own. We need each other. The whole is almost always greater than the sum of its parts. And second, it pays to have a mission. In our case, we aimed to surprise and delight our customers, to do right by them. To make their lives just a little better. We could have set out simply to make a lot of money, and perhaps we would have. But had that been our sole mission, I don't believe we'd feel nearly as good about the experience as we do. Talk to Dollar Tree's old-timers and you'll detect an almost spiritual kinship to the company and the people they worked with—and a sense that we were up to something good.

I like to think that whatever the future holds for Dollar Tree, that focus will remain in place. That we'll always strive to surprise and delight our customers. That we'll consider it necessary to treat people fairly. That we'll keep our egos out of the business.

We've never let them get in the way before.

Why would we? We're running a *dollar store* here.

Acknowledgments

Any book is the collective effort of a great many people. That goes for memoirs as much as any other tale. Had I relied solely on my own recollections for this story, it would have been a thin one indeed. I owe a tremendous debt in recapturing the details of Dollar Tree's genesis to some of the people most responsible for the company's success.

First off, my friends and partners Doug Perry and Ray Compton trusted me to tell a story we experienced together, and could have experienced no other way. Both, in multiple interviews, shared their remembrances of our lives together, and were also kind enough to read over my manuscript, on the lookout for mistakes of fact or interpretation. This is their story as much as mine. I thank both of them.

I thank Robin Jernigan and Debbie Sorensen, two of the company's most senior employees, for consenting to interviews about their earliest days back at the five-and-dime with Alice, as well as about their more than four decades on the job since. Likewise, such influential pioneers as Kay Waters Bousman, Tom Bowyer, Eric Coble, LuAnne Cox McCarty, Lewis Mitchell, and Darcy Stephan were generous with their time and memories, which added detail, texture, and perspective. Steve White not only shared his recollections but arranged two intensive inspections of the company's distribution centers in Marietta, Oklahoma, and Olive Branch, Mississippi, which refreshed my understanding of the technological miracles those facilities pull off every day.

Tom Saunders and John Megrue offered their accounts of our uncertain negotiations, the philosophies that guided our partnership, and the almost unimaginable successes it spawned. I can't imagine a more impressive combination of smarts, instincts, and grace than what these two brought to the table.

Bob Sasser, a very busy man, took time from running the company to describe his past, his recruitment by Dollar Tree, and his vision for the chain in the years ahead—which further attests to our profound good fortune in finding him and luring him aboard.

Of all my colleagues who pitched in on this project, one stands out. Bryan Bagwell not only sat patiently for several interviews, he shared his trove of photographs from our many trips abroad, as well as the detailed notes he amassed on those buying missions. Bryan's attention to detail, always a great asset to Dollar Tree, was likewise vital to this book.

My coauthor, Earl Swift, helped me shape a formless mass of memories, company reports, and press clippings into what I hope is an interesting and entertaining narrative spanning more than seventy years. He also found a partner for this project in the good people at John F. Blair, Publisher, of Winston-Salem, North Carolina, who turned our manuscript into the carefully edited, designed, and printed book you hold in your hands.

My old friend Richard Barry helped usher this project to life and was my top adviser throughout its creation, for which I'm tremendously grateful. The *Virginian-Pilot*'s Maureen Watts and Jake Hays gave me a hand with research. The paper also loaned us its photographs, for which I thank Randy Greenwell, its photo chief. The contributions of Amy Walton and ace editor and storyteller Mark Mobley also made this a much better book.

I took ill while working on this story, and without a team of doctors at the justly famed Cleveland Clinic would not have survived to finish it. I quite literally owe my life to Dr. Marie Budev, director of the clinic's Lung Transplant Program, and Dr. Kenneth R. McCurry, the surgeon who gave me new lungs.

Finally, I want to thank two groups of people to whom I owe much of my career, as well as my happiness.

The first consists of the many thousands of men and women of Dollar Tree—those who helped us build this remarkable enterprise, who comprise its human face to our millions of customers every day, and without whom none of our success would have been possible. I wish I could name each and every one of them. They're the key to surprising and delighting our customers. They're the main ingredient in everything we do.

And without my family—my parents, my siblings, my children, and most especially my wife and best friend, Joan—I would have no story to tell. I am the person I am because of them. I owe them more than words can express.

Index